SKETCHES

OF

Western North Carolina,

HISTORICAL AND BIOGRAPHICAL.

ILLUSTRATING PRINCIPALLY

THE REVOLUTIONARY PERIOD

OF

MECKLENBURG, ROWAN, LINCOLN AND ADJOINING COUNTIES,
ACCOMPANIED WITH MISCELLANEOUS INFORMATION,
MUCH OF IT NEVER BEFORE PUBLISHED

BY

C. L. HUNTER,

MEMBER OF THE "HISTORICAL SOCIETY OF NORTH CAROLINA,"
AND MEMBER OF THE "MECKLENBURG
HISTORICAL SOCIETY."

RALEIGH
THE RALEIGH NEWS STEAM JOB PRINT.
1877.

Notice

In many older books, foxing (or discoloration) occurs and, in some instances, print lightens with wear and age. Reprinted books, such as this, often duplicate these flaws, notwithstanding efforts to reduce or eliminate them. The pages of this reprint have been digitally enhanced and, where possible, the flaws eliminated in order to provide clarity of content and a pleasant reading experience.

Sketches of Western North Carolina, Historical and Biographical

Originally published
Raleigh, North Carolina
1877

Reprinted by:

Janaway Publishing, Inc.
732 Kelsey Ct.
Santa Maria, California 93454
(805) 925-1038
www.janawaygenealogy.com

2014

ISBN: 978-1-59641-339-9

Made in the United States of America

DEDICATION.

TO THE DESCENDANTS OF
THE REVOLUTIONARY PATRIOTS OF NORTH CAROLINA,
WHETHER NOW ABIDING WITHIN HER BORDERS AND SHARING
HER PROSPERITIES AND ADVERSITIES, OR SCATTERED
ABROAD IN OTHER STATES OF THE AMERICAN
UNION, BUT WHO STILL CHERISH A LASTING
VENERATION FOR THE MEMORIES OF
THEIR HEROIC FOREFATHERS:

AND

TO THE YOUNG MEN OF THE STATE GENERALLY,
WHO WOULD DRAW LESSONS OF WISDOM, PATIOTISM AND EN-
DURANCE FROM THE EXAMPLES HEREIN DE-
SCRIBED, THIS VOLUME IS RESPECT-
FULLY DEDICATED BY

THE AUTHOR.

PREFACE.

History has been defined, "Philosophy teaching by example." There is no branch of literature in a republic like ours, that can be cultivated with more advantage to the general reader than history. From the infinite variety of aspects in which it presents the dealings of Providence in the affairs of nations, and from the immense number of characters and incidents which it brings into view, it becomes a source of continuous interest and enjoyment.

The American Revolution is undoubtedly the most interesting event in the pages of modern history. Changes equally great and convulsions equally violent have often taken place in the Old World; and the records of former times inform us of many instances of oppression, which, urged beyond endurance, called forth the spirit of successful resistance. But in the study of the event before us—the story of the Revolution—we behold feeble colonies, almost without an army—without a navy—without an established government—without a good supply of the munitions of war, firmly and unitedly asserting their rights, and, in their defence, stepping forth to meet in hostile array, the veteran troops of a proud and powerful nation. We behold too, these colonies, amidst want, poverty and misfortunes, animated with the spirit of liberty and fortified by the rectitude of their cause, sustaining for nearly eight years, the weight of a cruel conflict upon their own soil. At length we behold them victorious; their enemies sullenly retiring from their shores, and these feeble colonies enrolled on the page of history as a *free, sovereign and independent nation.*

The American struggle for freedom, and its final achievement, was an act in the great drama of the world's history of such vast magnitude, and fraught with such momentous consequences upon the destinies of civilization throughout the world, that we can scarcely ever tire in contemplating the instrumentalities by which, under Divine guidance, it was effected. It has taught mankind that oppression and misrule, under any government, tends to weaken and ultimately destroy the power of the oppressor; and that a people united in the cause of freedom and their inalienable rights, are invincible by those who would enslave them.

No State in our Union can present a greater display of exalted patriotism, enduring constancy and persistent bravery than North Carolina. And yet, how many of our own people do we find who know but little of the early history of the State, her stern opposition to tyranny under every form, and her illustrious Revolutionary career.

On the shores of North Carolina the first settlement of English colonists was made; within her borders the most formidable opposition to British authority, anterior to the Revolution, was organized; by her people the *first declaration* of independence was proclaimed, and some of the

PREFACE.   vii

most brilliant achievements took place upon her own soil.

For several years, at intervals, the author has devoted a portion of his time and attention to the collection of historical facts relating principally to Western North Carolina, and bordering territory of South Carolina, to whom, as a sister State, and having a community of interests, North Carolina frequently afforded relief in her hour of greatest need.

Such materials, procured at this late day—upon the arrival of our National Centennial year, are often imperfect and fragmentary in character—merely scattered facts and incidents gathered here and there from the traditional recollections of our oldest inhabitants, or from the musty records of our State and county offices ; and yet, it is believed such facts, when truthfully transmitted to us, are worthy of preservation and rescue from the gulf of oblivion, which unfortunately conceals from our view much valuable information.

Being the son of a Revolutionary patriot, and accustomed in his boyhood to listen with enraptured delight to the narration of thrilling battle-scenes, daring adventures, narrow escapes and feats of personal prowess during the Revolution, all tending to make indelible impressions upon the tablet of memory, the author feels a willingness to "contribute his mite" to the store of accumulated materials relating to North Carolina, now waiting to be moulded into finished, hostoric shape by some one of her gifted sons.

Several of the sketches herein presented are original,

and have never before been published. Others, somewhat condensed, have been taken from Wheeler's "Historical Sketches," when falling within the scope of this work. To the venerable author of that compilation, the author also acknowledges his indebtedness for valuable information furnished from time to time from the "Pension Bureau" at Washington City, relating to the military services of several of our Revolutionary patriots.

The author and compiler of these sketches only aspires to the position of a historian in a limited sense. It cannot be denied that the history of our good old State, modest in her pretensions, but filled with grand, patriotic associations, has never been fully written. Acting under this belief, he feels tempted to say, like Ruth following the reapers in the time of Boaz, he has "gleaned in the field until even," and having found a few "handfuls" of *neglected* grain, and beaten them out, here presents his "ephah of barley"—plain, substantial food it is true, but yet may be made useful *mentally* to the present generation, as it was *physically* of old, to the inhabitants of Palestine.

In conclusion, the author cherishes the hope that other sons, and daughters too, of North Carolina—some of them forming with himself, *connecting links of the past with the present*—will also become *gleaners* in the same field of research, abounding yet with scattered grains of neglected and unwritten history worthy of preservation.

If the author's efforts in this direction shall impart additional information, and assist in elucidating "liberty's story" in the Old North State, his highest aspirations will be gratified, and his agreable labors amply rewarded.

CONTENTS.

INTRODUCTORY CHAPTER.

ORIGINAL SETTLEMENTS IN NORTH CAROLINA AND CHARACTER OF THE PEOPLE, ... 1

CHAPTER I.

MECKLENBURG COUNTY, ... 19
    The Mecklenburg Declaration of Independence,................. 24
    A brief account of the Mecklenburg Centennial,................ 31
    The Grand Procession,... 33
    Exercises at the Fair Grounds,... 34
    James Belk—A Veteran Invited Guest,.................................. 38
    Signers of the Mecklenburg Declaration of Independence,...... 39
    Origin of the Alexander Families of Mecklenburg County,.... 59
    Jack Family,.. 61
    Captain Charles Polk's "Muster Roll,"................................... 89
    President James K. Polk,.. 92
    General William Davidson,... 95
    General George Graham,.. 98
    William Richardson Davie,... 99
    Battle of the Hanging Rock,... 106
    General Michael McLeary,... 112
    Major Thomas Alexander,.. 113
    Captain William Alexander,.. 115
    Elijah Alexander,... 116
    Captain Charles Alexander,... 117
    Joseph Kerr—"The Cripple Spy,"... 120
    Robert Kerr, ... 122
    Henry Hunter,.. 123
    James Orr,.. 125
    Skirmish at Charlotte; or, First attack of the "Hornets,"..... 126
    Surprise at McIntire's; or, the "Hornets" at work,............. 136
    Judge Samuel Lowrie,... 141

CONTENTS.

The Ladies of the Revolutionary Period,............................. 142
Mrs. Eleanor Wilson,.. 146
Queen's Museum,... 152

CHAPTER II.

CABARRUS COUNTY,.. 157
   The "Black Boys" of Cabarrus,..................................... 158
   Dr. Charles Harris,... 162
   Captain Thomas Caldwell,.. 164

CHAPTER III.

ROWAN COUNTY,... 166
   Route of the British Army through Mecklenburg and Rowan
     Counties,... 172
   General Griffith Rutherford,...................................... 176
   Locke Family,... 178
   Hon. Archibald Henderson,... 179
   Richard Pearson,.. 180
   Mrs Elizabeth Steele,... 183

CHAPTER IV.

IREDELL COUNTY,... 186
   Col. Alexander Osborn... 186
   Captain William Sharpe,... 187
   Major William Gill, Captain Andrew Carson, and others,............ 189
   Captain Alexander Davidson,....................................... 194
   Captain James Houston,.. 194
   Captain James Houston's Muster Roll,.............................. 196
   Rev. James Hall,.. 196
   Hon. Hugh Lawson White,... 202

CHAPTER V.

LINCOLN COUNTY,... 205
   Battle of Ramseur's Mill,... 206
   Route of the British Army through Lincoln County,................. 218
   Gen. Joseph Graham,... 225

CONTENTS. xi

Brevard Family,.. 232
Col. James Johnston,... 238
Genealogy of Col. James Johnston,............................ 247
Jacob Forney, Sr.,.. 251
Gen. Peter Forney,.. 258
Major Abram Forney,.. 264
Remarks, ... 269
Genealogy of the Forney Family,............................... 270

CHAPTER VI.

GASTON COUNTY,.. 278
  Rev. Humphrey Hunter,... 278
  Dr. William McLean,... 285
  Major William Chronicle,.. 289
  Captain Samuel Martin,.. 291
  Captain Samuel Caldwell,... 294
  Captain John Mattocks,.. 295
  William Rankin,... 297
  General Jonn Moore... 299
  Elisha Withers,.. 300

CHAPTER VII.

CLEAVELAND COUNTY,.. 301
  Battle of King's Mountain,.. 301
  Colonel William Campbell,.. 312
  Colonel Isaac Shelby,... 314
  Colonel James D. Williams,...................................... 321
  Colonel William Graham,.. 322
  Lieutenant-Colonel Frederick Hambright,................. 324

CHAPTER VIII.

BURKE COUNTY,... 328
  Battle of the Cowpens,... 329
  General Daniel Morgan,.. 335
  General Charles McDowell and Brothers,................. 337

CONTENTS.

CHAPTER IX.

WILKES COUNTY, ... 342
    Colonel Benjamin Cleaveland, ... 342
    Colonel John Sevier, ... 344
    General William Lenoir, ... 346

CHAPTER X.

MISCELLANEOUS, ... 350
    Lord Cornwallis, ... 350
    Calonel Tarleton, ... 351
    Cherokee Indians, ... 352
    Conclusion, ... 357

CHRONOLOGICAL TABLE.

DATE		EVENTS.
1492	October 12,	Columbus discovered America.
1584	July 4,	Amadas and Barlow approach the coast of North Carolina.
1663		Charter of Charles II, William Drummond, first Governor of North Carolina.
1678		John Culpeper's Rebellion.
1693		Carolina divided into North and South Carolina.
1705		First Church erected in North Carolina.
"		First Newspaper published in the United States.
1710		Carey's Rebellion.
1729		Charter of Charles II, surrendered.
1765		Stamp Act passed.
1771	May 16,	Battle of Alamance.
1774	August 25,	Popular Assembly at Newbern.
1775	May 20	Mecklenburg Declaration of Independence.
"	June,	General Washington commander-in-chief.
"	June 17,	Battle of Bunker's Hill.
"	August,	Josiah Martin, Royal Governor, retreated.
"	December 9,	Battle of Great Bridge, near Norfolk, Va.
1776	February 27,	" of Moore's Creek, N. C.
"	August 27,	" of Long Island.
"	December 12,	Constitution of North Carolina formed at Halifax.
"	December 26,	Battle of Trenton.
"	Aug. & Sept.,	General Rutherford subdues the Cherokees.
1777	January 3,	Battle of Princeton.
"	September 11,	" of Brandywine.
"	October 4,	" of Germantown.
"	October 7,	" of Saratoga.
1778	June 28,	" of Monmouth
1779	March 3,	Ashe defeated at Brier Creek.
"	June 20,	Battle of Stono, near Charleston.
1780	May 12,	Surrender of Charleston.
"	June 20,	Battle of Ramsour's Mill.
"	August 7,	" of the Hanging Rock.
"	August 16,	Gates defeated at Camden.
"	October 7,	Battle of King's Mountain.
1781	January 17,	" of the Cowpens.
"	March 15,	" of Guilford Court House. —
"	September 8,	" of Eutaw.
"	October 19,	" of Yorktown.
1783	January 20,	Treaty of peace at Versailles.
"	September 3,	England recognizes the Independence of the United States.
1787	May.	Constitution of the United States formed.

INTRODUCTORY CHAPTER.

ORIGINAL SETTLEMENTS IN NORTH CAROLINA, AND CHARACTER OF THE PEOPLE.

North Carolina, in the days of her colonial existence, was the asylum and the refuge of the poor and the oppressed of all nations. In her borders the emigrant, the fugitive, and the exile found a home and safe retreat. Whatever may have been the impelling cause of their emigration—whether political servitude, religious persecution, or poverty of means, with the hope of improving their condition, the descendants of these enterprising, suffering, yet prospered people, have just reason to bless the kind Providence that guided their fathers, in their wanderings, to such a place of comparative rest.

On the sandy banks of North Carolina the flag of England was first displayed in the United States. Roanoke Island, between Pamlico and Albemarle Sounds, afforded the landing place to the first expedition sent out under the auspices of Sir Walter Raleigh, in 1584. "The fragrance, as they drew near the land, says Amadas in his report, was as if they had been in the midst of some delicate garden, abounding in all manner of odoriferous flowers." Such, no doubt, it seemed to them during the first summer of their residence in 1584; and, notwithstanding the disastrous termination of that, and several succeeding expeditions, the same maritime section of North Carolina has presented its peculiar features of attractiveness to many generations which have since arisen there, and passed away. In the same report, we have the first notice of the celebrated Scuppernong grape, yielding its most abundant crops under the saline atmospheric influence, and semi-tropical climate of eastern Carolina.

From the glowing description of the country, in its primitive abundance, transmitted to Elizabeth and her court, they gave it the name *Virginia*, being discovered in the reign of a *virgin Queen*. But having failed in this and several other attempts of a similar kind, Sir Walter Raleigh surrendered his patent, and nothing more was done in colonizing Virginia during the remainder of that century.

In 1607, the first permanent settlement was made by the English at Jamestown, Va., under the charter of the London or Southern Company. This charter contained none of the elements of popular liberty, not one elective franchise, nor one of the rights of self-government; but religion was especially enjoined to be established according to the rites and doctrine of the Church of England. The infant colony suffered greatly for several years from threatened famine, dissensions, and fear of the Indians, but through the energy and firmness of Capt John Smith, was enabled to maintain its ground, and in time, show evident signs of prosperity. The jealousy of arbitrary power, and impatience of liberty among the new settlers, induced Lord Delaware, Governor of Virginia in 1619, to reinstate them in the full possession of the rights of Englishmen; and he accordingly convoked a Provincial Assembly, the *first* ever held in America. The deliberations and laws of this infant Legislature were transmitted to England for approval, and so wise and judicious were these, that the company under whose auspicies they were acting, soon after confirmed and ratified the groundwork of what gradually ripened into the *American representative system*. The guarantee of political rights led to a rapid colonization. Men were now willing to regard Virginia as their home. "They fell to building houses and planting corn." Women were induced to leave the parent country to become the wives of adventurous planters; and during the space of three years thirty-five hundred persons of both sexes, found their way to Virginia. By various modifications of their charter, the colonists, in a few years, obtained nearly all the civil rights and privileges which they could claim as British subjects; but the church of England was "coeval with the settlement of Jamestown, and seems to have been considered from the beginning as the established religion." At what time settlements were first permanently made within the present limits of North Carolina, has not been clearly ascertained. In 1622, the Secretary of the colony of Virginia traveled overland to Chowan River, and described, in glowing terms, the fertility of the soil, the salubrity of the climate, and the kindness of the natives. In 1643, a company obtained permission of the Virginia Legislature to prosecute discoveries on the great river South of the Appomatox of which they had heard, under a monopoly of the profits for fourteen years, but with what measure of success has not been recorded. These early exploring parties to the South, bringing back favorable reports of the fertile lands of the Chowan and the Roanoke could not fail to excite in the colony of Jamestown a spirit of emigration, many of whose members were already suffering under the baneful effects of intolerant legislation. In 1643, during the administration of Sir William Berkeley, it was specially "ordered that no minister should preach or teach, publicly or privately, except in conformity to the constitutions of the church of England, and non-conformists were banished from the colony."* It is natural to suppose that individuals as well as families, who were fond of a roaming life, or who disliked the religious persecution to which they were subjected, would descend the banks of these streams until

---

* Bancroft, I., p. 270.

they found on the soil of Carolina suitable locations for peaceable settlements.

In 1653, Roger Green led a company across the wilderness from Nansemond, in Virginia, to the Chowan River, and settled near Edenton. There they prospered, and others, influenced by similar motives, soon afterward followed. In 1662, George Durant purchased of the Yeopim Indians the neck of land, on the North-side of Albemarle Sound, which still bears his name. It was settled by persons driven off from Virginia through religious persecutions. In 1663, King Charles II, granted to the Earl of Clarendon and seven other associates, the whole of the region from the thirty-sixth degree of north latitude to the river San Matheo, (now the St. John's) in Florida; and extending westwardly, like all of that monarch's charters, to the Pacific Ocean.

At the date of this charter, (1663,) Sir William Berkeley, Governor of Virginia, visited the infant settlement on the Chowan, and being pleased with its evident signs of prosperity, and increasing importance, appointed William Drummond the *first Governor* of the Colony of Carolina. Drummond was a Scotch Presbyterian, and, inheriting the national characteristics of that people, was prudent, cautious, and deeply impressed with the love of liberty. Such were the pioneer settlements, and such was the first Governor of North Carolina. The beautiful lake in the centre of the Dismal Swamp, noted for its healthy water, and abundantly laid in by sea-going vessels, perpetuates his name.

In 1665, it being discovered that the "County of Albemarle," as the settlement on the Chowan was called, was not in the limits of the Carolina charter, but in Virginia, King Charles, on petition, granted an enlargement of that instrument so as to make it extend from twenty-nine degrees to thirty-six degrees and thirty minutes, north latitude. These charters were liberal in the concession of civil rights, and the proprietors were permitted to exercise toleration towards non-conformists, if it should be deemed expedient. Great encouragement was held forth to immigrants from abroad, and settlements steadily increased. They were allowed to form a representative government, with certain limitations; and thus a degree of popular freedom was conceded, which it seems, was not intended to be permanent, but it could *never be recalled;* and had an important influence in producing the results which we now enjoy. As the people were chiefly refugees from religious oppression, they had no claims on government, nor did they wish to draw its attention. They regarded the Indians as the true lords of the soil; treated with them in that capacity; purchased their lands, and obtained their grants. At the death of Governor Drummond in 1667, the colony of Carolina contained about four thousand inhabitants.

The first assembly that made laws for Carolina convened in the Fall of 1669. "Here," says Bancroft, "was a colony of men scattered among forests, hermits with wives and children resting on the bosom of nature, in perfect harmony with the wilderness of their gentle clime. The planters of Albemarle were men led to the choice of their residence from a hatred of restraint. Are there any who doubt man's capacity for self-government? Let them study the history of North Carolina. Its inhabitants were restless and turbulent in their imperfect submission to a government imposed from abroad; the administration of the colony was firm, humane, and tranquil when they were left to take care of themselves. Any government but one of their own institution was oppressive. North Carolina was settled by the freest of the free. The settlers were gentle in their tempers, of serene minds, enemies to violence and bloodshed. Not all the successive revolutions had kindled vindictive passions; freedom, entire freedom was enjoyed without anxiety as without guarantees. The charities of life were scattered at their feet like the flowers of their meadows."* No freer country was ever organized by man. Freedom of conscience, exemption from taxation, except by their own consent; gratuities in land to every emigrant, and other wholesome regulations claimed the prompt legislative action of the infant colony." "These simple laws suited a simple people, who were as free as the air of their mountains; and when oppressed, were as rough as the billows of the ocean." †

In 1707, a company of Huguenots, as the French Protestants were called, settled on the Trent. In 1709, the Lords Proprietors granted to Baron de Graffenreidt ten thousand acres of land on the Neuse and Cape Fear rivers for colonizing purposes. In a short time afterward, a great number of Palatines (Germams) and fifteen hundred Swiss followed the Baron, and settled at the confluence of the Trent and the Neuse. The town was called New Berne, after Berne, in Switzerland, the birth-place of Graffenreidt. This was the first important introduction into Eastern Carolina of a most excellent class of liberty-loving people, whose descendants wherever their lots were cast, in our country, gave illustrious proof of their valor and patriotism during the Revolutionary war.

In 1729, the Lords Proprietors (except Lord Granville) surrendered the government of the province, with all the franchises under the charter of Charles II, and their property in the soil, to the crown for a valuable consideration. The population at that time did not exceed ten thousand inhabitants. George Burrington, Governor of the province under the Lords Proprietors, was re-appointed to the same office by the King. In February, 1731, he thus officially writes to the Duke of New Castle. "The inhabitants of North Carolina are not industrious, but

---

* Bancroft, Vol. II., p. 158. † Wheeler's Sketches, I., p. 30.

subtle and crafty to admiration ; always behaved insolently to their Governors; some of them they have imprisoned ; drove others out of the country ; and at other times have set up a governor of their own choice, supported by men under arms. These people are neither to be cajoled nor outwitted. Whenever any governor attempts to effect anything by these means, he will lose his labor, and show his ignorance." Lord Granvil'e's part of the colony of North Carolina (one-eighth) was not laid off to him, adjoining Virginia, until 1743. At that date, a strong tide of emigration was taking place from the Chowan and Roanoke, the pioneer attractive points of the colony, as well as from abroad, to the great interior, and Western territory, now becoming dotted with numerous habitations. The Tuscarora Indians, the terrible scourge of Eastern Carolina, having been subdued. and entered into a treaty of peace and friendship in 1718, no serious obstacle interposed to prevent a Western extension of settlements. Already adventurous individuals, and even families of hardy pioneers had extended their migrations to the Eastern base of the " Blue Ridge," and selected locations on the head-waters of the Yadkin and Catawba rivers. In 1734, Gabriel Johnston was appointed Governor of North Carolina. He was a Scotchman by birth, a man of letters and of liberal views. He was by profession a physician, and held the appointment of Professor of Oriental Languages in the University of Saint Andrews. His addresses to the Legislature show that he fully appreciated the lamentable condition of the colony through the imprudence and vicious conduct of his predecessor (Burrington) and his earnest desire to promote the welfare of the people. Under his prudent administration, the province increased in population, wealth and happiness. At the time of its purchase by the crown, its population did not exceed thirteen thousand ; it was now upwards of forty five thousand.

In 1754, Arthur Dobbs was appointed Governor by the crown. His administration of ten years presented a continued contest between himself and the Legislature on matters frivolous and unimportant. His high-toned temper for royal prerogatives was sternly met by the indomitable resistance of the colonists. The people were also much oppressed by Lord Granville's agents, one of whom (Corbin) was seized and brought to Enfield, where he was compelled to give bond and security, produce his books, and disgorge his illegal fees. But notwithstanding these internal commotions and unjust exactions, always met by the active resistance of the people, the colony continued to increase in power, and spread abroad its arms of *native inherent protection*. During the entire administrations of Governors Johnston and Dobbs, commencing in 1734 and ending in 1765, a strong tide of emigration was setting into North Carolina from two opposite directions. While one current from Pennsylvania passed down through Virginia, forming settlements in its course, another current met it from the South, and spread itself over the inviting lands and expansive domain of the Carolinas and Georgia. Near the close of Governor Johnston's administration (1750) numerous settlements had been made on the beautiful plateau of country between the Yadkin and Catawba rivers. At this time, the Cherokee Indians, the most powerful of the Western tribes, still claimed the territory, as rightful "lords of the soil," and were committing numerous depredations and occasional murders. In 1756, Fort Dobbs, about twenty miles West of Salisbury, was built for the protection of the small neighborhood of farmers and graziers around it. Even the thriving colony of "Albemarle County" on the seaboard now felt its growing importance, was beginning to call for "more room," and seek new possessions in the interior, thus unconsciously fulfilling the truth of the poet's prediction, "Westward the course of empire takes its way."

On the 3d of April, 1765, William Tryon qualified as Commander-in-chief, and Captain-General of the Province of North Carolina. The administration of Governor Tryon embraces an important period in the history of the State. He was a soldier by profession, and being trained to arms, looked upon the sword as the true scepter of government. "He knew when to flatter, and when to threaten. He knew when 'discretion was the better part of valor,' and when to use such force and cruelty as achieved for him from the Cherokee Indians, the bloody title of the 'Great Wolf of North Carolina.' He could use courtesy tawards the Assembly when he desired large appropriations for his magnificent palace; and knew how to bring to bear the blandishments of the female society of his family, and all the appliances of generous hospitality."* Governor Tryon first met the Assembly in the town of Wilmington on the 3d of May 1765. "In his address, he opposed all religious intolerance, and, although he recommended provision for the clergy out of the public treasury, yet he advised the members of the Church of England of the folly of attempting to establish it by legal enactment. Under such recommendations, a law was passed legalizing the marriages (which before were denounced as illegal) performed by Presbyterian ministers, and authorizing them and other dissenting clergymen to perform that rite."†

On the 22nd of March, 1765, the Stamp Act was passed. This act produced great excitement throughout the whole country, and no where was it more violently denounced than in North Carolina. The Legislature was then in session, and so intense and wide-spread was the opposition to this odious measure, that Governor Tryon, apprehending the passage of denunciatory resolutions, prorogued that body after a session of fifteen

---

* Wheeler's Sketches, I., p. 49. † Wheeler's Sketches, I., p. 50.

days. The speaker of the House, John Ashe, informed Governor Tryon that this law "would be resisted to blood and death.

Early in the year 1766, the sloop-of-war, Diligence, arrived in the Cape Fear River, having on board stamp paper for the use of the province. The first appearance and approach of the vessel had been closely watched, and when it anchored before the town of Brunswick, on the Cape Fear, Col. John Ashe, of the county of New Hanover, and Col. Hugh Waddell, of the county of Brunswick, marched at the head of the brave sons of these counties to Brunswick, and notified the captain of their determination to resist the landing of the stamps. They seized one of the boats of the sloop, hoisted it on a cart, fixed a mast in her, mounted a flag, and marched in triumph to Wilmington. The inhabitants all joined in the procession, and at night the town was illuminated. On the next day, Col. Ashe, at the head of a great concourse of people, proceeded to the Governor's house and demanded of him to desist from all attempts to execute the Stamp Act, and to produce to them James Houston, a member of the Council, who had been appointed Stamp Master for the Province. The Governor at first refused to comply with a demand so sternly made. But the haughty representative of kingly power had to yield before the power of an incensed people, who began to make preparations to set fire to his house. The Governor then reluctantly produced Houston, who was seized by the people, carried to the market-house, and there compelled to take a solemn oath never to perform the duties of his office. After this he was released and conducted by a delighted crowd, to the Governor's Palace. The people gave three cheers and quietly dispersed. Here we have recorded an act far more daring in its performance than that of the famous Tea Party of Boston, which has been celebrated by every writer of our national history, and
"Pealed and chimed on every tongue of fame."

It is an act of the sons of the "Old North State," not committed on the crew of a vessel, so disguised as to escape identity; but on royalty itself, occupying a palace, and in open day, by men of well known person and reputation.

Another event of great historic importance occurred during the administration of Governor Tryon. On the 16th of May, 1771, the battle of Alamance was fought. It is here deemed unnecessary to enter into a detail of the circumstances leading to this unfortunate conflict. Suffice it to say the Regulators, as they were called, suffered greatly by heavy exactions, by way of taxes, from the Governor to the lowest subordinate officer. They rose to arms—were beaten, but theirs was the *first blood shed* for freedom in the American colonies Many true patriots, who did not comprehend the magnitude of their grievances, fought against them. But the principles of right and justice for which they contended could never die. In less than four years, all the Colonies were found battling for the same principles, and borne along in the rushing tide of revolution! The men on the seaboard of Carolina, with Cols. Ashe and Waddell at their head, had nobly opposed the Stamp Act in 1765, and prevented its execution; and in their patriotic movements the people of Orange sustained them, and called them the "*Sons of Liberty.*" Col. Ashe, in 1766, had led the excited populace in Wilmington, against the wishes and even the hospitality of the governor. The assembled patriots had thrown the Governor's roasted ox, provided for a barbecue feast, untasted, into the river. Now, these patriotic leaders are found marching with this very Governor to subdue the *disciples of liberty* in the west. The eastern men looked for evils from across the waters, and were prepared to resist oppression on their shores before it should reach the soil of their State. The western men were seeking redress for grievances that oppressed them at home, under the misrule of the officers of the province, evils scarcely known in the eastern counties, and misunderstood when reported there. Had Ashe, and Waddell, and Caswell understood all the circumstances of the case. they would have acted like Thomas Person, of Granville. and favored the distressed, even though they might have felt under obligations to maintain the peace of the province. and due subordination to the laws. Herman Husbands, the head of the Regulators, has been denounced by a late writer, as a "turbulent and seditious character." If such he was, then John Ashe and Hugh Waddell, for opposing the stamp law, were equally turbulent and seditious. Time, that unerring test of principles and truth, has proved that the spirit of liberty which animated the Regulators, was the true spirit which subsequently led to our freedom from foreign oppression.

On the 24th of May, Tryon, after committing acts of revenge, cruelty and barbarity succeeding the Alamance battle, returned to his palace at Newbern, and on the 30th took shipping for New York, over which State he had been appointed Governor. Josiah Martin was appointed by the crown, Tryon's successor as Governor of North Carolina. He met the Legislature, for the first time, in the town of Newbern, in November, 1771. Had he lived in less troublesome times, his administration might have been peaceful and prosperous. Governor Martin had the misfortune to differ very soon with the lower House of the Assembly; and during the whole of his administration, these difficulties continued and grew in magnitude. helping, at last, to accelerate the downfall of the royal government. In this Assembly we find the names of a host of distinguished patriots, as John Ashe, Cornelius Harnett, "the Samuel Adams of North Carolina," Samuel Johnson,. Willie Jones, Joseph Hews, Abner Nash John Harvey, Thomas Person, Griffith Rutherford, Abraham Alexander, Thomas Polk, and many others.

showing that, at that early date, the Whig party had the complete control of the popular House of the Assembly. In accordance with the recommendation of Governor Martin, the veil of oblivion was drawn over the past unhappy troubles, and all the animosities and distinctions which they created. The year 1772 passed by without a meeting of the Assembly; and the only political event of any great importance, which occurred in the Province, was the election of members to the popular House. Such was the triumph of the Whig party, that in many of the counties there was no opposition to the election of the old leaders, nor could the Governor be said to have a party sufficiently powerful to effect an election before the people, or the passage of a bill before the Assembly. The Assembly, however, in consequence of two dissolutions by the Governor, did not convene in Newbern until the 25th of January, 1773, and the popular House illustrated its political character by the election of John Harvey to the office of Speaker. To this new Assembly many of the leading members of the House in 1771, were returned. Thomas Polk and Abraham Alexander were not members; the former having been employed in the service of the Governor, as surveyor, in running the dividing line between North and South Carolina, and the latter not having solicited the suffrages of the people. The county of Mecklenburg was, in the Assembly, represented by Martin Pheifer and John Davidson.

The Speaker of the House of Commons, John Harvey, laid before that body resolutions of the House of Burgess of Virginia (1773) of the 12th of March last; also, letters from the Speakers of the lower houses of several other provinces, requesting that a committee be appointed to inquire into the encroachments of England upon the rights and liberties of America. The House passed a resolution that "such example was worthy of imitation, by which means communication and concert would be established among the colonies; and that they will at all times be ready to exert their efforts to preserve and defend their rights." John Harvey, (Speaker) Robert Howe, Cornelius Harnet, William Hooper, Richard Caswell, Edward Vail, John Ashe, Joseph Hewes and Samuel Johnston were this committee. This is the first record of a legislative character which led to the Revolution.

During the summer of 1774 the people in all parts of the province manifested their approbation of the proposed plan of calling a Congress or Assembly, to consult upon common grievances; and in nearly all the counties and principal towns meetings were held, and delegates appointed to meet in the town of Newbern on the 25th of August, 1774.

On the 13th of August, Governor Martin issued a proclamation complaining that meetings of the people had been held without legal authority, and that resolutions had been passed derogatory to the authority of the King and Parliament. He advised the people to forbear attending any such meetings, and ordered the King's officers to oppose them to the utmost of their power. But the delegates of the people attended on the day appointed without any obstruction from the "king's officers." The proclamation of Governor Martin availed nothing. (*Vox et praetera nil.*) Excited at this state of affairs, Governor Martin consulted his council on the steps most proper to be taken in the emergency. They advised him that "nothing further could be done." This first Assembly, or Provincial Congress, independent of royal authority, in Newbern, on the 25th of August, 1774, is an important epoch in our history. It was the first act of that great drama of revolutionizing events which finally achieved our independence.

After the adjournment of this Provincial Congress, Governor Martin visited New York, ostensibly for the "benefit of his health," and, perhaps, for the benefit of his government. The tumults of the people at Newbern, that raged around him, and which threatened to overthrow his power, were, by his own confession, "beyond his control"; but he hoped the influence of Governor Tyron, who still governed New York, might assist him in restoring peace and authority in North Carolina. Vain, delusive hope, as the sequel proved!

The year 1775 is full of important events, only a few of which can be adverted to in this brief sketch. In February, 1775, John Harvey issued a notice to the people to elect delegates to represent them in a second Provincial Congress at Newbern on the 3rd of April, being the same time and place of the meeting of the Colonial Assembly. This roused the indignation of Governor Martin, and caused him to issue, on the 1st of March, 1775, his proclamation denouncing the popular Convention.

In his speech to the Assembly, Governor Martin expressed "his concern at this extraordinary state of affairs. He reminded the members of their oath of allegiance, and denounced the meeting of delegates chosen by the people, as illegal, and one that he should resist by every means in his power." In the dignified reply of the House, the Governor was informed that the right of the people to assemble, and petition the throne for a redress of their grievances was undoubted, and that this right included that of appointing delegatss for such purpose. The House passed resolutions approving of the proceedings of the Continental Congress at Philadelphia (4th of Sept. 1774) and declared their determination to use their influence in carrying out the views of that body. Whereupon, the Governor, by advice of his council, dissolved the Assembly, by proclamation, after a session of four days.

Thus ceased forever all legislative action and intercourse under the Royal government. Indeed, from the organization of the first Provincial Congress or Convention, in Newbern (Aug. 25th, 1774) composed of delegates "fresh from the people" the pioneers in our glorious revolution, until Governor Martin's expulsion, North Carolina was enjoying and exercising an almost unlimited control of *separate governmental independence.* After the dissolution of the Assembly on the 8th of April, 1775, Governor Martin lingered only a few days, first taking refuge in Fort Jonston, and afterwards, on board of the ship of war, the Cruiser, anchored in the Cape Fear River. Only one more frothy proclamation (8th of Aug., 1775,) appeared from Governor Martin, against the patriotic leaders of North Carolina, issued this time, not from "the palace," at Newbern, but from a *cruising* source and out-look, and on a river, whose very name typified the real origin of his departure, and present retirement.

These glimpses of the colonial history of North Carolina, necessary to a proper understanding of the following sketches, will serve to illustrate, in a limited degree, the character of her people, and their unyielding opposition to all unjust exactions, and encroachment of arbitrary power. While these sterring transactions were transpiring in eastern Carolina, the people of Mecklenburg county moved, in their sovereign capacity, the question of independence, and took a much bolder, and more decided stand than the Colonial or Continental Congress had as yet assumed. This early action of that patriotic county, effected after mature deliberation, is one of the ever-memorable transactions of the State of North Carolina, worthy of being cherished and honored by every lover of patriotism to the end of time. The public mind had been much excited at the attempts of Governor Martin to prevent the meeting of the Provincial Congress at Newbern, and his arbitrary conduct in dissolving the Assembly, when only in session four days, leaving them unprotected by courts of law, and without the present opportunity of finishing many important matters of legislation. In this state of affairs, the people began to think that, since the proper, lawful authorities failed to perform their legitimate duty, it was time to provide safe-guards for themselves, and to throw off all allegiance to powers that cease to protect their liberties, or their property.

A late author has truly said, "Men will not be fully able to understand North Carolina until they have opened the treasures of history, and become familiar with the doings of her sons, previous to the revolution; during that painful struggle; and the succeeding years of prosperity. Then will North Carolina be respected as she is known."*

---

* Foote's Sketches of North Carolina, p. 83.

SKETCHES
OF
Western North Carolina.

CHAPTER I.

MECKLENBURG COUNTY.

Mecklenburg county was formed in 1762 from Anson county, and named in honor of the native place of the new Queen, Princess Charlotte, of Mecklenburg, one of the smaller German States.

This county has a peculiar historical interest. It is the birth-place of liberty on American soil. No portion of the State presents a more glowing page of unflinching patriotic valor than Mecklenburg, always taking an active part in every political movement, at home or abroad, leading to independence.

The temper and character of the people were early shown. In 1766, George A. Selwyn, having obtained, by some means, large grants of lands from the British Crown, proceeded to have them surveyed, through his agent, Henry E. McCullock, and located. On some of these grants, the first settlers had made considerable improvements by their own stalwart arms, and persevering industry. For this reason, and not putting much faith in the validity of Selwyn's claims, they seized John Frohock, the surveyor, and compelled him to desist from his work, or *fare worse*. Here was manifested the early *buzzing* of the "Hornets' Nest," which, in less than ten years, was destined to *sting* royalty itself in these American colonies.

The little village of Charlotte, the seat of justice for Mecklenburg county, was in 1775, the theater of one of the most memorable events in the political annals of the United States. Situated on the beautiful and fertile champaign, between the Yadkin and Catawba Rivers, and on the general route of the Southern travel, and among the earliest settlements in the Carolinas and Georgia, it soon became the centre of an enterprising and prosperous population. The fertility of the soil, the healthfulness of the climate, and abundance of cheap and unappropriated lands, were powerful inducements in drawing a large influx of emigrants from the Northern colonies, and from the Old World. These natural features of middle and western Carolina, in particular, were strongly attractive, and pointed out, under well-directed energy, the sure road to prospective wealth and prosperity.

The face of the country was then overspread with wild "pea vines," and luxuriant herbage; the water courses bristled with cane brakes; and the forest abounded with a rich variety and abundance of food-producing game. The original conveyance for the tract of land, upon which the city of Charlotte now stands, contained 360 acres, and was made on the 15th day of January, 1767, by Henry E. McCullock, agent for George A. Selwyn, to "Abraham Alexander, Thomas Polk, and John Frohock, as Trustees and Directors, of the town of Charlotte, and their successors." The consideration was "ninety pounds, lawful money." The conveyance was witnessed by Matthew McLure and Joseph Sample.

A few words of explanation, as to one of the Trustees, may be here appropriate. The Frohock family resided in Rowan county, and, before the revolution, exerted a considerable influence, holding places of profit and trust. William Frohock was Captain of a military company, and at one time, (1771) Deputy Sheriff under General Rutherford. Thomas Frohock was Clerk of the Superior Court, in Rowan, and Senator to the State Legislature from the town of Salisbury, in 1785 and 1786 John Frohock, named in the conveyance, was, for several years, Clerk of the County Court, an active Surveyor, and resided, during much of his time in Mecklenburg. employed in the duties of his profession.

Soon after the town of Charlotte was laid out, a log building was erected at the intersection of Trade and Tryon streets, and in the centre of the space now known as "Independence Square." This building was placed upon substantial brick pillars, ten or twelve feet high, with a stairway on the outside, leading to the court room. The lower part, in conformity with primitive economy and convenience, was used as a Market House; and the upper part as a Court House, and frequently for church, and other public meetings. Although the original building has long since passed away, yet it has historic associations connected with its colonial and revolutionary existence, which can never cease to command the admiration of every true patriot.

In May, 1775, its walls resounded with the *tones of earnest debate and i d p ndence*, proclaimed from the court house steps. In September, 1780, its walls resounded with the *tones of the market*, by the same people, who "knew their rights, and knowing, dared maintain."

At this period, there was no printing press in the upper country of Carolina, and as no regular post traversed this region, a newspaper was seldom seen among the people. Important information was transmitted from one colony to another by express messengers on horse-back, as was done by Captain Jack in bearing the Mecklenburg Declaration to Philadelphia. The people were accustomed to assemble at stated places to listen to the reading of printed hand-bills from abroad, or to obtain verbal intelligence of passing events.

Charlotte early became the central point in Mecklenburg county for these assemblages, and there the leading men often met at Queen's Museum or College, to discuss the exciting topics of the day. These meetings were at first irregular, and without system. It was finally agreed that Thomas Polk, Colonel of the militia, long a surveyor in the province, frequently a member of the Colonial Assembly, and a man of great excellence of character should be authorized to call a convention of the Representatives of the people whenever circumstances seemed to require it. It was also agreed that such Representatives should consist of two delegates from each Captain's Company, chosen by the people of the several militia districts, and that their decisions, when thus legally convened, should be binding upon the whole county.

When it became known that Governor Martin had attempted, by his proclamation, issued on the 1st of March, 1775, to prevent the Assembling of a Provincial Congress at Newbern, on the 3d of April following; and when it was recollected that, by his arbitrary authority, he had dissolved the last Provincial Assembly, after a session of only four days, and before any important business had been transacted, the public excitement became intense. and the people were clamorous for some decisive action, and a redress of their grievances. A large majority of the people were willing to incur the dangers incident to revolution, for the sake of themselves, their posterity, and the sacred cause of liberty.

In this State of the public mind, Col. Polk issued his notice to the committee-men, two from each Captain's district, as previously agreed upon, to assemble in Charlotte on the 19th of May, 1775, to consult for the common good, and inaugurate such measures as would conduce to that desirable end. The notice of the appointed meeting spread rapidly through the county, and all classes of citizens, intuitively, as it were, partook of the general enthusiasm, and felt the importance of the approaching convention. On the appointed day, an immense concourse of people, consisting of gray-haired sires. and vigorous youths from all parts of the county, assembled in the town of Charlotte, then containing about twenty-five houses, all anxious to know the result of that ever-memorable occasion. After assembling in the court house, Abraham Alexander, a venerable citizen and magistrate of the county, and former member of the Legislature, was made chairman; and John McKnitt Alexander, assisted by Dr. Ephraim Brevard, Secretaries, all men of business habits, and of great popularity. A full, free and animated discussion upon the exciting topics of the day then ensued, in which Dr. Ephraim Brevard, a finished scholar; Col. William Kennon, an eminent lawyer of Salisbury, and Rev. Hezekiah J. Balch, a distinguished Presbyterian preacher, were the chief speakers. During the session of the convention, an express messenger arrived, bearing the news of the wanton and cruel shedding of blood at Lexington on the 19th of April, just one month preceeding. This intelligence served to increase the general patrotic ardor, and the assembly, as with one voice, cried out, "Let us be independent. Let us declare our independence, and defend it with our lives and fortunes." The speakers said, his Majesty's proclamation had declared them out of the protection of the British Crown, and they ought, therefore, to declare themselves out of his protection, and be independent of his government. A committee consisting of Dr. Brevard, Col. Kennon, and the Rev. Mr. Balch, was then appointed to prepare resolutions suitable to the occasion. The excitement of the people continued to increase, and the deliberations of the convention, including the framing of by-laws, and regulations by which it should be governed, as a standing committee, were not completed until after midnight. showing the great interest which every one felt, and that a solemn crisis had arrived which demanded firm and united action for the common defence. Upon the return of the committee, the chairman proceeded to submit the resolutions of independence to the vote of the convention. All was silence and stillness around (*intentique ora tenebant*)

The question was then put, "Are you all agreed." The response was one universal "aye," not one dissenting voice in that immense assemblage. It was then agreed that the proceedings should be read to the whole multitude. Accordingly at noon, on the 20th of May, 1775, Colonel Thomas Polk ascended the steps of the old court house, and read, in clear and distinct tones, the following patriotic resolutions, constituting,

THE MECKLENBURG DECLARATION OF INDEPENDENCE.

"*Resolved*, 1. That whoever directly or indirectly abetted, or in any way, form or manner, countenanced the unchartered and dangerous invasion of our rights, as claimed by Great Britain, is an enemy to this country, to America, and to the inherent, and inalienable rights of man.

Resolved, 2. That we, the citizens of Mecklenburg county, do hereby dissolve the political bands which have connected us to the mother country, and hereby absolve ourselves from all allegiance to the British Crown and abjure all political connection, contract, or association with that nation, who have wantonly trampled on our rights and liberties, and inhumanly shed the blood of American patriots at Lexington.

Resolved, 3. That we do hereby declare ourselves a free and independent people; are, and of right ought to be a sovereign, and self-governing association, under the control of no power, other than that of our God, and the general government of the congress; to the maintenance of which independence, we solemnly pledge to each other our mutual co-operation, our lives, our fortunes, and our most sacred honor.

Resolved, 4. That, as we acknowledge the existence and control of no law, or legal officer, civil or military, within this county, we do hereby ordain and adopt, as a rule of life, all, each, and every one of our former laws; wherein, nevertheless, the crown of Great Britain never can be considered as holding rights, privileges, immunities, or authority therein..

Resolved, 5. That it is also further decreed that all, each, and every military officer in this county is hereby retained in his former command and authority, he acting conformably to these regulations. And that every member present of this delegation shall henceforth be a civil officer, viz: a justice of the peace, in the character of a committeeman, to issue process, hear and determine all matters of controversy, according to said adopted laws; and to preserve peace, union and harmony in said county; and to use every exertion to spread the love of country, and fire of freedom throughout America, until a more general and organized government be established in this province."

After the reading of these resolutions, a voice from the crowd called out for "three cheers," and soon the welkin rang with corresponding shouts of applause. The resolutions were read again and again during the day to different parties, desirous of retaining in their memories sentiments of patriotism so congenial to their feelings.

A copy of the proceedings of the convention was then drawn off, and sent by express to the members of congress from North Carolina, at that time in session at Philadelphia. Captain James Jack, a worthy and intelligent citizen of Charlotte, was chosen as the bearer; and in a few days afterward, set out on *horse-back* in the performance of his patriotic mission. Of his journeyings, and *perilous adventures* through a country, much of it infested with Tories, we know but little. Having faithfully performed the duties of his important trust, by delivering the resolutions into the hands of the North Carolina Delegation at Philadelphia (Caswell, Hooper and Hews,) he returned to his home in Charlotte. He reported that our own Delegation, and several members of Congress, manifested their entire approbation of the earnest zeal and patriotism of the Mecklenburg citizens, but deemed it premature to lay their resolutions before their body, as they still entertained some hopes of reconciliation with the mother country.

A copy of the foregoing resolutions were also transmitted to the Provincial Congress, at Hillsboro, and laid before that body on the 25th of August, 1775, but for the same prudential reasons as just stated, they declined taking any immediate action.

It has been deemed proper to present this summarized statement of the circumstances leading to the Mecklenburg Convention of the 19th and 20th of May, 1775, as a source of reference for those who have no other history of the transaction before them. For a more extended account of its proceedings, the reader is referred to the pamphlet published by State authority in 1831, and to the exhaustive treatise of the late Ex-Governor Graham on the authenticity of the Meclenburg resolutions, with notices of the principal actors and witnesses on that ever-memorable occasion.

Since the publication of Governor Graham's pamphlet shortly before the Centennial Celebration in Charlotte another copy of the Mecklenburg resolutions of the 20th of May, 1775, has been found in the possession of a grandson of Adam Brevard, now residing in Indiana. This copy has all the outward appearances of age, has been sacredly kept in the family, and is in a good state of preservation. Adam Brevard was a younger brother of Dr. Ephraim Brevard, the reputed author of these resolutions, frequently performed his brother's writing during the active discharge of his professional duties, and was himself, a man of cultivated intellect, and christian integrity. He kept a copy of these patriotic resolutions, mainly with the view of preserving a memento of his brother's hand writing, and vigor of composition— not supposing for a moment, their authenticity would ever be called into question. This venerable patriot, in a manuscript account of a celebration in Iredell county on the 4th of July, 1824, in discoursing on a variety of revolutionary matters, says among other things, he was in Salisbury in June 1775, attending to his professional duties as a lawyer, and that during the sessions of the General Court in that place, the bearer of the Mecklenburg Declaration arrived on his way to Philadelphia. When the object of his mission became known, and the Mecklenburg resolutions of independence were read in open court, at the request of Col. Kennon, several Tories who were present said they were treasonable, and that the framers of them were "rushing headlong into an abyss where Congress had not dared to pass. Their intemperance, however, was suddenly arrested by a gentleman from the same county, who had entered with all his powers into the impending contest and offered to rest the propriety and justness of the proceedings, both of Mecklenburg and the Delegate, upon a decission by the *arm of flesh* with any one inclinable to abide the result. Matters, which threatened a conflict of arms were soon hushed up by this direct argument *ad hominem*, the Delegate retired to rest for the night, and, on the next morning, resumed his journey to Philadelphia."

He also states, in the same manuscript, that in the autumn of the year 1776, he was one of the number who composed the College of Queen's Museum, and lived with his brother, Dr. Ephraim Brevard, and that in ransacking a number of his brother's papers thrown aside as useless, he came across the fragments of a Declaration of Independence by the people of Mecklenburg. Upon inquiry, his brother informed him they were the rudiments out of which a short time before, he had framed the instrument despatched to Congress. The same authority states that he was in Philadelphia in the latter part of the year 1778, and until May of the year 1779. During that time, William Sharp, Esq., of Rowan county, arrived in Philadelphia, as a Delegate to Congress from North Carolina. Amidst a variety of topics introduced for discussion was that of the Mecklenburg Declaration of Independence. Hon. John Penn, of North Carolina, said in presence of several members of Congress, that he was "highly pleased with the bold and distinguished spirit with which so enlightened a county of the State he had the honor to represent had *exhibited to the world;* and, furthermore, that the bearer of the instrument to Congress had conducted himself very judiciously on the occasion by previously opening his business to the Delegates of his own State, who assured him that the other States would soon act in the same patriotic manner as Mecklenburg had done.

This important and additional testimony, here slightly condensed, but facts not changed, is extracted from a communication in the *Southern Home,* by Dr. J. M. Davidson, of Florida, a gentleman of great moral worth and christian integrity, and grandson of Adam Brevard, a brother of Dr. Ephraim Brevard, the reputed author of the Mecklenburg Declaration of Independence.

A brief extract from Governor Martin's dispatch to the British Secretary of State, dated 30th of June, 1775, as found in Wheeler's "Historical Sketches," will now be given, which cannot be viewed in any other light than that of disinterested evidence. The Governor proceeds by saying, "the situation in which I find myself at present is indeed, my Lord, most despicable and mortifying. * * * * I live, alas! ingloriously, only to deplore it. * .* The resolves of the Committee of Mecklenburg, which your Lordship will find in the enclosed newspaper, surpass all the horrid and treasonable publications that the inflamatory spirits of the continent have yet produced; and your Lordship may depend, its authors and abettors will not escape, when my hands are sufficiently strengthened to attempt the recovery of the lost authority of the Government. A copy of these resolves was sent off, I am informed, by express, to the Congress at Philadelphia, as soon as they were passed in the committee."

The reader will mark, in particular, the closing sentence of this extract, as confirmatory of what actually took place on the 20th of May, 1775. Captain James Jack, then of Charlotte, a worthy and patriotic citizen, did set out a few days after the Convention adjourned, on *horse back*, as the "express" to Congress at Philadelphia, and faithfully executed the object of his mission. (For further particulars, see sketch of the Jack Family.)

The resolutions passed by the county committtee of safety on the 31st of May following, and which some have erroneously confounded with those of the 20th of May, were a necessary consequence. embracing simply "rules and regulations" for the internal government of the county, and hence needed no "express" to Congress.

The preceding testimony, conjoined with that of Gen Joseph Graham, Rev. Humphrey Hunter, Captain James Jack, the bearer of the Mecklenburg Declaration to Congress, Rev. Francis Cummins, Mayor John Davidson, Isaac Alexander and others, previously referred to in the State pamphlet of 1831, and the exhaustive "Memoir" of the late Ex-Governor Graham—all men of exalted worth and christian integrity, ought to be "sufficient to satisfy incredulity itself," as to the genuineness of the Mecklenburg Declaration of Independence, and of its promulgation to the world on the 20th of May, 1775. And yet, in the face of this strong phalanx of unimpeachable testimony, there are a few who have attempted to rob North Carolina of this brightest gem in the crown of her early political history, and tarnish, by base and insidious cavilsthe fair name and reputation of a band of Revolutionary patriots, whose memories and heroic deeds the present generation and posterity will ever delight to honor.

Mecklenburg sent as a Delegate to the first Provincial

Congress direct from the people, which met at Newbern on the 25th of August, 1774, Benjamin Patton.

To the meeting at Hillsboro', on the 21st of August, 1775, Thomas Polk, John Phifer, Waightstill Avery, John McKnitt Alexander, James Houston, and Samuel Martin.

To the meeting at Halifax on the 4th of April, 1776, John Phifer, Robert Irwin and John McKnitt Alaxander.

To the meeting at Halifax, on the 12th of November, 1776 (which formed the first State Constitution) John Phifer, Robert Irwin, Waightstill Avery, Hezekiah Alexander and Zaccheus Wilson.

All of these Delegates were unwavering patriots, and nearly all were signers of the Mecklenburg Declaration of Independence. Not only were the patriotic sons of Mecklenburg county active and vigilant in those trying times, but no portion of our State was more constantly the theater of stirring events during the drama of the American Revolution. "Its inhabitants," says Tarleton in his campaigns, "were more hostile to England than any others in America."

A BRIEF ACCOUNT OF THE MECKLENBURG CENTENNIAL.

The Mecklenburg Declaration of Independence, proclaimed to the world on the 20th of May, 1775, was celebrated in Charlotte on the 20th of May, 1875, with all the honors and ceremonies befitting such an important occasion. A vast assemblage of at least 25,000 persons were present to enjoy the "welcome" extended to all, and participate in the festivities of this gala day of North Carolina. For three days preceding the grand holiday, (17th, 18th and 19th) visitors were continually pouring into the city. Enthusiastic excitement and necessary preparations were everywhere visible. Flags and streamers greeted the eye in every direction. Many private residences were handsomely decorated. One of the most exalted ideas was a Centennial pole, 115 feet high, erected by Capt. Thos. Allen, in the centre of Independence Square, from the top of which floated to the breeze a large flag, capped with a huge *hornet's nest* from Stokes county. To preserve the *Centennial* feature as far as possible of the Convention of the 19th of May, 1775, called out by Col. Thos. Polk, accordingly, on the 19th of May, 1875, a procession was formed, and the military companies formed into a hollow sqare around the Cencennial pole, the bands, in the meantime, rendering sweet music, and the artillery firing minute guns. The Mayor, Col. William Johnston, then addressed the multitude, extending to them a cordial welcome in behalf of the citizens and authorities of Charlotte; after which Governor Brogden was introduced, and spoke substantially as follows: He said the principles of liberty enunciated by the fathers of the revolution, one hundred years ago, upon the spot he then occupied would live throughout all time. Here, as free

American citizens, they had proclaimed the principles which North Carolina had ever since upheld, and of which this glorious flag, which waves protection to American citizens on land and sea was the star-gemmed type. Under this old flag we have a duty to perform in peace as well as in war. We have the principles of the fathers of the Mecklenburg Declaration to maintain. All should remember the sacrifices which gave us the right to that standard of our country; and we should not forget our duty to North Carolina, and her daughter, Tennessee, to the sister State of South Carolina, and to the whole country. Alluding to the growth of the United States in one hundred years, the Governor said that at the date of the Mecklenburg declaration of Independence, there were not more than six post-offices in North Carolina; now there are nine hundred post-offices; then here was no steam traveling; now there are twelve hundred miles of rail-way in this State alone. He hoped the country would go on to prosper in the fulness of civil liberty until there was no opposition to the principles we cherish. In the name of North Carolina he welcomed all her sons to this festival, and the sons of all other sister States.

May 20th, 1875—Centennial morning! Of the large number of illustrious patriots who participated in the exercises of the Mecklenburg Convention of the same date, 1775, not one was present to animate us with their counsel, or speak of the glorious deeds of the Revolutionary period—all having succumbed to the irrevocable fiat of nature, and passed to "that bourne whence no traveler returns." Their example, their precepts, and sacrifices in the cause of freedom, constitute their rich and instructive heritage to us. A cloudless sky, a balmy atmosphere, and a glow of patriotic feeling beaming on every countenance, all conspired to add impressiveness to the scene, and awaken hallowed remembrances of the past. Agreeably to the published programme, the day was ushered in by the ringing of bells, and a salute of one hundred guns by the Raleigh and Richmond artillery. From six o'clock in the morning until several hours afterward, the whistles of locomotives every few minutes told of the arrival of trains, packed with visitors, firemen, military and bands of music. The various committees were kept busy in directing the movements and assigning quarters for the organized bodies; while landlords and keepers of boarding-houses showed an accommodating spirit, and received visitors until their utmost capacity for room was more than exhausted—full to overflowing. And, although some difficulty was observed in procuring bed room, yet an abundance of provisions was everywhere exhibited for the comfort and well-being of the "inner man."

THE GRAND PROCESSION.

General Joseph E. Johnston, Chief Marshal, having been prevented from attending on account of severe sickness, General W. R. Cox, of Raleigh, was selected to fill his place. General Bradley T. Johnston, of Richmond, was placed in charge of the Military Department, and John C. Gorman of the Fire Department. The soldiers were nearly all dressed in gray suits, and the firemen in red and black, except the Wilmington company, which also appeared in gray. While the Chief Marshal and his assistants were endeavoring to bring order out of the immense mass of humanity in the streets, six splendid bands from Richmond, Newbern, Raleigh, Wilmington, Fayetteville and Salem, besides the Cadet band of the Carolina Military Institute, were exerting their sonorous energies to move the listening million by "concord of sweet sounds," and thereby prevent them from ever becoming subjects "fit for treason, stratagems and spoils."

At half-past ten o'clock the grand pageant was fully displayed. As far as the eye could reach the brilliant procession filled the streets, presenting a glittering, undulating line of infantry, artillery, firemen, laddermen, axemen, zouaves, cadets, grangers, masons, templars, highlanders, citizens, &c., with gleaming arms, rustling flags, soul-stirring music, and other manifestations of patriotic enthusiasm. Nearly every window, piazza and house-top was crowded with feminine loveliness, to cheer with their smiles and lend their graceful approbation to the moving exhibitions of the occasion. On the side-walks " miles of spectators" were seen submitting to the stifling effects of clouds of dust, with the laudable desire " to see and be seen." While immense flags were floating to the breeze across the principal streets, countless numbers of miniature ones, in red, white and blue, fluttered from windows and porches. A large number of military and fire companies followed by delegations of the Masonic Order, Good Templars, Odd Fellows, Caledonian Clubs, Grangers, invited guests, visitors, &c., all joined in the grand procession to the fair grounds.

EXERCISES AT THE FAIR GROUNDS.

Arriving at the Fair Grounds, the immense concourse of people gathered around the large stand, which had been erected amidst a clump of trees, for the ladies and invited guests. The stand was beautifully decorated with evergreens, festoons, flags, hornets' nests, and other emblematic devices. The ladies of the city had been diligently weaving these evergreen and floral adornments for several days preceding the Centennial. A precious bouquet and wreath, sent by Mrs. L. H. Walker, from the grounds of Washington's tomb at Mt. Vernon, added a venerated sanctity to the whole.

At 11 o'clock, Rev. Dr. A. W. Miller, of the First Presbyterian Church, opened the exercises with an eloquent prayer. The "Old North State" was then rendered in stirring tones by the Citizens' Band.

Ex-Gov. Graham then called the assembly to order, and

said there was cause to congratulate the vast assemblage of patriotic citizens convened on this centennial occasion, for the bright, auspicious weather that prevailed, and for the general health and prosperity of the country. He felt highly gratified with the patriotic demonstration, and rejoiced to see in our midst so many prominent citizens from sister States. The Governor of North Carolina, and several of the Judges of her Courts were present. The Governor of the far-off State of Indiana, (Mr. Hendricks,) was here, representing one of the great Western States which sprung from old Virginia. There was a representative present (Mr. Bright) from Tennessee, the daughter of North Carolina. The Governor (Mr. Chamberlain) of South Carolina; the ex-Governor (Mr. Walker) of Virginia, and a large delegation from both of these States were all present to participate in the centennial festivities. In the name of North Carolina, he bade all a hearty welcome.

After the conclusion of ex-Gov. Graham's remarks, Maj. Seaton Gales, of Raleigh, was introduced to the audience, who, previous to the reading of the Mecklenburg Resolves, delivered a short address expressing his entire confidence in their authenticity.

The orator of the day, Judge John Kerr, of the fifth Judicial District, was then introduced amidst loud applause. He spoke for half an hour in stirring, eloquent language, worthy of his high reputation as an impressive speaker.

Hon. John M. Bright, of Tennessee, was next introduced. He delivered an address of great power, abounding with many interesting historical facts relating to the early history of North Carolina, and the character of her people. As these speeches will be published, it is deemed unnecessary to present a synopsis of their contents.

The speeches being concluded, the invited guests, firemen, military, &c., marched into Floral Hall, and were entertained with toasts, short addresses and music, while the cravings of hunger were rapidly dispelled by the sumptuous food, and rich viands set before them.

On Thursday night, a stand having been erected around the Centennial Pole in Independence Square, a number of short and stirring addresses were made by ex-Gov. Hendricks, of Indiana ; ex-Gov. Walker, of Virginia ; Gov. Chamberlain, of South Carolina ; Gov. Brogden, of North Carolina ; ex-Gov. Vance, Gen. W. R. Cox, Gen. T. L. Clingman, Judge Davidson and Col. H. M. Polk, the latter two of Tennessee.

Gov. Hendricks, at the commencement of his address, spoke substantially as follows : "This is one of the greatest celebrations that has ever taken place in this country. Here your fathers, and mine, one hundred years ago, declared themselves free of the British crown. I need not refer to the events since. In intelligence, wealth and power, we are ahead of the world. Right here I must tell you that the fame of the Mecklenburg Declaration belongs not to the people of Mecklenburg alone, nor to the State of North Carolina, but its fame belongs to Indiana as well—in fact, to all the States of the Union. I claim a common participation in the glory of this great event. They were not only patriots, these Mecklenburgers of 1775, but they were also wise statesmen. One has but to carefully read this Declaration to discern the truth of this statement. The resolutions looked to a delegation of powers in the Continental Congress for their protection against enemies abroad, and all general purposes of nationality, but they assert most unequivocally the right of local self-government, and all the reserved powers not plainly granted to the general government. These old patriots showed their wisdom by providing against an interim of anarchy for want of lawful officers to protect life and property ; so they resolved that each military and civil officer under the Provincial government should retain all their authority. I ask the people of North Carolina to join with us in the National celebration, to take place in Philadelphia in 1876. Shall I see North Carolina represented there? (Cries of yes! yes!) What a lesson it will be to the whole country! The troubles of the war can be yet settled by a system of good government." Other speakers indulged in similiar patriotic sentiments.

After the speaking was over on Centennial night, the Mayor (Colonel Johnston) ascended the stand, and congratulated the large audience upon the excellent order and good feeling which had prevailed from the beginning to the end of the exercises. He thanked those present for their attendance and participation in the honors and festivities of the occasion.

Then commenced the pyrotechnical display which had been witnessed to some extent during the intervals of the addresses. The "rocket's red glare," without the "bumbs bursting in air," gave proof *on that night* our people were there. The streets, and the houses in the vicinity were never before so handsomely illuminated, and a brilliant and appropriate closing scene of "the day we celebrate" conspicuously displayed on a broad waving banner. Hundreds of the descendants of the patriots of Mecklenburg, and surrounding country, were present, as well as a goodly number of descendants of kindred spirits from the Cape Fear region, whose ancestors proved themselves "rebels" by *stamping under foot the stamp paper* intended for the use of the Colony—an act "worthy of all Roman, or Grecian fame." The celebration of the 20th of May, 1875, was a grand success—such a celebration as has never before occurred in the history of North Carolina, and will never again be witnessed by the present generation. May the Centennial of the 20th of May, 1975, be still more successful, pass off with the same degree of order and good feeling, and be attended with all the blessings of enlightened civil and religious liberty!

JAMES BELK—A VETERAN INVITED GUEST.

Among the honored invited guests of the Mecklenburg Centennial, on the 20th of May, 1775, was James Belk, of Union county (formerly a part of Mecklenburg), now upwards of one hundred and ten years old! As recorded in a family Bible, printed in Edinburg in 1720, he was born on the 4th of February, 1765. He still resides on the same tract of land upon which he was born and raised, his father being one of the original settlers of the country. He is a man of fine intelligence; acted for many years as one of the magistrates of Mecklenburg county, and is still well preserved in mind and body. He recollects the death of his father, who was mortally wounded in the Revolutionary war, near the North Carolina line, and knows that his mother, fearing the mournful result, visited the place of conflict, and found him, severely wounded, in the woods near the road-side. She assisted him to their home, but soon afterward had him transferred to the residence of his grandfather for better attention, where he died.

He remembers distinctly the great meeting in Charlotte (then upwards of ten years old) on the 20th of May, 1775, when a Declaration of Independence was read by Colonel Polk, and heard his father speak of it, in presence of the family, after his return from Charlotte. His mother seemed to be greatly disturbed, supposing it would bring on war. Although then but a youth of tender years, the *scene* and the *declaration* made an indellible impression upon his memory. He says his recollection of events of that period, and a few years subsequently, is more vivid and distinct than those which transpired thirty years ago.

He has been twice married, having ten children by the first, and twelve by the last wife. He was accompanied to the centennial meeting by one of his younger sons, a lad *forty-one years* of age. His oldest child, a daughter, is still living, aged *eighty-eight years!* He named one of his sons Julius Alexander, an intimate friend and junior schoolmate. As he and Alexander grew up, they frequently heard the two meetings of the 20th and 31st of May, 1775, spoken of as being separate and distinct. Having already attained a longevity seldom allotted to frail humanity, may continued health, prosperity, and, above all, the consolations of the Gospel, attend him in his remaining days upon earth!

P. S.—Thus the author wrote soon after the centennial celebration in Charlotte, on the 20th of May, 1875, but before these sketches go to the press, he is informed of the death of this veteran and worthy citizen; passing away calmly and peacefully, at his home in Union county, N. C., on the 9th of May, 1876, at the extreme old age of *one hundred and eleven years three months and five days!*

SIGNERS OF THE MECKLENBURG DECLARATION OF INDEPENDENCE.

Abraham Alexander, the Chairman of the Mecklenburg Convention of the 19th and 20th of May, 1775, was born in 1718, and was an active and influential magistrate of the county before and after the Revolution, being generally the honored chairman of the Inferior Court. He was a member of the popular branch of the Assembly in 1774-'75, with Thomas Polk as an associate; also one of the fifteen trustees of Queen's Museum, which institution, in 1777, was transformed into "Liberty Hall Academy."

After the involuntary retreat of Josiah Martin, the royal Governor, in June, 1775, from the State, its government was vested in—1. A Provincial Council for the whole province. 2. A District Committee of Safety for each county, of not less than twenty-one persons, to be elected annually by the people of each county. The members of the Provincial Council for the Salisbury district were Samuel Spencer and Waightstill Avery. . The members of the District Committee of Safety were John Brevard, Griffith Rutherford, Hezekiah Alexander, James Auld, Benjamin Patton, John Crawford, William Hill, John

Hamilton, Robert Ewart, Charles Galloway, William
Dent, Maxwell Chambers. The county committee, elected
annually by the people in each county, executed such
orders as they received from the Provincial Council, and
made such rules and regulations as the internal condition
of each county demanded. They met once in three months
at the Court-house of their respective counties, to consult
on public measures, to correspond with other committees,
to disseminate important information, and thus performed
the duties and requirements of courts. The county committees exercised these important functions until justices
of the peace were appointed by the Legislature and duly
commissioned by the Governor.

It was this committee which met in Charlotte on the
31st of May, 1775, and passed a series of rules and regulations for the internal government of the county—a necessary sequel, as previously stated, of the more important
meeting of the 20th of May preceding. This statement is
strongly corroborated by a communication published last
summer in the "Charlotte Observer," by D. A. Caldwell,
Esq., one of Mecklenburg's most aged, intelligent and
worthy citizens. The portion of the communication most
pertinent to our subject reads thus: "I was born and
raised in the house of my maternal grandfather, Major
John Davidson, who was one of the signers of the Mecklenburg Declaration. I have often heard him speak of
the 20th of May, 1775, as the day on which it was signed,
and the 31st of the same month as the time of an adjourned meeting. The "20th of May" was a household
word in the family. Moreover, I was present (and am
now the only surviving witness of the transaction) when
he gave a certificate of the above dates to Dr. Joseph
McKnitt Alexander, whose father, John McKnitt Alexander, was also a signer, and the principal secretary of the
meeting. This certificate was called forth by the celebrated attempt of Thomas Jefferson to throw discredit on
the whole affair. A certificate to the same effect was

given on that occasion by Samuel Wilson, a brother-in-law of Major Davidson, and a man of undoubted integrity. Mr. Wilson, although not a signer, was present at the signing on the 20th of May. I often heard my grandfather allude to the date in later years, when he lived with his daughter, Mrs. William Lee Davidson, whose husband was the son of General Davidson, who fell at Cowan's Ford."

Under the administration of Abraham Alexander as Chairman of the Committee of Safety, the laws passed by that body of vigilant observers of the common good were strictly enforced; and each citizen, when he left the county, was required to carry with him a certificate of his *political standing*, officially signed by the chairman.

Abraham Alexander was a most worthy, exemplary and influential member of society; was, for many years, a Ruling Elder of the Presbyterian Church, and lies buried in the graveyard of Sugar Creek Church. On his gravestone is this brief record:

" Abraham Alexander,
" Died on the 22nd of April, 1786,
" Aged 68 years.
"'Let me die the death of the righteous, and let my last end be like his.'"

Adam Alexander was chiefly known by his military services He was appointed Lieutenant Colonel of a battalion of minute men, with Thomas Polk as Colonel, and Charles M'Lean as Major, by the Provincial Council held at Johnston Court-house, on the 18th of December, 1775 ; and Colonel of Mecklenburg county, with John Phifer as Lieutenant Colonel, and John Davidson and George A. Alexander as Majors, by the Provincial Congress, held at Halifax on the 4th of April, 1776.

He was a brave and energetic officer; and his name will be found in nearly every expedition which marched from Mecklenburg county to oppose the enemies of his country. He was for many years, before and after the war, an acting

Justice of the Peace, and tradition speaks of him as bearing an excellent character. He died in 1798, aged seventy years, and is buried in the old graveyard of Rock Spring, seven miles east of Charlotte. Many of his descendants lie buried in the graveyard at Philadelphia Church, two miles from Rock Spring, at which latter place the congregation worshipped before the Revolution, mingling with their pious devotion many touching and prayerful appeals for the final deliverance of their country from the storms of the approaching conflict of arms in a righteous cause.

Hezekiah Alexander was more of a statesman than a soldier. He was born in Pennsylvania in 1728. He was appointed a member of the Committee of Safety for the Salisbury district by the Provincial Congress which met at Hillsboro on the 21st of August, 1775, with General Griffith Rutherford, John Brevard, Benjamin Patton and others—a position of much responsibility and power. He was appointed by the Provincial Congress, in April, 1776, with William Sharpe, of Rowan county, on the Council of Safety. He was elected a member of the Provincial Congress from Mecklenburg county, which met at Halifax on November 12th, 1776, and framed the first Constitution of the State, with Waightstill Avery, Robert Irwin, John Phifer, and Zaccheus Wilson, as colleagues. At the Provincial Congress, which met at Halifax on the 4th of April, 1776, he was appointed Paymaster of the Fourth Regiment of North Carolina Continentals—Thomas Polk, Colonel, James Thackston, Lieut. Colonel, and William Davidson, Major. He was the treasurer of " Liberty Hall Academy" (formerly " Queen's Museum") during its existence. He died on the 16th of July, 1801, and lies buried in the graveyard of Sugar Creek Church, of which he had long been an active and worthy member. The inscription on his tombstone reads thus:

" In memory of Hezekiah Alexander,
" Who departed this life July 16th, 1801,
" Aged 73 years."

John McKnitt Alexander, of Scotch-Irish ancestors, was born in Pennsylvania, near the Maryland line, in 1733. He served as an apprentice to the trade of tailor, and when his apprenticeship expired, at the age of twenty-one, he emigrated to North Carolina, joining his kinsmen and countrymen in seeking an abode in the beautiful champaign between the Yadkin and Catawba rivers—the land of the deer and the buffalo; of " wild pea-vines" and canebrakes, and of peaceful prosperity. In 1759 he married Jane Bain, of the same race, from Pennsylvania, and settled in Hopewell congregation. Prospered in his business, he soon became wealthy and an extensive landholder, and rising in the estimation of his fellow-citizens, was promoted to the magistracy and the Eldership of the Presbyterian Church. He was a member of the Provincial Assembly in 1772, and one of the Delegates to the Convention which met at Hillsboro, on the 21st of August, 1775.

He was also a member of the Provincial Congress, which met at Halifax on the 4th of April, 1776, with John Phifer and Robert Irwin as colleagues. In 1777, he was elected the first Senator from Mecklenburg county, under the new Constitution. He was an active participator in the Convention of the 19th and 20th of May, 1775, and preserved for a long time, the records, as being its principal secretary, and the proper custodian of its papers. He gave copies of its important and ever-memorable proceedings to Gen. William R. Davie, Dr. Hugh Williamson, then *professing* to write a history of North Carolina, and others. Unfortunately, the original was destroyed in 1800, when the house of Mr. Alexander was burned, but Gen. Davie's copy has been preserved. He was one of the Trustees of the ' College of Queen's Museum," the name of which was afterward changed to "Liberty Hall." He was for many years, a ruling Elder of the Presbyterian Church, and by his walk and conversation, its firm supporter.

By the east wall of the grave-yard at Hopewell Church, is a row of marble slabs, all bearing the name of Alexander. On one of them, is this short inscription :
"John McKnitt Alexander,
"Who departed this life July 10th, 1817,
"Aged 84."
It is a singular fact, that the signers of the Mecklenburg Declaration were all, with perhaps one or two exceptions, members of the Presbyterian Church. One of them, Rev. Hezekiah J. Balch, was a Presbyterian preacher, and nine others Elders of that Church, which may be truly styled, at and before the Revolution, the "nursing mother of freemen."

Waightstill Avery was an eminent lawyer, born in the town of Groton, Connecticut, in 1747, and graduated at Princeton College in 1766. There were eight brothers of this family, and all true patriots; some of them were massacred at Fort Griswold, and some perished at Wyoming Valley. Some of the descendants still reside at Groton, Conn., and others at Oswego, and Seneca Lake, N. Y. He studied law on the eastern shore of Maryland, with Littleton Dennis. In 1769, he emigrated to North Carolina, obtained license to practice in 1770, and settled in Charlotte. By his assiduity and ability, he soon acquired numerous friends. He was an ardent advocate of liberty, but not of licentiousness.

In 1778, he married near Newbern, Mrs. Leah Frank, daughter of William Probart, a wealthy merchant of Snow Hill, Md., who died on a visit to London. He was a member of the Provincial Congress which met at Hillsboro on the 21st of August, 1775. In 1776, he was a delegate to the Provincial Congress which met at Halifax to form a State Constitution, with Hezekiah Alexander, Robert Irwin, John Phifer and Zaccheus Wilson as colleagues. He was appointed to sign proclamation bills by this body. On the 20th of July, 1777, with William Sharpe, Joseph Winston and Robert Lanier, as associates, he made the treaty of the Long Island of the Holston with the Cherokee Indians. This treaty, made without an oath, is one that has never been violated. In 1777, he was elected the first Attorney General of North Carolina.

In 1780, while Lord Cornwallis was encamped in Charlotte, some of the British soldiery, on account of his well-known advocacy of independence, set fire to his law office, and destroyed it, with all his books and papers. In 1781, he moved to Burke county, which he represented in the Commons in 1783–'84–'85 and '93; and in the Senate in 1796. He was held in high esteem by all who knew him, and died at an advanced age, in 1821. At the time of his death he was the "Patriarch of the North Carolina Bar;" an exemplary Christian, a pure patriot, and of sterling integrity. He left a son, the late Colonel Isaac T. Avery, who represented Burke county in the Commons in 1809 and 1810, and three daughters, one of whom married William W. Lenoir; another, Thomas Lenoir, and the remaining one, Mr. Poor, of Henderson county.

Rev. Hezekiah J. Balch was born at Deer Creek, Harford county, Md., in 1748. He was said to be the brother of Col. James Balch, of Maryland, and the uncle of the late distinguished Rev. Stephen B. Balch, D. D., of Georgetown, D. C. He graduated at Princeton in 1766, when not quite eighteen years old, in the class with Waightstill Avery, Luther Martin, of Maryland, Oliver Ellsworth, of Connecticut, and others. He came to North Carolina in 1769, as a missionary, being appointed for this work by the Synod of New York and Philadelphia. Although ordained before the war, he served four years as Captain of a company in Maryland, under General Somerville. Soon after this service, he removed to North Carolina, and settled on "Irish Buffalo Creek," in Cabarrus county. He was the first Pastor of Rocky River and Poplar Tent Churches, where he continued to faithfully labor in the cause of his Divine Master, until the time of his death. Abundant in every good word and work, he took an active part in moulding the popular mind for the great struggle of the approaching Revolution. He combined in his character, great enthusiasm with unflinching firmness He looked to the achievement of principles upon which a government of well-regulated law and liberty could be safely established, and which should be removed from its strong foundations no more forever. Hence, he was a prominent actor in the Convention at Charlotte on the 19th and 20th of May, 1775, which declared independence of the British crown. But in the inscrutable ways of Providence, he did not live long enough to see the warmest wish of his heart gratified—the independence of his country, for which he was ready, if necessary, to yield up his life in its achievement. He died in the spring of 1776, in the midst of his usefulness, and his mortal remains repose in the old grave-yard of Poplar Tent Church.

On the occasion of a railroad meeting at Poplar Tent Church in 1847, attention was called to the fact that no monument of any kind marked the grave of this eminent divine and patriot; whereupon, a voluntary subscription was immediately made, and the necessary funds promptly raised to build a suitable monument to his memory. Fortunately, Abijah Alexander, then ninety years of age, was still living, a worthy citizen, and long a member of Poplar Tent Church, who was present at the burial of his beloved pastor, and who could point out the precise spot of sepulture, near the centre of the old graveyard. The following is a copy of the inscription over his grave:

"Beneath this marble are the mortal remains of the Rev. Hezikiah J. Balch, first pastor of Poplar Tent congregation, and one of the original members of Orange Presbytery. He was licensed a preacher of the everlasting gospel, of the Presbytery of Donegal in 1766, and rested from his labors A. D. 1776; having been pastor of the united congregations of Poplar Tent and Rocky River, about seven years. He was distinguished as one of the Committee of Three who prepared the Declaration of In dependence, and his eloquence, the more effectual from his acknowledged wisdom, purity of motive and dignity of character, contributed much to the unanimous adoption of that instrument on the 20th of May, 1775."

Dr. Ephraim Brevard, the reputed author of the Mecklenburg Declaration of Independence, proclaimed on the 20th of May, 1775, was born in Maryland in 1744. He came with his parents to North Carolina when about four years old. He was the son of John Brevard, one of the earliest settlers of Iredell, then Rowan, county, and of Huguenot descent. At the conclusion of the Indian war in 1761, he and his cousin, Adlai Osborne, were sent to a grammar school in Prince Edward county, Va. About a year later, he returned to North Carolina and attended a school of considerable notoriety in Iredell county, conducted successively by Joseph Alexander, (a nephew of John McKnitt Alexander) David Caldwell, then quite young, and Joel Benedict, from the New England States. Adlai Osborne, Ephraim Brevard and Thomas Reese (a brother of David Reese, one of the signers), graduated at Princeton College in 1768, and greatly contributed by talents and influence to the spread and maintenance of patriotic principles. Soon after graduation, Ephraim Brevard commenced the study of medicine under the celebrated Dr. Alexander Ramsey, of South Carolina, a distinguished patriot and historian of the Revolutionary war.

In 1776, Dr. Brevard joined the expedition of General Rutherford in his professional capacity, during the Cherokee campaign. Soon after this service he settled in Charlotte, where he married a daughter of Col. Thomas Polk, and rapidly rose to eminence in his profession. He had one child, Martha, who married Mr. Dickerson, the father of the late James P. Dickerson, a Lieutenant-Colonel in the South Carolina regiment in the Mexican war, and who died from a wound received in a battle near the City of Mexico. After the death of his beloved and youthful wife, Dr. Brevard again entered the Southern army, as "surgeon's mate," or assistant surgeon, under General Lincoln, in 1780, and was made a prisoner at the surrender of Charleston.

While engaged as one of the teachers in the Queen's Museum he raised a company, from the young men of that institution, to assist in putting down the Tories assembled on Cape Fear River. Of this company he was made captain. They marched immediately in the direction of Cross Creek (Fayetteville), but, on learning of the dispersion of the Tories, they returned home. Inheriting from his family a devotion to liberty and independence, he early became distinguished for his patriotic ardor and decision of character. He was a fine scholar, fluent writer, and drew up the resolutions of independence which the Convention of the 20th of May, 1775, adopted, with very slight alteration, acting as one of the secretaries. During his confinement in Charleston, as a prisoner of war, he suffered so much from impure air and unwholesome diet that his health gave way, and he returned home only to die. He reached the house of his friend and fellow patriot, John McKnitt Alexander, in Mecklenburg county, where he soon after breathed his last. He lies buried in Charlotte, in the lot now owned by A. B. Davidson, Esq., near the grave of his beloved wife, who, a short time before, preceded him to the tomb. Upon this lot was located the Queen's Museum College, receiving, in 1777, the more patriotic name of "Liberty Hall Academy." Within its walls were educated a Spartan band of young men, who afterward performed a noble part in achieving the independence of their country.

Richard Barry was born in Pennsylvania, of Scotch-Irish descent, and joining the great southern emigration of that period, he settled in Mecklenburg county, in the bounds of the Hopewell congregation, many years previous to the Revolution. In this vicinity he married Ann Price, and raised a numerous family. A. M. Barry, Esq., who now (1876) resides at the old homestead, is the only surviving grandson. Mrs. A. A. Harry, Mrs. G. L. Sample and Mrs. Jane Alexander, are the only surviving grand-daughters. He acted for many years as one of the magistrates of the county, and was a worthy and useful member of society. He was a true patriot and soldier, and was present at the affair of Cowan's Ford, where General Davidson was killed, on the 1st of February, 1781. After this short conflict he, David Wilson and a few others, secured the body of General Davidson, conveyed it to the house of Samuel Wilson, Sen., where, after being properly dressed, it was moved by these devoted patriots to the graveyard of Hopewell Church, and there buried by *torch-light.*

John Davidson was born in Pennsylvania in 1736. He performed much civil and military service to secure the independence of his country. He was appointed by the Provincial Congress, which met at Halifax on the 4th of April, 1776, a field officer (Major) with Adam Alexander as Colonel, John Phifer as Lieutenant Colonel, and George A. Alexander as second Major. He was with General Sumpter in August, 1780, at the battle of the Hanging Rock, and was a General in the State militia service. He was enterprising, and successful in business. With Alexander Brevard, and Joseph Graham, his sons-in-law, he established Vesuvius Furnace and Tirza Forge iron works in Lincoln county. He married Violet, daughter of Samuel Wilson, Sr., and raised a large family. His daughter, Isabella, married Joseph Graham; Rebecca married Alexander Brevard; Violet married William Bain Alexander, son of John McKnitt Alexander; Elizabeth married William Lee Davidson, son of General Davidson, who fell at Cowan's Ford; Mary married Dr. William McLean; Sallie married Alexander Caldwell, son of Rev. David Caldwell, of Guilford county; Margaret married Major James Harris. He had only two sons. John (or "Jackey") and Robert: John married Sallie Brevard, daughter of Adam Brevard; Robert married Margaret Osborne, daughter of Adlai Osborne, grandfather of the late Judge James W. Osborne, of Charlotte. Major Davidson's residence was about one mile east of Toole's Ford, on the Catawba river. A large Elm, of his own planting, is now growing in front of the old family mansion, with over-arching limbs, beneath whose beneficent shade the old patriot could quietly sit in summer, (*sub tegmine patulæ ulmi*) whilst surrounded with some of his children, grand-children, and other blessings to cheer his earthly pilgrimage to the tomb.

Robert Irwin was a distinguished officer, and performed important military service during the Revolutionary War. In 1776, he and William Alexander each, commanded a regiment under General Rutherford, in the expedition from Mecklenburg, Rowan, Lincoln, and other counties, to subdue the Cherokee Indians, who were committing murders and numerous depredations upon the frontier settlements.

After the fall of Charleston many of the unsubdued Whigs sought shelter in North Carolina. Early in July, 1780, General Sumter had taken refuge in Mecklenburg county, and having enlisted a considerable number of brave and dashing recruits in that chivalric region, returned to South Carolina prepared for new and daring exploits. Soon thereafter, accompanied by Colonels Neal, Irwin, Hill and Lacy, he made a vigorous assault against the post of Rocky Mount, but failed in reducing it for the want of artillery. After this assault General Sumter crossed the Catawba, and marched with his forces in the direction of Hanging Rock. In the engagement which took place there, and, in the main successful, the right was composed of General Davie's troops, and some volunteers under Major Bryan; the centre consisted of Colonel Irwin's Mecklenburg Militia, which made the first attack; and the left included Colonel Hill's South

SKETCHES OF WESTERN NORTH CAROLINA. 51

Carolina Regulars.* In 1781 Colonel Irwin commanded a regiment under General Rutherford, in the Wilmington campaign. He was a delegate to the Provincial Congress, which met at Halifax, on the 4th of April, 1776, with John McKnitt Alexander and John Phifer as colleagues. He was again a delegate to the Provincial Congress which met at Halifax, on the 12th of November, 1776, which body formed our first Constitution. His last civil services were as Senator from Mecklenburg county, in 1797,-'98-'99 and 1800. For many years he was a worthy and influential Elder of the Presbyterian Church at Steele Creek. He died on the 23rd of December, 1800, aged sixty-two years.

William Kennon was an early and devoted friend of liberty. He was an eminent lawyer, resided in Salisbury, and had a large practice in the surrounding counties. He was one of the prominent advocates for *absolute independence* at the Convention in Charlotte, on the 19th and 20th of May, 1775. He, with Mr. Willis, a brother-in-law, Adlai Osborne, and Samuel Spencer (afterward Judge Spencer), took an active part in arresting two obnoxious lawyers, John Dunn and Benjamin Booth Boote, preceding the Revolution, in giving utterance to language inimical to the cause of American independence.

They were conveyed to Charlotte for trial, and being found guilty of conduct inimical to the American cause, they were transported to Camden, S. C., and finally to Charleston, beyond the reach of their injurious influence. Colonel Kennon was a member of the first Congress which met at Newbern on the 25th of August, 1774, in opposition to royalty, and "fresh from the people," with Moses Winslow and Samuel Young as colleagues. He

---

* General Moultrie, in speaking of this engagement in his "Memoirs of the American Revolution," says: "When General Sumter began this attack he had not more than ten rounds of ball to a man; but before the action was over, he was amply supplied with arms and ammunition from the British and Tories that fell in the beginning."

was also a delegate to the same place in April, 1775, with
Griffith Rutherford and William Sharpe as colleagues:
and to the Provincial Congress at Hillsboro, in August,
1775, associated with William Sharpe, Samuel Young and
James Smith. In 1776, he was appointed commissary of
the first regiment of State troops. He was ever active and
faithful in the discharge of his duties. Soon after the
Revolutionary war he moved to Georgia, where he died
at a good old age.

Benjamin Patton was one of the earliest settlers in the
eastern part of Mecklenburg county (now Cabarrus). He
was a man of iron firmness and of indomitable courage.
Descended from the blood of the Covenanters, he inherited
their tenacity of purpose, sagacity of action and purity of
character. He was an early and devoted friend of liberty.

He was a delegate to the Provincial Congress which met
at Newbern on the 25th of August, 1774. This was the
first meeting of representatives direct from the people.
The royal Governor, Josiah Martin, issued his proclamation against its assembling, as being without legal authority. It constitutes an illustrious epoch in our colonial
history, transpiring nearly two years before Congress
would dare to pass a national declaration Although it was
not a battle, or conflict of arms, yet it was the first and
leading act in a great drama, in which battles and blood
were the *direct and inevitable consequences*. Had Governor
Martin the power at that time, he would have seized every
member of this "rebellious" body and tried them for
treason. In this dilemma, he summoned his ever obsequi-
ous Council for consultation, who, becoming alarmed at
the "signs of the times," declared "nothing could be
done."

Tradition informs us that Mr. Patton, not being able to
procure a horse, or any conveyance, walked all the way
from Charlotte to Newbern, about three hundred miles,
rather than not be present to vote with those determined
on *liberty* or *death*. Although then advanced in years, he

showed all the enthusiasm of youth. At the Provincial Congress which met at Hillsboro on the 21st of August, 1775, he was appointed Major of the second Continental regiment, with Robert Howe as Colonel, and Alexander Martin as Lieutenant Colonel. Of his military record, in such high position, little is known, but we find him acting as a member of the Committee of Safety for Mecklenburg county, with very full powers, associated with John Paul Barringer and Martin Phifer. They were a "terror unto evil doers." He was a man of considerable learning, of ardent temperament, and of Christian integrity. He died near Concord, in Cabarrus, county, at a good old age, and is buried on the banks of Irish Buffalo Creek. No monument marks his grave :

> "They carved not a line, they raised not a stone,
> But left him alone in his glory."

John Phifer was born in Cabarrus county (when a part of Bladen) in 1745. He was the son of Martin Phifer, a native of Switzerland, and of Margaret Blackwelder. He raised a numerous family, who inherited the patriotic spirit of their ancestors. The original spelling of the name was *Pfeifer*. He resided on "Dutch Buffalo" Creek, at the Red Hill, known to this day as "Phifer's Hill." He was the father of General Paul Phifer, grandfather of General John N. Phifer of Mississipi, and great grandfather of General Charles H. Phifer, a distinguished officer in the battle of "Shiloh," in the late war between the States. At the Provincial Council, held at Johnston Court House in December, 1775, he was appointed Lieutenant Colonel of the first battalion of "Minute Men," in the Salisbury District; General Griffith Rutherford, Colonel, and John Paisley, Major. He was a member of the Provincial Congress which met at Hillsboro on the 21st of August, 1775, associated with Thomas Polk, Waightstill Avery, James Houston, Samuel Martin and John McKnitt Alexander; and also of the Congress which met at Halifax on the 4th of April, 1776, with Robert Irwin and John McKnitt Alexander.

By this latter body, he was appointed Lieutenant Colonel of the regiment commanded by Colonel Adam Alexander. He was also a member of the Provincial Congress which met at Halifax in November, 1776, which formed our first Constitution, associated with Hezekiah Alexander, Waightstill Avery, Robert Irwin and Zaccheus Wilson, as colleagues. He married Catharine Barringer, which latter name was originally spelled *Behringer*.

It was on the plantation of John Phifer, three miles west of Concord, that the gallant band of "Black Boys," headed by Captain "Black Bill Alexander" of Sugar Creek, aided by the Whites and others from the neighboring congregation of Rocky River, effected their memorable achievement in 1771, of destroying the king's powder, which was on its way from Charleston to Hillsboro, to be used by a tyrannical Governor. The reader should bear in mind this *blackening of faces*, to prevent detection, was in the spring of 1771, when the patriotic sentiment of this country had not ripened into that state of almost entire unanimity which characterized it, and the State generally, four years later. John Phifer filled an early grave, and lies buried at the "Red Hill," on the Salisbury road, where a decaying headstone, scarcely legible, marks the last resting-place of this true patriot.

Thomas Polk is a name of historic distinction in North Carolina, as well as in our nation. He was the early, constant, and enduring friend of liberty, and the unfaltering opponent of arbitrary power and oppression. He was a member of the Colonial Assembly in 1771 and 1775, associated with Abraham Alexander from Mecklenburg. In 1775, he was appointed Colonel of the second battalion of "Minute Men," with Adam Alexander as Colonel, and Charles McLean as Major.

As Colonel of the Mecklenburg militia, he issued orders

to the Captains of the several *beats*, or districts, to send two delegates each to the Convention in Charlotte on the 19th of May, 1775. This act alone, proceeding from patriotic motives, entitles him to our gratitude. In accordance with orders, and the anticipated discussion of political measures affecting the welfare of the country, a vast concourse of delegates, and of the citizens generally, from all parts of the country, as well as from the adjoining counties of Anson, Rowan and Tryon (afterward Lincoln) assembled on the appointed day—such a gathering as had never before met in Charlotte, preceding, or during the Revolution. It was not a small assemblage, like that of the 31st of the same month, composed entirely of the Committee of Safety, met for the purpose of passing such rules and regulations as the internal government of the county demanded.

At the Provincial Congress which met at Halifax on the 4th of April, 1776, he was appointed Colonel of the fourth regiment of Continental troops, with James Thackson as Lieutenant-Colonel, and William Davidson as Major. The last named officer was afterward appointed a Brigadier General, and was killed while disputing the passage of Cornwallis at Cowan's Ford, on the 1st of February, 1781. After the death of General Davidson, he was appointed Brigadier General in his stead. When General Greene took command of the Southern army in Charlotte on the 3rd of December, 1780, the commissary department was left vacant by the resignation of Colonel Polk. At the earnest solicitation of General Greene, Colonel Davie was induced to accept the position, an ungracious and troublesome office at any time, but then attended with peculiar difficulties, as the country had been lately devastated and stripped of its usual resources by a large invading army.

Colonel Thomas Polk married Susan Spratt, and left several children. He died in 1793, full of years and full of honors, and his mortal remains repose in the graveyard of the Presbyterian Church in Charlotte.

William Polk, son of Colonel Thomas Polk, was born in 1759, and was present at the Mecklenburg Convention of the 19th and 20th of May, 1775. He commenced his military career with his father in the expedition against the Scovillite Tories, in upper South Carolina, in the autumn of 1775. He was with General Nash when he fell at Germantown; with General Davidson, at Cowan's Ford; with General Greene, at Guilford Court House; and with the same officer at Eutaw Springs. In the last named battle he was severely wounded, the effects of which he carried with him to his grave. When the war closed, he held the rank of Lieutenant-Colonel. He settled in Charlotte, his place of nativity, and represented Mecklenburg county in the Commons in 1787-'90, and '91. Soon thereafter he removed to Raleigh, where he spent the remainder of his life. He was the last surviving field officer of the North Carolina line. He died on the 14th of January, 1835, in the seventy-sixth year of his age. He was the father of Bishop Leonidas Polk, a brave and meritorious officer, killed in the late civil war, while holding the position of Major General; of the late Thomas G. Polk, of Tennessee, and of Mrs. Rayner, wife of the Hon. Kenneth Rayner, of Washington City.

Ezekiel Polk, one of the older brothers of Colonel Thomas Polk, was the first clerk of the county court of Lincoln, after its separation from Mecklenburg in 1768; a Magistrate of Mecklenburg county at a later period; and was a man of considerable wealth and influence, owning much of the valuable lands around "Morrow's Turnout," now the flourishing village of "Pineville." He was the grandfather of James K. Polk, President of the United States in 1845, some of whose noblest traits of character were illustrated in *refusing to serve a second term*, and in being *never absent from his post of duty.* Well would it be for the best interests of our Republic if other occupants of the "White House" would imitate his noble example.

Zaccheus Wilson, was one of three brothers who moved from Pennsylvania and settled in Mecklenburg county about 1760. At the time of the Mecklenburg Convention on the 19th and 20th of May, 1775, he signed that instrument, pledging himself and his extensive family connections to its support and maintenance. He was said to be a man of liberal education, and very popular in the county in which he resided. He was a member of the Convention which met at Halifax on the 12th of November, 1776, to form a State Constitution, associated with Waightstill Avery, John Phifer, Robert Irwin and Hezekiah Alexander.

The Wilsons were Scotch-Irish Presbyterians, and were arrayed by early education, civil and religious, against tyranny in any form. The eldest brother, Robert Wilson, who lived for many years in Steele Creek congregation, was the father of eleven sons, seven of whom were at one time (all who were old enough) in the Revolutionary army. Shortly after the Revolution, Zaccheus Wilson moved to Sumner county, Tennessee, and there died at an advanced age.

Ezra Alexander was a son of Abraham Alexander, the President of the Mecklenburg Convention of the 20th of May, 1775. He and William Alexander each commanded a company in Colonel William Davidson's battalion, under General Rutherford, against the Tories assembled at Ramsour's Mill, near the present town of Lincolnton. He was also engaged in other military expeditions during the war, whenever the defence of the country demanded his services.

Charles Alexander and *John Foard*, two of the signers, served as privates in Captain Charles Polk's company of "Light Horse" in 1776, in the Wilmington campaign, and in other service during the war. John Foard was, for many years, one of the magistrates of Mecklenburg county, and both have descendants living among us.

David Reese was a son of William Reese, a worthy citizen of Western Rowan (now Iredell county), who died in April, 1808, aged *ninety-nine years*, and brother of the Rev. Thomas Reese, whose ministerial labors were chiefly performed in Pendleton District, S. C., where he ended his days, and is buried in the Stone Church graveyard.

James Harris was from Eastern Mecklenburg (now Cabarrus county), a neighborhood universally holding Whig principles. He was the Major in Colonel Robert Irwin's regiment at the battle of the Hanging Rock, and elsewhere performed important services during the war. Next to the Alexanders the name *Harris* was most prevalent in Mecklenburg county preceding the Revolution, and both still have numerous worthy descendants among us to perpetuate the fair name and fame of their distinguished ancestors.

Matthew McLure, one of the signers, was an early and devoted friend of liberty. Some of his worthy descendants are still living among us. Other descendants of the same patriotic family reside in Chester county, S. C. One of his daughters married George Houston, who, with a Spartan band of twelve or thirteen brave spirits, under Captain James Thompson, beat back a British foraging party of over four hundred soldiers, at McIntyre's Branch, on the Beattie's Ford road, seven miles north-west of Charlotte. His son, Hugh Houston, served throughout the Revolutionary war. The rifle used on that occasion by George Houston is still in possession of the family. His son, M. M. Houston, Esq., of Hopewell congregation, is one of the few grandsons now living of the original signers of the Mecklenburg Declaration.

William Graham, an Irishman by birth, was one of the early advocates of liberty in Mecklenburg county. He was intelligent and highly respected by all who knew him. He lived on the plantation now owned by Mrs. Potts, about four miles south-east of Beattie's Ford, on the public road leading to Charlotte, where he died at a good old age.

It is hoped others will prosecute this branch of historical research, here imperfectly sketched, supply omissions, and favor the public with the result of their investigations. In this Centennial year it is pleasant and profitable to revert to the deeds of noble daring and lofty patriotism of our forefathers, and strive to emulate their illustrious examples.

ORIGIN OF THE ALEXANDER FAMILIES OF MECKLENBURG COUNTY.

The name, Alexander, is of frequent mention among the nobility of Scotland. About the year 1735 John Alexander married Margaret Gleason, a "bonnie lassie" of Glasgow, and shortly afterward emigrated to the town of Armagh, in Ireland. About 1740, wishing to improve more rapidly his worldly condition, he emigrated with his rising family, two nephews, James and Hugh Alexander, and their sister, who was married to a Mr Polk, to America, and settled in Nottingham, Chester county, Pa. These two nephews, and their brother-in-law, Polk. soon afterward emigrated to Mecklenburg county, North Carolina, then holding forth flattering inducements for settlement. These families, of Scotch-Irish descent, there prospered in their several callings, and early imbibed those principles of civil and religious liberty which stamped their impress on themselves and their descendants, and shone forth conspicuously preceding and during the American Revolution.

About the time of this emigration of the Alexanders to North Carolina, John Alexander moved to Carlisle, Cumberland county, Pa. While he resided there his son James (James the first) married "Rosa Reed," of that place. Soon after his marriage he left Carlisle, and settled on "Spring Run," having purchased a tract of land which covered "Logan's Springs," where the celebrated Mingo chief, Logan, then lived. After Logan's death he moved to the Springs, which valuable property is still owned by the Alexander heirs.

John Alexander, partaking of the roving spirit of the age, left Carlisle, and finally settled in Berkeley county, Va., where he purchased a large farm, and spent the remainder of his days. His son James had twelve children, seven sons and five daughters. One of his daughters, Rachel, married Joseph Vance, of Virginia, the ancestor of ex-Governor Vance, of Ohio, and other descendants. He gave Vance a farm of three hundred acres as an inducement to settle near him. Vance accepted the gift, and soon afterward removed to the farm; but Indian troubles breaking out at that time, he sold his possession and returned to Virginia, selecting a location near Martinsburg.

James Alexander (James the second) had four sons and six daughters. The eldest son (James the third) married his cousin Celia, youngest daughter of Robert Alexander, of whom was a descendant, Robert Alexander (perhaps a son), a captain in the Revolution, who married Mary Jack, third daughter of Patrick Jack, of Charlotte, and settled in Lincoln county, where he died in 1813.

James Porterfield Alexander (James the fourth), and son of James the third, married Annie Augusta Halsey, grand-daughter of the Hon. Jeremiah Morton, and resides, in this centennial year, on the St. Cloud plantation, Rapidan Station, Culpeper county, Va.

Hugh Alexander, son of James the first, married Martha Edmundson, settled in Sherman's Valley, Pa., and had a large family. He died at Independence Hall, Philadelphia, while sitting as a member to form a State Constitution.

Another prolific source of the Alexanders in America is traceable to the descendants of seven brothers, who fled from Scotland, on account of political troubles, to the north of Ireland, and passing through the Emerald Isle, sailed for America, and landed in New York in 1716. One of their descendants was William Alexander, born in New York in 1726, a son of James Alexander, of Scotland.

He became a distinguished officer in the Revolutionary war, known as "Lord Stirling." He married a daughter of Philip Livingston (the second lord of the manor), a sister of Governor Livingston, of New Jersey.

From these prolific sources (Scotch and Scotch-Irish) North Carolina, and other States of the American Union, have received their original supplies of Alexanders, embracing, in their expansion, many distinguished names.

In the list of the signers of the Mecklenburg Declaration of the 20th of May, 1775, six bear the name of Alexander, and a *host* of others, officers and privates, honored the name in their heroic achievements during the Revolutionary war. Two of the distinguished teachers in Rowan county, preceding the Revolution, were James Alexander and Robert Brevard.

It is also worthy of mention that one of the *twenty-six* persons who met in Charleston, in the fall of 1766, after the repeal of the Stamp Act, under the leadership of that early patriot, General Christopher Gadsden, rejoiced under the duplicated name of *Alexander Alexander*. He had strayed off from the paternal roof in North Carolina, and was employed there in the honorable calling of schoolmaster. Johnson, in his "Traditions and Reminiscences," thus speaks favorably of his eminent worth: "Alexander Alexander was a school-master of high character and popularity. He was a native of Mecklenburg, North Carolina, and educated in the Whig principles of that distinguished district."

JACK FAMILY.

At the commencement of the Revolutionary War, one of the worthy and patriotic citizens of the little town of Charlotte, in Mecklenburg county, N. C., was Patrick Jack. He was a native of Ireland, and emigrated to America, with several brothers, about 1730. He married Lillis McAdoo, of the same race, who is represented to have been, by all who knew her, as "one of the best of women," having an amiable disposition, frequently dispensing charities to the poor, and truly pious. Her Christian name, *Lillis*, in subsequent years, was softened into *Lillie*, by many of her descendants in adopting it. The descent of Patrick Jack is traceable to noble ancestors, one of whom was a ministerial sufferer in the reign of Charles II, in 1661. In that year, that despotic monarch, who, according to one of his own satirists, "Never said a foolish thing, nor ever did a wise one," ejected from their benefices or livings, under Jeremy Taylor, thirteen ministers of the Presbytery of Lagan, in the northern part of Ireland, for their non-conformity to the Church of England. The Puritans of England were called to the same trial, in August, 1662, and in the following October, the same scene of heroic suffering was exhibited in Scotland.

Among the honored names of these thirteen ejected ministers, were Robert Wilson, ancestor of the Rev. Francis McKemie, who, twenty years later, was the first Presbyterian preacher that had ever visited the Western Continent, and near relative of George McKemie, of the Waxhaw settlement, and a brother-in-law of Mrs. Elizabeth Jackson, the mother of General Andrew Jackson: Robert Craighead, ancestor of the Rev. Alexander Craighead, the first settled pastor of Sugar Creek congregation, the early apostle of civil and religious liberty in Mecklenburg county, and who ended his days there in 1766: Thomas Drummond, a near relative of William Drummond, the first royal Governor of North Carolina; Adam White, ancestor of Hon. Hugh Lawson White, a native of Iredell county, and William Jack, ancestor of Patrick Jack, of Charlotte, Charles Jack, of Chambersburg, Pennsylvania, and others, whose descendants are now found in ten or twelve States of the American Union.

In the list of tax-payers for Chambersburg, Pa., during the latter half of the last century, the "Chief Burgess," or Mayor of that place, informs the author the name of Jack (especially John, James, Charles, and William) is of frequent occurrence; but, at the present time, not one of the name is to be found there One of these, (James) probably a nephew of Patrick and Charles Jack, served five years with distinction in the Revolutionary army, and others are traditionally spoken of as actively engaged in the same patriotic duty. Several of the elder members of the family are buried in the graveyard of Chambersburg, others in Williamsport, Md., and elsewhere in western Pennsylvania.

Several years previous to the Revolution, there also came over from the north of Ireland to America, at least two brothers of the name of Jack, distant relatives of Patrick and Charles Jack, and settled in western Pennsylvania. When the county town of Westmoreland (Hannastown) was burned by the Indians in 1783, one of this family distinguished himself by saving the lives of the women and children. After the burning of that place, the name of the town was changed to Greensburg, and a new location selected on land donated by William Jack, who had become quite wealthy, and one of the Associate Judges of Westmoreland county. He had five sons, four of whom died bachelors; the elder married, but none of his descendants are now (1876) living, except a grand-son, (William Jack,) who resides near Greensburg, Pa. The only daughter of Judge William Jack, married *John Cust*, who fled from Ireland soon after the rebellion in 1798.

About 1760, animated with the hope of more rapidly improving his worldly condition, Patrick Jack joined the great tide of emigration to the Southern colonies, and shortly after his arrival in North Carolina purchased a tract of land between Grant and Second Creeks, in the Cathey settlement (now Thyatira) in Rowan county. After remaining there for about two years, he sold his land and moved to the adjoining county of Mecklenburg. Here, by strict economy and industry, he was "blest in his basket and his store," and enabled to make more enlarged possessions. This improvement in his pecuniary condition and prosperity may be inferred from the fact that in 1775, and a few years subsequently, he and his eldest son, Capt. James Jack, who, about this time united in business with his father, became the owners of some of the finest lots, or rather blocks, in Charlotte. Among the valuable lots they are recorded as owning, may be briefly named: No. 25, the present Irwin corner; No. 26, the Parks lot; No. 27, the whole space, or double block, from the Irwin corner to the Court House lot; No. 29, the space from the Parks lot to the corner embracing the Brown property; and several lots on Trade street, opposite the First Presbyterian Church. On one of these last named lots (the old Elms property, on the corner next to the Court House) Patrick Jack and his son Capt. James Jack, resided when the delegates from the militia districts of the county assembled, on the 19th and 20th of May, 1775, and kept a public house of entertainment. Here Patrick Jack, on suitable occasions, was accustomed to "crack" many an Irish joke, to the infinite delight of his numerous visitors: and by his ready wit, genial good humor and pleasantry, greatly contributed to the reputation of his house, and inculcated his own patriotic principles. The house soon became the favorite place of resort for the students of the collegiate institute known as "Queen's Museum," and of other ardent spirits of the town and country, to discuss the political issues of that exciting period, all foreboding the approach of a mighty revolution.

Patrick Jack had four sons, James, John, Samuel and Robert, and five daughters, Charity, Jane, Mary, Margaret and Lillis, named in the order of their ages. Capt. James Jack, the eldest son, married Margaret Houston, on the 20th of November, 1766. The Houston family came South nearly at the same time with the Alexanders, Polks, Pattons, Caldwells, Wallaces, Wilsons, Clarkes. Rosses, Pattersons, Browns, and many others, and settled mostly in the eastern part of Mecklenburg county (now

Cabarrus), and in neighborhoods convenient to the old established Presbyterian churches of the country, under whose guidance civil and religious freedom have ever found ardent and unwavering defenders. The late Archibald Houston, who served Cabarrus county faithfully in several important positions, and died in 1848, was one of this worthy family,

On the 2nd of October, 1768, Captain James Jack, as stated in his own family register, moved to his own place, on the head of the Catawba river, then receiving a considerable emigration. He had five children: 1. Cynthia, born on the 20th of September, 1767. 2. Patrick, born on the 27th of September, 1769. 3. William Houston, born on the 6th of June, 1771. 4. Archibald, born on the 20th of April, 1773 (died young); and 5. James, born on the 20th of September, 1775.

On the 4th of August, 1772, Captain Jack left his mountain home and moved to the residence of his father, Patrick Jack, in Mecklenburg county. On the 16th of February, 1773, he and his father moved from the country, where they had been temporarily sojourning, into "Charlotte town," prospered in business, and soon became useful and influential citizens.

On the 26th of Sept., 1780, Lord Cornwallis, elated with his victory at Camden, entered Charlotte, with the confident expectation of soon restoring North Carolina to the British Crown. Patrick Jack was then an old and infirm man, having given up the chief control of his public house to his son, Captain James Jack; but neither age nor infirmity could enlist the sympathies of the British soldiery. The patriotic character of the house had become extensively known through Tory information, and its destruction was consequently a "foregone conclusion." The British soldiers removed its aged owner from the feather bed upon which he was lying, emptied its contents into the street, and then set the house on fire! The reason assigned for this incendiary act was, "all of old Jack's sons were in the rebel army," and he himself had been an active promoter of American independence.

The loss to Patrick Jack of his dwelling-house and much furniture, accumulated through many years of patient toil and industry, was a severe one. The excitement of the burning scene, consequent exposure, and great nervous shock to a system already debilitated with disease, a few months afterward brought to the grave this veteran patriot. His aged partner survived him a few years. Both were worthy and consistent members of the Presbyterian Church, and their mortal remains now repose in the old graveyard in Charlotte.

By the last will and testament of Patrick Jack, made on the 19th of May, 1780, he devised the whole of his personal estate and the " undivided benefit of his house and lots to his beloved wife during her life-time." After her death they were directed to be sold, and the proceeds divided among his five married daughters, viz.: Charity Dysart, Jane Barnett, Mary Alexander, Margaret Wilson and Lillie Nicholson. James Jack and Joseph Nicholson were appointed executors. It is related of Dr. Thomas Henderson, a former venerable citizen of Charlotte, that, on his death-bed, he requested to be buried by the side of Patrick Jack, "one of the best men he had ever known."

At the Convention of Delegates in Charlotte on the 19th and 20th of May, 1775, Capt. James Jack was one of the deeply interested spectators, and shared in the patriotic feelings of that ever memorable occasion. He was then about forty-three years of age—brave, energetic and ready to engage in any duty having for its object the welfare and independence of his country. After the passage of the patriotic resolutions, elsewhere given in this volume, constituting the Mecklenburg Declaration of Independence, Capt. Jack, for his well-known energy, bravery and determination of character, was selected to be the bearer of them to Congress, then in session in Philadelphia. Accordingly, as soon as the necessary preparations for traveling could be made, he set out from Charlotte on that long, lonesome and perilous journey, *on horseback.* There were then nowhere in the American colonies, *stages* or *hacks* to facilitate and expedite the weary traveler. Express messengers were alone employed for the rapid transmission of all important intelligence. On the evening of the first day he reached Salisbury, forty miles from Charlotte, before the General Court, then in session, had adjourned. Upon his arrival, Colonel Kennon, an influential member of the Court, who knew the object of Captain Jack's mission, procured from him the copy of the Mecklenburg resolutions of independence he had in charge, and read them aloud in open court. All was silence, and all apparent approval (*intentique ora tenebant*) as these earliest key-notes of freedom resounded through the hall of the old court house in Salisbury. There sat around, in sympathizing composure, those sterling patriots, Moses Winslow, Waightstill Avery, John Brevard, William Sharpe, Griffith Rutherford, Matthew Locke, Samuel Young, Adlai Osborne, James Brandon, and many others, either members of the court, or of the county "Committee of Safety." The only marked opposition proceeded from two lawyers, *John Dunn* and *Benjamin Booth Boote*, who pronounced the resolutions *treasonable*, and said Captain Jack ought to be detained. These individuals had previously expressed sentiments "inimical to the American cause." As soon as knowledge of their avowed sentiments and proposed detention of Captain Jack reached Charlotte, the patriotic vigilance of the friends of liberty was actively aroused, and a party of ten or twelve armed horsemen promptly volunteered to proceed to Salisbury, arrest said Dunn and Boote, and bring them before the Committee of Safety of Mecklenburg for trial. This was accordingly done (George Graham, living near Charlotte, being one of the number), and both being found guilty of conduct inimical to the cause of American freedom, were transported, first to Camden, and afterward, to Charleston, S. C. They never returned to North Carolina, but after the war, it is reported, settled in Florida, and died there, it is hoped not only repentant of their sins, as all should be, but with chastened notions of the reality and benefits of American independence.

On the next morning, Captain Jack resumed his journey from Salisbury, occasionally passing through neighborhoods, in and beyond the limits of North Carolina, infested with enraged Tories, but, intent on his appointed mission, he faced all dangers, and finally reached Philadelphia in safety.

Upon his arrival he immediately obtained an interview with the North Carolina delegates (Caswell, Hooper and Hewes), and, after a little conversation on the state of the country, then agitating all minds, Captain Jack drew from his pocket the Mecklenburg resolutions of the 20th of May, 1775, with the remark: "Here, gentlemen, is a paper that I have been instructed to deliver to you, with the request that you should lay the same before Congress."

After the North Carolina delegates had carefully read the Mecklenburg resolutions, and approved of their patriotic sentiments so forcibly expressed, they informed Captain Jack they would keep the paper, and show it to several of their friends, remarking, at the same time, they did not think Congress was then prepared to act upon so important a measure as *absolute independence.*

On the next day, Captain Jack had another interview with the North Carolina delegates. They informed him that they had consulted with several members of Congress, (including Hancock, Jay and Jefferson,) and that all agreed, while they approved of the patriotic spirit of the Mecklenburg resolutions, it would be premature to lay them officially before the House, as they still entertained some hopes of reconciliation with England. It was clearly perceived by the North Carolina delegates and other members whom they consulted, that the citizens of Mecklenburg county were *in advance* of the general sentiment of Congress on the subject of independence; the phantasy of "reconciliation" still held forth its seductive allurements in 1775, and even during a portion of 1776; and hence, no record was made, or vote taken on the patriotic resolutions of Mecklenburg, and they became concealed from view in the blaze of the National Declaration bursting forth on the 4th of July, 1776, which only re-echoed and reaffirmed the truth and potency of sentiments proclaimed in Charlotte on the 20th of May, 1775.

Captain Jack finding the darling object of his long and toilsome journey could not be then accomplished, and that Congress was not prepared to vote on so bold a measure as *absolute independence*, just before leaving Philadelphia for home, somewhat excited, addressed the North Carolina delegates, and several other members of Congress, in the following patriotic words: "*Gentlemen, you may debate here about 'reconciliation,' and memorialize your king, but, bear it in mind, Mecklenburg owes no allegiance to, and is separated from the crown of Great Britain forever*"

On the breaking out of hostilities with the mother country, no portion of the Confederacy was more forward in fulfilling the pledge of "life, fortune and sacred honor," in the achievement of liberty, previously made, than Mecklenburg and several adjacent counties. Upon the first call for troops, Captain Jack entered the service in command of a company, and acted in that capacity, with distinguished bravery, throughout the war, under Colonels Polk, Alexander, and other officers. He uniformly declined promotion when tendered, there being a strong reciprocal attachment between himself and his command, which he highly appreciated, and did not wish to sunder. At the commencement of the war he was in "easy" and rather affluent circumstances—at its close, comparatively a poor man. Prompted by patriotic feelings for the final prosperity of his county, still struggling for independence, he loaned to the State of North Carolina, in her great pecuniary need, $4,000, for which, unfortunately, he has never received a cent in return. As a partial compensation for his services the State paid him a land warrant, which he placed in the hands of a Mr. Martin, a particular friend, to be laid at his discretion. Martin moved to Tennessee, and died there, but no account of the warrant could be afterward obtained.

Soon after the war he sold his house and lots in Charlotte, and moved with his family to Wilkes county, Ga. Here he is represented, by those who knew him, as being a " model farmer," with barns well filled, and surrounded with all the evidences of great industry, order and abundance. Here, too, he was blest in enjoying for many years the ministerial instructions of the Rev. Francis Cummins, a distinguished Presbyterian clergyman, who, at the youthful age of eighteen, joined his command in Mecklenburg county, and had followed him to his new home in Georgia —formerly a gallant soldier for his country's rights, but now transformed into a "soldier of the cross," on Christian duty in his Heavenly Master's service.

The latter years of Captain Jack's life were spent under the care of his second son, William H. Jack, long a successful and most worthy merchant of Augusta, Ga. In 1813 or 1814, Captain Jack moved from Wilkes to Elbert county, of the same State. There being no Presbyterian church in reach, of which he had been for many years a devout and consistent member, he joined the Methodist church, with which his children had previously united. He was extremely fond of meeting with old friends, and of narrating incidents of the Revolution in which he had actively participated, and for its success freely contributed of his substance. In the serenity of a good old age, protracted beyond the usual boundaries of life, he cared but little for things of this world, and took great delight in reading his Bible, and deriving from its sacred pages those Christian consolations which alone can yield true comfort and happiness, and cheer the pathway of our earthly pilgrimage to the tomb. He met his approaching end with calm resignation, and died on the 18th of December, 1822, in the ninety-first year of his age. His wife, the partner of his joys and his sorrows through a long and eventful life, survived him about two years, and then passed away in peace.

Cynthia Jack, eldest child and only daughter of Capt. James Jack, married A. S. Cosby, and settled in Mississippi. After his death the widow and family settled in Louisiana, about 1814. Their descendants were: 1. Margaret. 2. Cynthia. 3. James; and 4. Dr. Charles Cosby. Patrick Jack, eldest son of Captain James Jack, was Colonel of the 8th Regiment U. S. Infantry, in the war of 1812, stationed at Savannah. He sustained an elevated position in society, frequently represented Elbert county in the State Senate, and died in 1820. His children were: 1. Patrick. 2. William H.; and 3. James W. Jack. Patrick Jack, the eldest son, married Miss Spencer, and, in turn, had two daughters, Harriet and Margaret, and six sons: 1. James. 2. William H. 3. Patrick C. 4. Spencer H. 5. Abner; and 6. Churchill Jack. Abner died several years ago in Mississippi—a planter by occupation, and a man of wealth.

James Jack, eldest son of Col. Patrick Jack, married, in 1822, Ann Scott Gray, who died in 1838. In 1847, he married Mary Jane Witherspoon, having by the first wife ten, and by the second, eleven children, of whom at present (1876) twelve are living. In 1823, he moved to Jefferson county, Ala., and one year afterward to Hale county, in the same State, where he ended his days. During the fall of the last year (1875) the author received from him two interesting letters respecting the history of his ever-memorable grandfather, Capt. James Jack, after his removal from North Carolina to Georgia. But alas! the uncertainty of human life! Before the year closed this venerable, intelligent, and truly christian man was numbered with the dead! He was a successful farmer, the prudent counsellor of his neighborhood, good to the poor, dispensing his charities with a liberal hand, and was universally beloved by all who knew him. On the 27th of November he had a severe stroke of paralysis, from which he never recovered. On the 27th of December, 1875, like a sheaf, ripe in its season, he was cut down, and gathered to his fathers, quietly passing away in the seventy-sixth year of his age, with the fond hope of a blissful immortality beyond the grave.

Churchill Jack, youngest son of Col. Patrick Jack, is a farmer in Arkansas, and the only one of this family now (1876) living. William H., Patrick C. and Spencer H. Jack, all young and adventurous spirits, emigrated from Alabama to Texas in 1831, and cast their lots with the little American colony which was then just beginning to establish itself. They were all three lawyers by profession, and took an active interest and part in the difficulties with Mexico, which were sure to result in open hostilities and the independence of Texas. Spencer H. Jack died young and without issue.

Patrick C. Jack played a prominent part in one of the earliest acts "rebellion" against the Mexican authorities. He, Travis and Edward, at Anahuac, smarting under the tyranny of the Mexican General, Bradburn, then commanding the post, denounced and rebelled against his usurpations and oppression. For this they were seized and imprisoned by Bradburn, and held as *captive traitors*, until released by a company of armed Texans, who demanded their *immediate surrender or a fight*. Bradburn, not having a particular fondness for *leaden arguments*, and well knowing the message *meant business*, reluctantly yielded to the stern demand. But this chivalric rescue, as might be expected, was regarded by Mexico *as treason*, and war soon afterward followed.

After the close of the Mexican war Patrick C. Jack returned to his profession, which he pursued successfully. At the time of his death, in 1844, though still a young man, he was one of the Judges of the Supreme Court of the Republic of Texas. His brother, William H. Jack, also participated prominently in council, and in the field in the Revolution of Texas, and served as a private in the battle of San Jacinto, which sealed the independence of the "Lone Star" Republic. He achieved distinction in his profession as a lawyer and advocate, and served repeatedly as Representative and Senator in the Congress of the young Republic. Under President Burnet's administration he became Secretary of State. He, too, died in 1844, not having attained his fortieth year. He left a widow and three children, two of the latter being daughters. His elder daughter is the wife of Hon. W. P. Ballinger, of the city of Galveston, lately appointed to the bench of the Supreme Court of Texas, which position he declined. His second daughter (now deceased) married the Hon. Grey M. Bryan, of Galveston, who represented his district in Congress before the war, and was Speaker of the House of Representatives of Texas in 1875.

Colonel Thomas M. Jack, only son of William H. Jack, and great-grandson of Captain James Jack, of Mecklenburg memory, is an eminent lawyer and advocate, also of Galveston (of the firm of Ballinger, Jack and Mott), to whom the author acknowledges his indebtedness for many particulars respecting the Texan members of the Jack family.

William Houston Jack, second son of Captain James Jack, was one of the first settlers, and successful merchants of Augusta, Ga. After his withdrawal from the mercantile business, he settled in Wilkes county, taking care of his aged father and mother until their death. He married Frances Cummins, a daughter of the Rev. Francis Cummins, one of the witnesses of the Mecklenburg Declaration of Independence. He was universally beloved by all who knew him, and sustained through life a character of unsullied integrity. He left one son, William Cummins Jack, a teacher by profession, a fine classical scholar, and a gentleman of culture and great moral worth. He is now

(1876) residing with his second son, William H. Jack, a distinguished lawyer (of the firm of "Jack and Pierson") of Natchitoches, La. His eldest son, Dr. Samuel Jack, is an eminent physician, of extensive practice, residing in Columbia county, Arkansas. Two other sons are industrious farmers, and all are pursuing successfully their several vocations of life. For the patriotic services, civil and military, performed by different members of the Jack family, Texas, in her formation stage, honored one of her counties with their name.

James W. Jack, third son of Captain James Jack, married Annie Barnett, a daughter of John Barnett and Ann Spratt. He was a farmer by profession, of unblemished character, and extensive influence, residing and ending his days in Wilkes county, Ga. He had the following children: 1. Samuel T.; 2. Jane; 3. James, (killed at the massacre of the Alamo, under Col. Fannin) 4. Lillis; 5. Patrick, and 6. Cynthia Jack. Samuel T. Jack married Martha Webster, of Mississippi; Jane Jack married Dr. James Jarratt; Lillis Jack married Osborne Edwards, Esq., and Patrick Jack married Emily Hanson, of Texas.

John Jack, second son of Patrick Jack, of Charlotte, preceding and during the Revolutionary War, lived on McAlpine's Creek, in Mecklenburg county. He performed a soldier's duty during the war, and soon after its termination, moved to Wilkes county, Ga. Of his further history and descendants, little is now known.

Samuel Jack, third son of Patrick Jack, of Charlotte, was also a soldier of the Revolution, and commanded an artillery company. He lived in the Sugar Creek neighborhood, and married, 1st. Miss Knight, of Mecklenburg county, by whom he had two children, 1. Eliza D. Jack, who married the Rev. Mr. Hodge, a Presbyterian minister, and settled in Athens, Ga., and 2. James Jack, who died when a young man. A few years after her death, he married Margaret Stewart, of Philadelphia, Pa., by whom he had five children: 1. Samuel Stewart; 2. John McCormick; 3. William D.; 4. Mary E., and 5. Amanda M. Jack. Samuel S. Jack married Elizabeth Meredith, of Walton county, Ga., in 1831. None of the other children ever married. He had five children: 1. William Howard; 2. Amanda E.; 3. James Mortimer; 4. Joseph Henry, and 5. Sarah M. Jack. Of these, William Howard Jack, in 1860, married Mary Lunsdale, by whom he had five children. He was a printer and editor, and highly respected by all who knew him. He died in April, 1876, in Rome. Ga., aged forty-two years. His son, James Mortimer Jack, was killed in the late war. Amanda E. Jack, a worthy lady, is now (1876) living in the country with her brother, Joseph Henry Jack.

Robert Jack, the fourth and youngest son of Patrick Jack, of Charlotte, remained in Chambersburg, Pa., where his father had resided many years previous to his removal to North Carolina. He had the following children: 1. James; 2. John; 3. Cynthia, and 4. Margaret Jack. John Jack was the only one of this family who married. He was born in Chambersburg, on the 29th of December, 1763. At the age of sixteen, he went to Baltimore, engaged as a clerk in a mercantile house, and there acquired those correct business habits and educational training which qualified him for future usefulness. Near the close of the last century, when quite a young man, he settled in Romney, Hampshire county, Va. He there became a successful merchant, and sustained, through a long and busy life, an unblemished reputation for honesty, integrity and general uprightness of character. He married Rebecca Singleton, an estimable lady who survived him a few years.

In 1823, he was appointed Cashier of the Romney Branch of the Valley Bank of Virginia, which position he held until his death, with distinguished ability. The former intelligent Mayor of Romney, (A. P. White, Esq.,) in writing to the author, says: "John Jack, when young, was of a gay and festive disposition. After he joined the church, he sobered down to great calmness and evenness. He was always exceedingly neat in his person, courteous in his manners, and kind and charitable to the poor. He bore through life, the character of an earnest, honest, and upright man of business, was an Elder of the Presbyterian Church, and a good Christian." He died on the 28th of September, 1837, in the seventy-fourth year of his age. He had the following children : 1. Robert Y.; 2. Carlton T.; 3. James R.; 4. John ; 5. Margaret ; 6. Juliette M.; 7. John G., and 8. Edward W. Jack. The last named son is now (1876) the only one of the family living. Robert Y. Jack settled in Winchester, Va., and engaged in merchandising. In the war of 1812, he raised a company which was stationed at Craney Island, and participated in the battle at that place.

Robert Y. Jack died near Charleston, Jefferson county, Va., in 1834, leaving an only child, Frances Rebecca, who married Thomas J. Manning, of the U. S. Navy. They both died previous to the late Confederate war, leaving three sons : 1. Charles J.; 2. George Upshur, and 3. Frank Jack Manning. Each one of these brave youths joined the Confederate army, all under the age of eighteen years. George Upshur was killed in the cavalry charge under General Stewart at Brandy Station. Frank Jack was shot through the body, but recovered of his severe wound and continued in the army. They all three served under General (Stonewall) Jackson, through his campaigns, and after his death, under General Early.

John G. Jack settled in Louisville, Ky., and died there, leaving three daughters and one son, Robert Bruce Jack.

Edward W. Jack, youngest son of John Jack, of Romney, now lives near Salem, Roanoke county, Va., in the quiet fruition of all that pertains to an honorable *bachelor's* life. All the members of this family have sustained exemplary characters, and now occupy fair and eminent positions in society.

Charity Jack, eldest daughter of Patrick Jack, of Charlotte, married Dr. Cornelius Dysart, a distinguished physician and surgeon of the Revolutionary army. The Dysart family, at that time, resided in Mecklenburg county. Dr. Dysart is said to have built the first house on the "Irwin corner," assisted by his brother-in-law, Captain Jack, who owned the lot until his removal to Georgia, shortly after the war. Dr. Dysart died comparatively young, leaving a widow and two children, James and Robert Dysart, who settled in Georgia. Of their subsequent history little is known. Jane (or "Jean,") Jack, second daughter of Patrick Jack, married William Barnett, son of John Barnett and Ann Spratt, of Scotch-Irish descent. The name Spratt is generally spelled "Sprot," or "Sproat," in the old records. Thomas Spratt is said to have been the *first person* who crossed the Yadkin river, *with wheels;* and his daughter Ann the *first child* born in the beautiful champaign country between the Yadkin and Catawba rivers. He first intended to settle on Rocky River (now in Cabarrus county), but Indian disturbances occurring there near the time of his arrival, induced him to select a home in the vicinity of the place which afterward became the "town of Charlotte." At his humble dwelling, one mile and a half south of Charlotte, was held the *first Court* of Mecklenburg county. Abraham Alexander, the Chairman of the Mecklenburg Convention of the 20th of May, 1775, and Colonel Thomas Polk, its "herald of freedom" on the same occasion, were then prominent and influential members of this primitive body of county magistrates. Near the residence of Thomas Spratt is one of the oldest private burial grounds in the county, in which his mortal remains repose. Here are found the grave-stones of several members of the Spratt, Barnett and Jack families, who intermarried; also those of the Binghams, McKnights, and a few others. On the head-stone of Mary Barnett, wife of William Barnett, it is recorded, she died on the 4th of October, 1764, aged forty-five years. A hickory tree, ten or twelve inches in diameter, is now growing on this grave, casting around its beneficent shade. The primitive forest growth, once partially cut down, is here fast assuming its original sway, and peacefully overshadowing the mortal remains of these early sleepers in this ancient graveyard.

The descendants of William Barnett and Jane Jack were: 1. Annie Barnett, married James Jack, third son of Captain James Jack, of Mecklenburg memory, whose genealogy has been previously given. 2. Samuel Barnett, married, 1st, Eliza Joyner; descendants: 1. Jane Barnett, married A. S. Wingfield. 2. Sarah J. Barnett, married Alexander Pope, Sen. Descendants of Samuel Barnett (second marriage) and Elizabeth Worsham were: 1. Samuel Barnett (Washington, Ga.), married Elizabeth A. Stone. Descendants: 1. Annie Barnett, married Rev. William S. Bean. 2. Frank W. 3. Samuel (Davidson College.) 4. Osborne S. 5. Edward A. 6. Hattie A.; and 7. Susan Barnett.

The descendants of John Jack and Mary Barnett were: 1. Ann Jack, married Moses Wiley. 2. Mary A. Jack, married John J. Barnett. 3. Dr. Thomas Jack. 4. John Jack. 5. Samuel Jack, married Annie Leslie. 6. Susan Jack, married Alexander Bowie, formerly Chancellor of Alabama.

The descendants of Moses Wiley and Ann Jack were: 1. Leroy M. Wiley. 2. Mary Wiley, married Thomas Baxter. 3. Thomas Wiley. 4. Eliza Wiley, married Mr. Carnes. 5. Sarah Ann, married John R. Hays. 6. Laird Wiley; and 7. Jack Wiley.

The descendants of Susan Barnett and George W. Smart were five children, of whom only two arrived at the years of maturity, Albert W. and Thomas B. Smart.

George W. Smart represented Mecklenburg county in the House of Commons in 1805, and again in 1808. He died in May, 1810. Mrs. Smart survived her husband many years, and was one of the *remarkable women* of her age. She was long known and highly esteemed in Mecklenburg and surrounding country for her general intelligence, ardent piety, and retentive memories of Revolutionary events. At the great gathering of delegates and people in Charlotte, on the 20th of May, 1775, she was present (then thirteen years old), and still retained a distinct recollection of some of the thrilling scenes of that memorable occasion, not the least of which was "the throwing up of hats," in the universal outburst of applause, when the resolutions of independence were read by Colonel Thomas Polk, from the Court-house steps.

She died on the 28th of November, 1851, aged ninety years, and is buried, with other members of the family, in a private cemetery on her own farm, nine miles from Charlotte, on the Camden road. It should be stated, the grandfather of L. M. Wiley and others, (John Jack) was a *cousin* and not a brother, as some have supposed, of Capt. James Jack, of Charlotte.

Our prescribed limits forbid a more extended genealogical, notice of the Barnett family and their collateral connections, many of whom performed a conspicuous part in the Revolutionary War. Capt. William Barnett was a bold, energetic officer, and was frequently engaged, with his brothers, and other ardent spirits of Mecklenburg, in that species of partisan warfare which struck terror into the Tory ranks, checked their atrocities, and gave celebrity to the dashing exploits of Col. Sumpter and his brave associates.

Mary Jack, third daughter of Patrick Jack, of Charlotte, married Captain Robert Alexander, of Lincoln county, who emigrated from Pennsylvania to North Carolina about 1760. He commanded a company during the Revolution, in the Cherokee expedition, under General Rutherford; acted for several years as Commissary, and performed other minor, but important trusts for the county. He was one of the early band of patriots who met at Newbern on the 25th of August, 1774, and again attended the Convention at Hillsboro, on the 21st of August, 1775. After the war, he settled on his farm, one mile northwest of Tuckasege Ford, on the Catawba River. His residence was long a general stopping-place for travelers, and painted red—hence, it was widely known as the "Red House Place."

He was elected to the State Legislature consecutively from 1781 to 1787; and acted, for many years, as one of the magistrates of the county, showing the general acceptance with which his services were held. He died in 1813, aged about seventy years, and is buried in Goshen graveyard, Gaston county, N. C. His descendants by the first wife, Mary Jack, were: 1. Margaret, married Judge Samuel Lowrie; 2. Lillis, married Capt. James Martin; 3. Robert W., married Louisa Moore; 4. Mary, married, 1st. James J. Scott, and 2nd. General John Moore; 5. Annie, married John Sumter, (nephew of Gen. Sumter.) His descendants by the second wife, Margaret Reily, were: 1. Eliza 2. Evaline; 3. Amanda, married Dr. J. C. Rudisill, of Lincolnton.

Descendants of Judge Lowrie and Margaret Alexander were: 1. Mary, married Dr. David R. Dunlap, of Charlotte; 2. Eliza, died unmarried; 3. Margaret, do.; 4. Lillis, married B. Oates; 5. Robert B., married Ann Sloan; 6. Samuel, married Mary Johnson.

Margaret Jack, fourth daughter of Patrick Jack, married Samuel Wilson, of Mecklenburg. (For his descendants, see "Genealogy of Samuel Wilson, Sr.")

Lillis Jack, the fifth and youngest daughter of Patrick Jack, married Joseph Nicholson. He left the State, and is reported as having a family of six children, but of their subsequent history little is known.

Colonel Patrick Jack, a brave and meritorious officer under the Colonial Government, and during the Revolutionary war, was the son of Charles Jack, who lived on the Conococheague river, near Chambersburg, Pa., and was probably the brother of Patrick Jack, of Charlotte, N. C., whose family history has just been given.

Colonel Jack lived an active and adventurous life, and was born about 1730. He was much engaged, when a young man, in assisting to subdue the Indians in Pennsylvania, and commanded a company of Rangers, under Generals Braddock and Washington, in the Indian and French war of 1755. He also commanded a regiment, and participated actively in the Revolutionary War He was in the Cherokee country many years anterior to the Revolution.

He was at the massacre of the garrison in Fort London, on the Tennessee River in 1760, and was one of three persons who survived, his life having been saved through the influence of the Indian chief, *Atta-kulla-kulla*, the "Little Carpenter." He had three children; Mary, Jane, and John Finley Jack. John was educated at Dickinson College, Carlisle, Pa. He studied law, and emigrated to Knoxville, then the capital of Tennessee, where he soon acquired eminence, and a lucrative practice in his profession. He afterward removed to Rutledge, in Grainger county, East Tennessee, where he associated himself in the same profession with his brother-in-law, the late General John Cocke, a son of General William Cocke, one of the distinguished characters in the early history of Tennessee. He took a prominent part in the politics of the country, filled the offices of Circuit Clerk, State's Attorney, served several times in both branches of the Legislature, and was finally elected Circuit Judge, which position he held for many years. When the infirmities of old age impeded his activity and usefulness, he retired from public life to his plantation near Bean's Station, East Tennessee, where he ended his days.

He was a profound lawyer, a Judge of great purity of character, of remarkable discrimination and integrity of purpose, evinced through a long, useful, and honorable life. He was a hard student, possessed fine colloquial powers, and was a man of eminent learning and research.

Judge John F. Jack married Elizabeth, next to the

youngest daughter of General William Cocke, previously mentioned, who was a Captain in the Revolutionary War, a companion of Daniel Boon from western North Carolina across the Alleghany mountains to the "wilderness of Kentu..," a prominent actor in the establishment of the Frankland Government," one of the first Senators to Congress from the new State of Tennessee, and afterward, one of the Circuit Judges of that State. He served in the Legislatures of Virginia, North Carolina, Tennessee and Mississippi. At the advanced age of sixty-five years, he volunteered in the war of 1812, and distinguished himself for his personal courage. He died on the 8th of August, 1828, in the eighty-seventh year of his age, universally lamented, and is buried in Columbus, Mississippi.

It has been previously stated that Col. Patrick Jack, the father of Judge John F. Jack, led an active and adventurous life. One of these adventures will be now narrated.

In Dr. Ramsey's "Annals of Tennessee," page 68, we have this record : "A grant, signed Arthur Dobbs, Governor of North Carolina; William Beamer, Sen., Superintendent and Deputy Adjutant in and for the Cherokee Nation; and William Beamer, Jun., Interpreter; and the "Little Carpenter," half king of the Cherokee Nation of the over-hill towns; and Matthew Toole, Interpreter, made to Captain Patrick Jack, of the province of Pennsylvania, is recorded in the Register's office of Knox county, Tennessee. It purports to have been made at a council held at Tennessee River, on the 1st of March, 1757. The consideration is four hundred dollars, and conveys to Capt. Jack *fifteen miles square* south of the Tennessee river. The grant itself, confirmatory of the purchase by Jack, is dated at a general council, met at the Catawba River, on the 7th of May, 1762, and is witnessed by Nathaniel Alexander."

Upon this speculative transaction it is proper to make a few explanatory remarks. About 1750, East Tennessee was beginning to be settled by adventurous individuals, principally from western North Carolina, south-western Virginia, and occasionally from more northern colonies. The Indians were still regarded as the rightful owners and proper "lords of the soil." At the date of the council held at the Tennessee River in 1757, only that portion of the country north of that stream had become sparsely settled, but soon thereafter purchases of land were sometimes made directly from the Indian chiefs themselves, as in the above instance, and settlements of whites speedily followed. Matthew Toole, one of the parties named, had lived among the Cherokee Indians, and taken to "bed and board," as a wife, one of the swarthy damsels of that tribe—hence his qualification as interpreter. He lived on the eastern bank of the Catawba river, in Mecklenburg county, giving origin to the name of the ford which still bears his name. Nathaniel Alexander, the subscribing witness, was then an acting magistrate of the county, and a man of extensive influence.

Colonel Patrick Jack, the father of Judge John F. Jack, died in Chambersburg, Pa., on the 25th of January, 1821, aged ninety-one years. His daughter, Jane Stewart, died in 1853, also aged ninety-one years. His daughter Mary (never married) died on the 29th of May, 1862, aged eighty-five years.

The family of Judge John F. Jack consisted of eight children, of whom, at the present time (1876) only four are living, viz.: Martha Mariah (Mrs. Dr. Rhoton), of Morristown, East Tennessee; William Pinkney Jack, of Russelville, Ala.; John F. Jack, of West Point, Mississippi, both worthy and eminent lawyers in their respective locations: and Sarah Anne (Mrs. Dr. Carriger), of Morristown, Tenn. Few persons, in the early history of East Tennessee, were held in as great estimation, and filled with universal acceptance as many important positions of public trust as Judge John F. Jack. The county seat of justice of Campbell county, Jacksboro, was named in his honor, and his descendants should hold in cherished remembrance his purity of life and unsullied integrity of character.

GENEALOGY OF SAMUEL WILSON, SEN.

Samuel Wilson, Sr., was one of the earliest settlers of Mecklenburg county, and the patriarchal ancestor of numerous descendants, who performed important civil and military services in the Revolutionary war. He emigrated from Pennsylvania about 1745, and purchased a large body of valuable lands in the bounds of Hopewell church, in Mecklenburg county. He was of Scotch-Irish descent, and inherited the peculiar traits of that liberty-loving people. He was married three times, and was the father of thirteen children. His first wife was Mary Winslow, a sister of Moses Winslow, one of the early and leading patriots of Rowan county, who died on the 1st of October, 1813, in the eighty-third year of his age, and is buried in the graveyard of Center Church.

Samuel Wilson, Sr., died on the 13th of March, 1778, in the sixty-eighth year of his age. His children, by the first wife, were: 1, Mary; 2, Violet; 3, Samuel; 4, John; 5, Benjamin Wilson. Mary, the eldest daughter, married Ezekiel Polk, the father of Samuel Polk, and grandfather of James K. Polk, President of the United States in 1845. Ezekiel Polk was a man of wealth and influence in Mecklenburg county preceding the Revolution, and owned a large body of the valuable lands in and around the present flourishing village of Pineville. Samuel Polk inherited a portion of this land, lying in the "horse shoe bend" of Little Sugar Creek, and immediately on the Camden road, over which Cornwallis marched with his army on his celebrated visit (the first and the last) to the "Hornet's Nest" of America.

2. Violet Wilson married Major John Davidson, one of the signers of the Mecklenburg Declaration of Independence.

3. Samuel Wilson, a soldier of the Revolution, married Hannah Knox, a daughter of Captain Patrick Knox, killed at the battle of Ramsour's Mill. He raised a large family, all of whom have passed away, falling mostly as victims of consumption. His daughter Mary (or "Polly") married her cousin Benjamin Wilson, (son of David Wilson) who was killed by Nixon Curry, because he was to appear in court as a witness against him.

4. *Major David Wilson*, an ardent patriot, and one of the heroes under Colonel Locke at Ramsour's Mill, married Sallie McConnell, a sister of Mrs. General James White, the father of the Hon. Hugh Lawson White. (See sketch of his life, under "Iredell County.")

Mrs. Adaline McCoy, of Lincolnton, is a daughter, and worthy descendant of Moses Winslow Wilson, a son of Major David Wilson. John and Benjamin Wilson, the remaining sons of Samuel Wilson, Sr., by the first wife, never married.

After General Davidson was killed at Cowan's Ford, on the morning of the 1st of February, 1781, Major David Wilson, and Richard Barry, Esq., both of whom participated in the skirmish at that place, secured the body of their beloved commander, and carried it to the residence of Samuel Wilson, Sr., to receive the usual preparatory attentions for burial. Mrs. Davidson, who resided about ten miles distant, in the vicinity of Center Church, was immediately sent for; she came as hastily as possible in the afternoon, under the charge of George Templeton, one of her neighbors, and received, on that solemn occasion, the heart-felt condolence and sympathy of numerous sorrowing friends and relatives. In consequence of this necessary delay, those true patriots and friends of the deceased (Wilson and Barry) moved with the body late in the evening of the same day, and committed it to the silent tomb, *by torchlight*, in Hopewell grave-yard.

7. *Rebecca Wilson*, the youngest daughter by the first wife, married John Henderson. After the birth of two

children, they set out from Mecklenburg, with the intention of moving to Tennessee, accompanied by a brother and sister of Henderson. On the way, while they were stopping for dinner, they were suddenly attacked by Indians. Henderson and his wife were killed. The brother and sister each seized a child and made their escape. The children were brought back to Mecklenburg county, and properly cared for by their relatives; but, after they grew up, and Indian outrages having subsided, they returned to Tennessee.

The second wife of Samuel Wilson, Sr., was a widow Potts. Having a feeble constitution, she lived but a short time, leaving a daughter, named Margaret, who married John Davidson, an uncle of the late William Davidson, Esq., of Charlotte. After she was left a widow, she moved with her three children, Samuel Wilson, John (or "Jackey") and Mary Davidson, to Alabama, where a large number of her descendants may be now found in Bibb and adjoining counties of that State.

The children of Major John Davidson and Violet Wilson were:

1. Isabella Davidson married Gen. Joseph Graham, of Lincoln county, the father of the late Hon. William A. Graham and others.

2. Rebecca Davidson married Capt. Alexander Brevard, a brother of Dr. Ephraim Brevard, the reputed author of the Mecklenburg Declaration of the 20th of May, 1775, and one of the "seven brothers in the rebel army," at one time.

3. Violet Davidson married William Bain Alexander, a son of John McKnitt Alexander, one of the secretaries of the Mecklenburg Convention.

4. Elizabeth Davidson married William Lee Davidson, a son of General Davidson, who fell at Cowan's Ford.

5. Mary Davidson married Dr. William McLean, a distinguished physician during and after the Revolution.

6 Sarah Davidson married Alexander Caldwell, a son of Dr. David Caldwell, an eminent Presbyterian minister of Guilford county.

7. Margaret Davidson married Major James Harris, of Cabarrus county.

8. John (or "Jackey") Davidson, married Sallie Brevard, a daughter of Adam Brevard, a brother of Dr. Ephraim Brevard.

9. Robert Davidson married Margaret Osborne, a daughter of Adlai Osborne, the grandfather of the late Jas. W. Osborne, of Charlotte.

10. Benjamin Wilson Davidson married Elizabeth Latta, a daughter of James Latta, Esq.

The third wife of Samuel Wilson, Sr., was Margaret Jack, a sister of Captain Jack, the bearer of the Mecklenburg Declaration to Congress. By this marriage there were five children:

1. *Sarah Wilson*, married Ben McConnell, who had three children, Charity, Latta and Wilson McConnell. Charity McConnell married Reese Davidson, a nephew of General Ephraim Davidson. This family, and also that of Wilson McConnell, moved to Tennessee.

2. *Charity Wilson*, died at the age of sixteen years.

3. *Robert Wilson*, married Margaret Alexander, a daughter of Major Thomas Alexander, and grand-daughter of Neil Morrison, one of the Mecklenburg signers. He left five daughters, and one son, who lost his life in the Confederate cause.

4. *Lillis Wilson*, (frequently written "Lillie,") married James Connor, who emigrated from Ireland when about twenty-one years of age; volunteered his services at the commencement of the Revolutionary War, and fought through the struggle to its close. He died in April, 1835, aged eighty-four years, and is buried in Baker's graveyard. He left two children, Henry Workman and Margaret Jack Conner. II. Workman Conner was a worthy and influential citizen of Charleston, S. C., where he spent

about fifty years of his life, and died in January, 1861. Margaret J. Connor married J. Franklin Brevard, a son of Capt. Alexander Brevard, of Lincoln county. She was an estimable Christian lady, survived her husband many years, was beloved by all who knew her, and died with peaceful resignation, on the 25th of October, 1866, in the sixty-eighth year of her age. Her only child, Rebecca, married Robert I. McDowell, Esq., of Mecklenburg county.

5. *William Jack Wilson*, youngest child of Samuel Wilson, Sr., by the third wife, married Rocinda Winslow, the youngest daughter of Moses Winslow. The house in which this old patriot then resided, has long since disappeared. It stood on the public road, about three miles southwest of Center Church. A large Honey Locust tree now (1876) nearly points out its original location.

William J. Wilson left four children: 1. Dovey A., (Mrs. Dougherty); 2. Robert; 3. LaFayette, and 4. James C. Wilson.

The house in which Samuel Wilson, Sr., resided, and to which the body of General Davidson was borne by David Wilson and Richard Barry, before sepulture, was a two-story frame building. No portion of it now remains, and the plow runs smoothly over its site. Robert and William J. Wilson built on the old homestead property. These two brothers were closely united in filial affection during their lives, and now lie, side by side, in Hopewell graveyard.

Mrs. Margaret Jack Wilson, third wife of Samuel Wilson, Sr., is described by all who knew her, as a woman of uncommon energy, of an amiable disposition, charitable to the poor, and a truly humble Christian. She died at the age of fifty-eight years, was never sick during her life, until a few days before her death, and is buried in Baker's graveyard. When drawing near to the close of her earthly existence, she was asked if she had a desire to live longer; she replied, "No; she was like a ship long tossed at sea and about to land at a port of rest."

In this same spot of ground, (Baker's graveyard,) five miles northeast of Beattie's Foard, on the Catawba, consecrated as the last resting-place of some of the earliest settlers of Mecklenburg county, repose the mortal remains of the Rev. John Thompson, one of the first Presbyterian missionaries in this section of the State, and who died in September, 1753. No monumental slab or head-stone is placed at his grave. Tradition says he built a cabin (or study-house) in the northwestern angle of the graveyard, and was buried beneath its floor, being the first subject of interment. John Baker, who lived in the immediate vicinity, married his daughter, and dying a few years later, gave the permanent name to the burial-ground. Here also repose the remains of *Hugh Lawson*, the grandfather of the Hon. Hugh Lawson White, a native of Iredell county. The only tablet to the memory of this early setler, is a rough slate rock, about one foot high and nine inches broad, on which are rudely chiseled the initial letters of his name, thus combined, I̵L. In subsequent years, after the erection of Hopewell Church, the most of the Wilson family and relatives were buried in the graveyard at that place.

CAPTAIN CHARLES POLK'S "MUSTER ROLL."

Among the interesting Revolutionary records of Mecklenburg county, which have been preserved, is the "Muster Roll" of Captain Charles Polk's Company of "Light Horse," with the time of service and pay of each member thereof, as follows:

"Dr. The Public of North Carolina,
To Captain Charles Polk, for services done by him and his Company of Light Horse, who entered the 12th of March, 1776.

Captain, Charles Polk.
1st Lieut., William Ramsey.
2nd Lieut., John Lemmond.
1st Sergt., John Montgomery
2nd Sergt., William Galbraith (erased).
Drummer, Hugh Lindsay.
John Smith.
John Polk, Sen. (erased).
John Wylie.
John Findley.
John Galbraith.
James Hall.
John Stansill.
William ―――― (illegible).
John Miller.
Humphrey Hunter.
Henry Carter.
James Maxwell.
John Maxwell.
Robert Galbraith.
John McCandlis.
Nicholas Siler.
Samuel Linton.
Thomas Shelby.
James Alexander.
Robert Harris, Jun.
John Foard.
Jonathan Buckaloe.
Charles Alexander, Sen.
Henry Powell.
William Rea.
Samuel Hughes.
Charles Alexander, Jun.
William Shields.
Charles Polk, Jun.
John Purser.
William Lemmond, 'Clerk to the said company, and Shurgeon to ye same.'"

Remarks.—The whole expense of Captain Polk's company in this campaign for sixty-five days, including the hire of three wagons at 16s. each per day, and two thousand and five rations, at 8d. each, amounted to £683 9s. 8d. The account was proven, according to law, before Colonel Adam Alexander, one of the magistrates of the county, and audited and countersigned by Ephraim Alexander, George Mitchell and James Jack, the bearer of the Mecklenburg Declaration to Congress. The pay of a Captain was then 10s. per day; of a 1st and 2nd Lieutenant, 7s. each; of a first Sergeant, 6s. 6d.; of a 2nd Sergeant, 5s. 6d.; of the Clerk and "Shurgeon," 6s. 6d.; and of each private, 5s.

James Hall, one of the privates in this expedition, afterward became a distinguished Presbyterian minister of the gospel, and was elected on two occasions by his own congregation, in pressing emergencies, to the captaincy of a company, and acted as chaplain of the forces with which he was associated. The late Rev. John Robinson, of Poplar Tent Church, in Cabarrus county, in speaking of him, said, "when a boy at school in Charlotte (Queen's Museum), I saw James Hall pass through the town, with his three-cornered hat, the captain of a company and chaplain of the regiment." In Captain Polk's manuscript journal of his march, under Gen. Rutherford, through the mountains of North Carolina, then the unconquered haunts of wild beasts and savage Indians, he says: "On September 15th, 1776, Mr. Hall preached a sermon," prompted, as it appears, by the death of one of Captain Irwin's men on the day before.

This was probably the first sermon ever heard in those secluded mountainous valleys, now busy with the hum of civilized life. (See sketch of his services under "Iredell County.")

Humphrey Hunter, first a private and afterward lieutenant in Captain Robert Mebane's company in this expedition, also became an eminent minister of the gospel, and presided at the *semi-centennial* celebration of the Mecklenburg Declaration of Independence, on the 20th of May, 1825. (See sketch of his services under Gaston county.)

William Shields was the gallant soldier of General Sumter's command, who discovered a bag of gold in the camp of the routed enemy after the battle of Hanging Rock. Not less generous than brave, steady on the march, and true on the field, he voluntarily carried the gold to his commanding general, and requested him to use it in the purchase of clothing and shoes for his ragged and suffering fellow-soldiers. It is needless to say that this brave and meritorious officer faithfully applied it according to the request of the honest and generous soldier.

Thomas Shelby, a relative of Colonel Isaac Shelby, of King's Mountain fame, James Alexander, Charles Polk, Jun., Robert Harris, William Ramsey, John Foard (one of the Mecklenburg signers), John Lemmond, John Montgomery, William Rea, and others on the list, will awaken in the minds of their descendants emotions of veneration for their patriotic ancestors, who, one hundred years ago—at the very dawn of the Revolution, and before a *hesitating* Congress, proclaimed our National declaration, pledged their lives, fortunes and sacred honor in the cause of American freedom.

PRESIDENT JAMES K. POLK.

James Knox Polk, son of Samuel Polk, and grandson of Ezekiel Polk, was born on the 2nd of November, 1795 about eleven miles south of Charlotte, on the Camden road, on a plantation which, at his father's removal to Tennessee in 1806, became the property of Nathan Orr, and finally that of the late James Hennigan, Esq. The house in which James K. Polk was born, stood about two hundred yards south of the present crossing place of Little Sugar Creek, and about one hundred yards to the right of the public road in passing from Charlotte. The lingering signs of the old family mansion are still visible; and the plow, in this *centennial year*, runs smoothly over its site, presenting a more vigorous growth of the great Southern staple, *cotton*, than the adjoining lands. The plantation was a part of the valuable lands owned by Ezekiel Polk in the "Providence" settlement, and near the present flourishing village of "Pineville." The family mansion, around which "Jimmy Polk" sported with his younger brothers and sisters, and wended their way in frolicsome mood to a neighboring school, was an humble building, made by joining two hewn log houses together, with a passage between, in the common style of the first settlers. In 1851 Mr. Hennigan, the last owner of the property, moved one half of the building, apparently the better portion, but with a badly decayed roof, to his barn-yard, and near his handsome residence on the rising ground south-east of its original location, and re-covered it, where it may be seen at the present time.

Samuel Polk, the father of James K. Polk, married Jane, a daughter of James Knox, a soldier of the Revolution, who lived at a place about midway between the residences of the late Rev. John Williamson and Benjamin Wilson Davidson, Esq., youngest son of Major John Davidson. He had ten children, of whom James K. was the eldest, and who early displayed quick, intuitive powers. He received the principal part of his education in North Carolina, and graduated in 1818 at the State University, with the highest honors of his class. While at college, he laid the foundations of his future fame and usefulness.

It is said he never missed a single recitation, or avoided a single duty during the whole course of his collegiate term. After graduating, he returned to Tennessee, his father's adopted state, commenced the study of law in the office of the Hon. Felix Grundy, and was admitted to the bar in 1820. In 1823, he entered the stormy sea of politics, in which he was destined to achieve a brilliant career. In 1825, he was elected to Congress, and in 1835, was made Speaker of the House of Representatives, which honorable position he held for five sessions. After serving fourteen years, with distinguished ability and impartiality, he declined a re-election. During this long and laborious service, he was never known to be absent, for a single day, from the House. In 1839, after an animated contest, he was elected Governor of Tennessee. In May, 1844, he was nominated as a candidate for the Presidency of the United States. His majority in the Electoral College over Henry Clay for this high office was sixty-five votes. The great labor he performed at a period of unexampled danger to the republic, and of difficulties with foreign nations, operated seriously upon his debilitated system, and hastened his end.

In May, 1844, in accepting the nomination, he declared in advance, that, if elected, he would only serve *one term*. And in a letter addressed to the Convention, through Dr. J. G. M. Ramsey, of Knoxville, he re-iterated his determination, and voluntarily declined, when many of his friends deemed his name the only available means of success. His precarious and constantly declining state of health, forcibly admonished him of his early departure from the scenes of earth. He calmly met his approaching end, and died at Nashville, on the 15th of June, 1849, in the forty-fourth year of his age.

When the mists of party and prejudice shall have subsided, and the dispassionate verdict of posterity be given, the services of James K. Polk will be acknowledged as unsurpassed in the annals of our nation; and his noble and disinterested example of only serving *one term*, will be regarded by all pure-minded occupants of the Presidential Chair, as worthy of imitation.

Mecklenburg county is proud of her son!

In the old "Polk Graveyard," nine miles from Charlotte, is the tombstone of Mrs. Maria Polk, a grand-aunt of President Polk, containing a lengthy eulogy, in poetry and prose, of this good woman. The first sentence, "*Virtus non exemptio a morte,*"* is neatly executed on a semi-circle, extending over the prostrate figure of a departed female saint, sculptured with considerable skill on the soapstone slab, but now scarcely visible on account of the over-spreading moss and lichen. Immediately beneath the *sainted figure* is the expression, *Formosa etsi mortua.*† From the lengthy eulogy, the following extracts are taken:

"Here, unalarmed at death's last stroke,
Lies in this tomb, Maria Polk;
A tender mother, virtuous wife,
Resigned in every scene of life.
 * * * * *
To heavenly courts she did repair;
May those she loved all meet her there."

"Supported by the hope of a happy death, and a glorious resurrection to eternal life, she bore a tedious and painful illness with a truly christian fortitude. The last exercise of her feeble mind was employed in singing the 33rd of the second book of Dr. Watt's Hymns, in which, anticipating the blessed society above, she exchanged the earthly for the heavenly melody."

She died on the 29th of November, 1791, in the forty-fifth year of her age.

---

*"Virtue affords no exemption from death." †"Beautiful, although dead."

GENERAL WILLIAM DAVIDSON.

General William Davidson was the youngest son of George Davidson, and born in 1746. His father moved from Lancaster county, in Pennsylvania, in 1750, to North Carolina, and settled in the western part of Rowan county (now Iredell.) Here General Davidson received his earliest mental training, and subsequently his principal and final education at Queen's Museum College in Charlotte, where many of the patriots of Mecklenburg and surrounding counties were educated.

At the Provincial Congress which met at Halifax, on on the 4th of April, 1776, four additional regiments to the two already in service, were ordered to be raised, over one of which (the 4th) Thomas Polk was appointed Colonel, James Thackston Lieutenant Colonel, and William Davidson Major. With this regiment, under General Francis Nash, he marched to join the army of the North, under General Washington, where he served until November, 1779, when the North Carolina line was ordered south to reinforce General Lincoln, at Charleston. Previous to this time he had been promoted to the rank of Lieutenant Colonel in the line. As the troops passed through North Carolina, Colonel Davidson obtained a furlough for a few days to visit his family, whom he had not seen for three years. This saved him from the fate which befell Gen. Lincoln and his army at Charleston; for, when he approached that city, he found it so closely invested by the British Army that he was prevented from joining his regiment. When Lincoln surrendered, Davidson returned to Mecklenburg, and rendered important services in subduing the Tories, who, encouraged by the success of the British arms, became numerous, daring and oppressive.

A strong force of Tories having assembled at Coulson's Mill, General Davidson raised a troop of volunteers and marched against them. A fierce skirmish took place, in which he was severely wounded by a ball passing through his body near the kidneys. This wound nearly proved fatal, and detained him from the service about two months. After his recovery, he again took the field, having been promoted for his bravery to the rank of Brigadier-General in the place of General Rutherford, made a prisoner at the battle of Camden. He was active, with General Sumner and Colonel Davie, in checking the advance of the British, and throughout this darkest period of the Revolution gave ample evidence of his untiring zeal in the cause of his country.

After the battle of the Cowpens, on the 17th of January, 1781, in which General Morgan, with an inferior force, chastised the temerity and insolence of Tarleton, General Davidson was actively engaged in assembling the militia of his district to aid General Greene in impeding the advance of the British army in pursuit of General Morgan, encumbered with more than five hundred prisoners, on his way to Virginia. General Greene, accompanied by two or three attendants, left his camp near the Cheraws, rode rapidly through the country, and met General Morgan at Sherrill's Ford, on the eastern bank of the Catawba river, and directed his future movements.

General Davidson had placed guards at Tuckasege, Toole's, Cowan's and Beattie's Fords. When Cornwallis approached the Catawba, on the evening of the 28th of January, he found it considerably swollen and impassable for his infantry.

This Providential obstacle caused him to fall back five miles from the river to Jacob Forney's plantation, a thrifty farmer of that neighborhood. General Davidson had assembled a force of about three hundred and fifty men at Cowan's Ford. At half past two o'clock on the morning of the 1st of February, 1781, Cornwallis broke up his encampment at Forney's and reached Cowan's Ford at daybreak. It was a dark morning, accompanied with slight drizzling rain. The light infantry, under Colonel Hall, entered first, followed by the grenadiers and the battalions

The picquet of the Americans challenged the enemy: receiving no reply, the guard fired at the advancing enemy. This immediately called into action that portion of Davidson's forces placed near the river, who kept up a galling fire from the bank. According to Stedman, the English historian, who accompanied Cornwallis, the Tory guide, becoming alarmed at the firing, when the British army reached the middle of the river, turned about and left them. This caused Colonel Hall to lead them directly across to an unexpected landing-place. Colonel Hall was killed as he ascended the bank; the horse of Lord Cornwallis was shot in the river, and fell dead as he reached the bank; three privates were killed and thirty-six wounded. The diversion of the British army from the proper landing caused the Americans to fire angularly and not directly upon their enemy, and hence was less effective in its results. General Davidson, who was about half a mile in the rear with the larger portion of his forces, arrived at the scene of action just as the Americans were fleeing before the fire of the well-organized and greatly superior British forces.

In attempting to rally the Americans, and venturing too near the British army, he received a fatal shot in his breast, and fell dead almost instantly from his horse. The loss of the Americans in privates was only two killed and about twenty wounded.

The British infantry waded the river in platoons, and reserved their fire until they ascended the eastern bank, and thus effected their passage. Cornwallis remained only about three hours after the skirmish, for the purpose of burying his dead, and then proceeded in the direction of Salisbury. Soon after his departure David Wilson and Richard Barry, both of whom were in the skirmish, secured the body of their beloved commander, conveyed it to the house of Samuel Wilson, Sen., and buried it that night by *torch-light* in the graveyard of Hopewell Church.

Thus fell in the prime of life, and at a moment of great

usefulness to his country, this noble and patriotic soldier. Right worthily is his name bestowed upon one of the most fertile counties of our State, and upon a seat of learning, located near the scene of his death, which will perpetuate his fame as long as liberty has a votary throughout all succeeding time.

GENERAL GEORGE GRAHAM.

General George Graham was born in Pennsylvania in 1758, and came with his widowed mother and four others to North Carolina, when about six years old. He was chiefly educated at "Queen's Museum," in Charlotte, and was distinguished for his assiduity, manly behaviour and kindliness of disposition. He was early devoted to the cause of liberty, and was ever its untiring defender. There was no duty too perilous, no service too dangerous, that he was not ready to undertake for the welfare and independence of his country.

In 1775, when it was reported in Charlotte that two Tory lawyers, Dunn and Boothe, had proposed the detention of Capt. Jack on his way to Philadelphia, and had pronounced the patriotic resolutions with which he was entrusted, as "treasonable," George Graham was one of the gallant spirits who rode all night to Salisbury, seized said offending lawyers, and brought them them to Mecklenburg for trial. Here, after being found guilty of conduct "inimical to the cause of American freedom," they were transported to Camden, S. C., and afterward to Charleston, and imprisoned.

Such were the open manifestations of liberty and independence in different portions of North Carolina in 1775!

When Cornwallis lay at Charlotte in 1780, Graham took an active part in attacking his foraging parties, making it extremely difficult and hazardous for them to procure their necessary supplies. He was one of the thirteen brave spirits, under Capt. James Thompson, who dared to attack a foraging party of four hundred British troops at McIntire's Branch, seven miles northwest of Charlotte, on the Beattie's Ford road, compelling them to retreat, with a considerable loss of men and a small amount of forage, fearing, as they said, an ambuscade was prepared for their capture.

After the war, he was elected Major General of the North Carolina militia. For many years, he was clerk of the court of Mecklenburg county, and frequently a member of the State Legislature. He was the people's friend, not their flatterer, and uniformly enjoyed the confidence and high esteem of his fellow-citizens. He lived more than half a century on his farm, two miles from Charlotte. He died on the 29th of March, 1826, in the sixty-eighth year of his age, and is buried in the grave-yard of the Presbyterian Church at Charlotte.

WILLIAM RICHARDSON DAVIE.

General William R. Davie was born in Egremont, near White Haven, in England, on the 20th of June, 1756. When he was only five years of age, he emigrated, with his father, Archibald Davie, to America, and was adopted by his maternal uncle, Rev. William Richardson, who resided on the Catawba river, in South Carolina. After due preparation at "Queen's Museum" in Charlotte, he entered Princeton College, where, by his close application, he soon acquired the reputation of an excellent student. But the din of arms disturbed his collegiate studies, so auspiciously commenced, and he forthwith exchanged the gown for the sword. The studies of the College were closed, and Davie volunteered his services in the army of the north in 1776. The campaign being ended, he returned to College, and graduated in the Fall of that year with the first honors of the Institution.

He returned to North Carolina, and commenced the study of the law in Salisbury, but the struggle for life and liberty then going on, did not allow his chivalric spirit to repose in quietude while his country was in danger. Actuated by urgent patriotic motives, he induced William Barnett, of Mecklenburg county, to raise, with as little delay as possible, a troop of horsemen. Over this company. William Barnett was elected Captain, and Davie, Lieutenant. The commission of the latter is signed by Governor Caswell, and is dated the 5th of April, 1779. This company joined the southern army, and became attached to Pulaski's Legion. Davie's gallantry and activity were so conspicuous, that he soon rose to the rank of Major.

At the battle of Stono, near Charleston, he experienced his first serious conflict in arms, and was severely wounded in the thigh, which laid him up for some time in the hospital in that city. In this engagement, Major Davie also received a wound from a heavy cavalry charge of the enemy, which caused him to fall from his horse. He still held the bridle, but was so severely wounded that, after repeated efforts, he could not remount. The enemy was now close upon him, and in a moment more he would have been made a prisoner. Just at this time, a private, whose horse had been killed, and who was retreating, saw the imminent danger of his gallant officer, and returned at the risk of his life to save him. With great composure he raised Major Davie on his horse, and safely led him from the bloody field. "An action of courage worthy of Rome in her palmiest days." In the haste and confusion of the retreat, this brave soldier disappeared. Major Davie made frequent inquiries for his preserver, to evince his gratitude to him and his family, for his timely and heroic aid; but in vain.

At the siege of Ninety-Six, when Davie was acting as Commissary-General of the Southern army, on the morning of the attack, a soldier came to his tent, and made himself known as the man who had assisted him in mounting his horse at Stono. The soldier promised to call again, but, alas! he fell soon after in battle, which deprived Major

Davie of the pleasure of bestowing upon him substantial tokens of his lasting gratitude.

After his recovery, Major Davie returned to Salisbury, and resumed the study of law. In 1780, he obtained his license to practice, and soon became distinguished in his profession. But the camp rather than the Court-house still demanded his services. In the winter of 1780, he obtained authority from the General Assembly of North Carolina to raise a troop of cavalry, and two companies of mounted infantry. But the authority only was granted. The State being too poor to provide the means, Major Davie, with a patriotism worthy of perpetual remembrance, disposed of the estate acquired from his uncle, and thus raised funds to equip the troops. With this force, he proceeded to the southwestern portion of the State and protected it from the predatory incursions of the British and Tories. Charleston having surrendered on the 12th of May, 1780, and Tarleton's butchery of Colonel Buford's regiment, in the Waxhaws, on the 29th, induced General Rutherford to order out the militia in mass, to oppose the advance of the conquerors. On the 3rd of June, nine hundred men assembled at Charlotte, ready to defend their country. The militia were reviewed by General Rutherford, and, after being addressed in strong, patriotic language by Dr. Whorter, President of the College in Charlottee, were dismissed, with directions to hold themselves in readiness at a moment's warning.

Lord Rawdon having advanced with the British army to Waxhaw Creek, General Rutherford issued, on the 10th of June, his orders for the militia to rendezvous at McKee's plantation, eighteen miles north-east of Charlotte. The orders were obeyed, and on the 12th eight hundred men were in arms on the ground. On the 14th the troops were organized. The cavalry, under Major Davie, was formed into two troops under Captains Lemmonds and Martin; a battalion of three hundred light infantry was placed under Colonel William Davidson, a regular officer, and the remainder under the immediate command of General Rutherford.

On the 15th of June General Rutherford marched within two miles of Charlotte. Here he learned that Lord Rawdon had retrograded from the Waxhaws to Camden. He then resolved to advance on the Tories, who, it was well known, had assembled in strong force at Ramsour's Mill, near the present town of Lincolnton. Having issued orders on the 14th to Colonel Francis Locke, Captains Falls and Brandon, of Rowan, and to Major David Wilson, of Mecklenburg, and to other officers, to raise men and attack this body of Tories, he marched on the 18th eleven miles, to Tuckasege Ford, on the Catawba River. He sent an express on the same day to Colonel Locke to meet him with his forces three miles north-west of the river, at Colonel Dickson's plantation. The express, for some unknown reason, never reached Colonel Locke. This officer, failing to secure the co-operative aid of General Rutherford, marched from Mountain Creek late on the evening of the 19th of June, and early on the morning of the 20th attacked and routed the Tories before the arrival of General Rutherford's forces. (For further particulars, see the "Battle of Ramsour's Mill," under the head of Lincoln County.)

After the battle of Ramsour's Mill, General Rutherford marched against the Tories assembled under Colonel Bryan in the forks of Yadkin River, while Major Davie was ordered to move with his mounted force and take position near the South Carolina line, to protect this exposed frontier from the incursions of the British and the Tories. He accordingly took position on the north side of Waxhaw Creek, where he was joined by Major Crawford, with a few South Carolina troops and thirty-five Indian warriors of the Catawba tribe, under their chief, New River, and the Mecklenburg militia under Colonel Hagins.

On the 20th of July Major Davie surprised and captured

at Flat Rock, a convoy of provisions, spirits and clothing, guarded by some dragoons and volunteers, on their way to the post at Hanging Rock, about four and a half miles distant. The capture was effected without loss; the spirits, provisions and wagons were destroyed, and the prisoners, mounted on the captured horses and guarded by dragoons under Captain William Polk, at dark commenced their retreat. On Beaver Creek, about midnight, they were attacked by the enemy in ambuscade, concealed under the fence in a field of standing corn. The rear guard had entered the lane when Captain Petit, the officer in advance, hailed the British in their place of concealment. A second challenge was answered by a volley of musketry from the enemy, which commenced on the right, and passed by a running fire to the rear of the detachment. Major Davie rode rapidly forward and ordered the men to push through the lane; but, under surprise, his troops turned back, and upon the loaded arms of the enemy. He was thus compelled to repass the ambuscade under a heavy fire, and overtook his men retreating by the same road they had advanced. The detachment was finally rallied and halted upon a hill, but so discomfited at this unexpected attack that no effort could induce them to charge upon the enemy.

A judicious retreat was the only course left to avoid a similar disaster, which was effected; and Major Davie, having passed the enemy's patrols, regained his camp early on the next day without further accident. In this attack, the fire of the enemy fell chiefly upon those in the lane, who were prisoners (confined two on a horse with the guard). These were nearly all killed, or severely wounded. Of the Whigs, Lieutenant Elliott was killed, and Captain Petit, who had been sent in advance by Major Davie to examine the lane, the ford of the creek and the houses, and failing to do so, as carefully as was proper, paid the penalty of neglect of duty by being wounded with two of his men. Major Davie, who was noted for his vigilance, anticipated some attempt by the British and Tories to recover the prisoners, and had taken, as he believed, all necessary precautions to prevent a surprise or ambuscade.

Major Davie, in a manuscript account of this affair, now on file in the archives of the Historical Society at Chapel Hill, leaves this judicious advice: "It furnishes a lesson to officers of partisan corps, that every officer of a detachment may, at some time, have its safety and reputation committed to him, and that the slightest neglect of duty is generally severely punished by an enemy."

Rocky Mount is on the west bank of the Wateree River (as the Catawba is called after its junction with Wateree Creek), thirty miles from Camden, and was garrisoned by Colonel Turnbull with one hundred and fifty New York volunteers and some militia. Its defences consisted of two log-houses, a loop-holed building and an *abattis*.*

On the 30th of July, 1780, General Sumter and Colonel Neal, from South Carolina, and Colonel Irwin, with three hundred Mecklenburg militia, joined Major Davie. A council was held, and it was determined that simultaneous attacks should be made upon the British posts at Rocky Mount and Hanging Rock. General Sumter was accompanied by Colonels Neal, Irwin and Lacy, and Captain McLure, and some of his kinsmen, the Gastons. Having crossed the Catawba at Blair's Ford, he arrived early on the next day, and made vigorous attacks against the fort, but failed in capturing it, mainly for the want of artillery. The attack elicited the praise of even the enemy. Early in the action, the gallant Colonel Neal was killed, with five whites and one Catawba Indian, and many were severely wounded. The British loss was ten killed, and the same number wounded. General Sumter ordered a retreat, which was effected without further annoyance or loss.

---

* Tarleton's Southern Campaigns, p. 91.

Major Davie, with about forty mounted riflemen, and the same number of dragoons, and some Mecklenburg militia, under Colonel Hagins, approached Hanging Rock on the same day. While he was reconnoitering the ground, previous to making the attack, he was informed that three companies of Bryan's Tory regiment, returning from a foraging expedition, were encamped at a farm-house near the post.

Major Davie, with his brave associates, immediately fell upon them with vigor, both in front and rear, and all but a few of them were either killed or wounded. No time could be spared to take prisoners, as the engagement at the farm-house was in full view of the British post at Hanging Rock. The fruits of this victory were sixty valuable horses, and one hundred muskets and rifles. The whole camp of the enemy instantly beat to arms, but this brilliant affair was ended, and Davie out of reach before the enemy's forces were in motion, or their consternation subsided from this daring and successful attack. Major Davie reached his camp safely without the loss of a single man.

General Sumter was thoroughly convinced that the ardent patriots of which his command consisted must be kept constantly employed, and that the minds of such men are greatly influenced by dashing exploits. He, therefore, resolved to unite with Major Davie and other officers, and make a vigorous attack against the post of Hanging Rock. This post derives its name from a huge conglomerate bowlder of granite, twenty-five or thirty feet in diameter, lying upon the eastern bank of Hanging Rock Creek, with a concavity sufficiently large to shelter fifty men from the rain. Near this natural curiosity Lord Rawdon, then commanding the British and Tories in that section, had established a post, garrisoned by Tarleton's Legion of infantry, a part of Brown's Corps of South Carolina and Georgia Provincials, and Colonel Bryan's

North Carolina Loyalists, the whole under the command of Major Carden.

BATTLE OF THE HANGING ROCK.

> "Catawba's waters smiled again
>   To see her Sumter's soul in arms!
> And issuing from each glade and glen,
>   Rekindled by war's fierce alarms,
> Thronged hundreds through the solitude
>   Of the wild forests, to the call
> Of him whose sp r t, unsubdued,
>   Fresh impulse gave to each, to all."

On the 5th of August, 1780, the detachments of the patriots met again at Land's Ford, on the Catawba. Major Davie had not lost a single man in his last dashing exploit. The North Carolina militia, under Colonel Irwin and Major Davie, numbered about five hundred men, officers and privates; and about three hundred South Carolinians under Colonels Sumter, Lacey and Hill. The chief command was conferred upon Colonel Sumter, as being the senior officer. Early in the morning, Colonel Sumter marched cautiously, and approached the British camp in three divisions, with the intention of falling upon the main body stationed at Cole's Old Field. The right was composed of Major Davie's corps, and some volunteers, under Major Bryan; the center, of the Mecklenburg militia, under Colonel Irwin; and the left, of South Carolina refugees, under Colonel Hill. General Sumter proposed that the detachments should approach in their divisions, march directly to the centre encampments, then dismount, and each division attack its camp. This plan was approved by all except Major Davie, who insisted on leaving their horses at their present position, and march to the attack on foot. He urged, as an objection against the former plan, the confusion always consequent upon dismounting under fire, and the certainty of losing the effect of a sudden and vigorous attack. He was, however, overruled, but the sequel proved he was right in his opinion. Through the error of his guides, Sumter came first upon Bryan's corps, on the western bank of the creek, half a mile from the British camp. Colonel Irwin's Mecklenburg militia commenced the attack. The Tories soon yielded, and fled toward the main body, many of them throwing away their arms without discharging them. These the patriots secured ; and, pursuing this advantage, Sumter next fell upon Brown's corps, which, by being concealed in a wood, poured in a heavy fire upon the Americans. The latter also quickly availed themselves of the trees and bushes, and returned the British fire with deadly effect. The American riflemen, taking deliberate aim, soon cut off all of Brown's officers and many of his soldiers; and at length, after a fierce conflict, his corps yielded, and dispersed in confusion. The arms and ammunition procured from the enemy were of great service, for when the action commenced, Sumter's men had not two rounds each.

Now was the moment to strike for decisive victory ; it was lost by the criminal indulgence of Sumter's men in plundering the portion of the British camp already secured, and drinking too freely of the liquor found there. Sumter's ranks became disordered, and while endeavoring to bring order out of confusion, the enemy rallied. Of his six hundred men only about two hundred, with Major Davie's cavalry, could be brought into immediate action. Colonel Sumter, however, was not to be foiled. With his small number of patriots he rushed forward, with a shout, to the attack. The enemy had formed a hollow square, with the field pieces in front, and in this position received the charge. The Americans attacked them on three sides, and for a while the contest was severe. At length, just as the British line was yielding, a reinforcement under Captains Stewart and McDonald, of Tarleton's Legion, made their appearance, and their number being magnified, Colonel Sumter deemed it prudent to retreat.

All this was done about mid-day, but the enemy had been so severely handled that they did not attempt a pursuit. A small party appeared upon the Camden road, but were soon dispersed by Davie's cavalry. Could Sumter have brought all of his forces into action in this last attack, the rout of the British would have been complete. As it was,

> "He beat them ! ack! beneath the flame
> Of valor quailing, or the shock!
> He carved, at last, a hero's name,
> Upon the glorious Hanging Rock!"

This engagement lasted about four hours, and was one of the best-fought battles between militia and British regulars during the war. Sumter's loss was twelve killed and forty one wounded. Among the killed were the brave Colonel McLure (lately promoted to that rank), of South Carolina, and Captain Reid, of North Carolina: Colonel Hill, Captain Craighead, Major Winn, Lieutenants Crawford and Fletcher, and Ensign McLure were wounded.

Colonel McLure, being mortally wounded, was conveyed under the charge of Davie's cavalry to Charlotte. He lingered until the 18th of August, on which day he died in Liberty Hall Academy. "Of the many brave men," said General Davie, "with whom it was my fortune to become acquainted in the army, he was one of the bravest; and when he fell we looked upon his loss as incalculable."

The British loss was much greater than that of the Americans. Sixty-two of Tartleton's Legion were killed and wounded. Bryan's regiment of Loyalists also suffered severely.

Major Davie's corps suffered much while tying their horses and forming into line under a heavy fire from the enemy, a measure which he had reprobated in the council when deciding on the mode of attack.

Having conveyed his wounded to a hospital in Charlotte, which his foresight had provided, Major Davie hastened to the general rendezvous at Rugely's Mill, under

General Gates. On the 16th of August, while on his way to unite his forces with those of General Gates, he met a soldier in great speed, about ten miles from Camden. He arrested him as a deserter, but soon learned from him that Gates was signally defeated by the British on that day.

Major Davie then retraced his steps and took post at Charlotte. On the 5th of September, he was appointed by Governor Nash, Colonel Commandant of Cavalry, with instructions to raise a regiment. He succeeded in raising only a part, and with two small companies, commanded by Major George Davidson, he took post at Providence.

On the 21st day of September, Colonel Davie attacked a body of Tories at the plantation of Captain Wahab (now written Walkup), in the southwestern corner of Union county (then a part of Mecklenburg), killed fifteen or twenty of their men, wounded about forty, and retreated in good order without any loss. In this dashing exploit, Davie brought off ninety-six horses, one hundred and twenty stands of arms, and reached his camp the same evening, after riding sixty miles in less than twenty-four hours.

Generals Sumner and Davidson, with their brigades of militia, reached his camp in Providence on the same evening. On the advance of the British army these officers retreated by way of Phifer's to Salisbury, ordering Colonel Davie, with about one hundred and fifty men, and some volunteers under Major Joseph Graham, to hover around the approaching enemy, annoy his foraging parties, and skirmish with his light troops.

On the night of the 25th of September, Colonel Davie entered the town of Charlotte, determined to give the British army, which lay a few miles from that place, a *hornets-like reception*. The brilliancy and patriotic spirit of that skirmish was appropriately displayed on the very ground which, in May, 1775, was the birth-place American independence. (See "Skirmish at Charlotte.")

On the next day, Colonel Davie joined the army at

Salisbury, where the men and officers to raise new recruits had assembled. Generals Davidson and Sumner continued their retreat beyond the Yadkin River, while Colonel Davie returned to Charlotte, around which place the activity of his movements, dashing adventures, and perfect knowledge of the country, rendered him extremely useful in checking the incursions of the enemy, repressing the Tories and encouraging the friends of liberty.

Lord Cornwallis sorely felt the difficulties with which his position at Charlotte was surrounded, and, on hearing of the defeat and death of Colonel Ferguson, one of his favorite officers, he left that town late on the evening of the 14th of October, in great precipitation, recrossed the Catawba at Land's Ford, and took position, for a few months, at Winnsboro, S. C.

The signal defeat of the British and Tories at King's Mountain—the conspicuous turning point of success in the American Revolution, and the retreat of Cornwallis, after his previous boast of soon having North Carolina under royal subjection, greatly revived the hopes of the patriots throughout the entire South.

General Smallwood, of Maryland, who had accompanied General Gates to the South, had his headquarters at Providence, and, in a short time, several thousand militia, under Generals Davidson, Sumner, and Jones, joined his camp. Colonel Davie, with three hundred mounted infantry, occupied an advanced post at Land's Ford.

When General Greene took command of the Southern Army in December, 1780, he and Colonel Davie met for the first time. The Commissary Department having become vacant by the resignation of Colonel Thomas Polk, General Greene prevailed upon Colonel Davie to accept this troublesome and important office. Although the duties of the office would prevent him from displaying that dashing patriotism so congenial to his chivalric spirit, yet he agreed to enter upon its arduous and unthankful responsibilities.

Colonel Davie accompanied General Greene in his rapid retreat from the Catawba to the Dan River. He was present at the battle of Guilford, in March, 1781; at Hobkirk's Hill, in April; at the evacuation of Camden, in May; and at the siege of Ninety-six, in June.

The war, having ended, Colonel Davie retired to private life and his professional pursuits. He took his first circuit in February, 1783, and near this time he married Sarah, eldest daughter of General Allen Jones, of Northampton county, and located himself at Halffax Courthouse, where he soon rose to the highest eminence in his profession.

Colonel Davie was a member of the Convention which met at Philadelphia, in May, 1787, to form the Federal Constitution. The late Judge Murphy, in speaking of Colonel Davie, bears this honorable testimony to his abilities: "I was present in the House of Commons, when Davie addressed that body (in 1789,) for a loan of money to erect the buildings of the University, and, although more than thirty years have elapsed, I have the most vivid recollections of the greatness of his manner and the power of his eloquence upon that occasion. In the House of Commons he had no rival, and on all questions before that body his eloquence was irresistible."

In December, 1798, he was elected Governor of the State. After fulfilling other important National and State trusts, and losing his estimable wife in 1803, Colonel Davie, under the increasing infirmities of old age, sought retirement. In 1805 he removed to Tivoli, his country seat, near Land's Ford, in South Carolina, where he died in 1820, in the sixty-fourth year of his age. He had six children: 1. Hyder Ali, who married Elizabeth Jones, of Northampton county, N. C.; 2. Sarah Jones, who married William F. Desaussure, of Columbia, S. C.; 3. Mary Haynes; 4. Martha; 5. Rebecca; 6. Frederick William.

GENERAL MICHAEL MCLEARY.

General Michael McLeary was born in 1762. He first entered the service as a private in Captain William Alexander's company, in the regiment commanded by Colonel Robert Irwin, William Hagins, Lieutenant Colonel, and James Harris, Major. The regiment was encamped on Coddle Creek, near which time Colonel William Davidson, a Continental officer, was appointed to the command of a battalion. In a short time afterward, his command marched to Ramsour's Mill, to disperse a large body of Tories, under Colonel John Moore, but failed to reach that place before they had been subdued and routed by Colonel Locke and his brave associates.

General McLeary was in the fight against a considerable body of Tories assembled at Coulson's Mill, at which place General Davidson was severely wounded.

After this service he again volunteered in Captain William Alexander's company, Colonel Irwin's regiment, watching the movements of the enemy. About two miles south of Charlotte, Lieutenant James Taggart captured two wagons loaded with valuable supplies from Camden for the British army, then encamped near the former place. In this dashing exploit, two of the British guard were killed, and the remainder made prisoners, who were afterward turned over to Colonel Davidson. At the same time, an express was captured from Lord Cornwallis to Colonel Turnbull, in command of the forces at Camden. Here, as elsewhere in the surrounding country, it will be seen the vigilant "hornets" of Mecklenburg were engaged in their accustomed work.

Captain Alexander's command continued to hang on the enemy's rear for the purpose of making rapid captures and picking up stragglers, and followed them to the Old Nation Ford, on the Catawba. Colonel Davidson having been promoted in the meantime to the rank of Brigadier General, marched down and encamped near Six Mile

Creek, where he was joined by Generals Morgan and Smallwood, in November, 1780. Near this time General Morgan was ordered to move with a detachment to the relief of the upper districts of South Carolina. He set off immediately, and remained there until after the battle of the Cowpens, on the 17th of January, 1781.

General McLeary again volunteered in Captain John Brownfield's company, in General Davidson's brigade, watching the movements of Lord Cornwallis in his pursuit of General Morgan, encumbered with five hundred prisoners on his way to a place of safety in Virginia.

General Davidson, anticipating the movements of Cornwallis, had placed guards at four or five crossing-places on the Catawba river, making his headquarters near the Tuckasege Ford, on the eastern bank of the river. On the 31st of January, he left his headquarters to inspect the position of his guard at Cowan's Ford. Here the British army crossed at dawn of day, on the 1st of February, 1781. At the close of the skirmish which ensued, General Davidson was killed. General McLeary continued in service until after the battle of Guilford, when he returned home, and was soon afterward discharged. He was highly respected, represented his county several times in the State Legislature, and died at a good old age.

MAJOR THOMAS ALEXANDER.

Major Thomas Alexander, born in 1758, was one of the earliest and most unwavering patriots of Mecklenburg county. He first entered the service in 1775, as a private, in Captain John Springs' company, and marched to the head of the Catawba river, to assist in protecting the frontier settlements, then greatly suffering from the murderous and depredating incursions of the Cherokee Indians. In 1775 he also volunteered in Captain Ezekiel Polk's company, and marched against the Tories assembled at the post of Ninety, in South Carolina.

In 1776 he volunteered in Captain William Alexander's company, under Colonels Adam Alexander and Robert Irwin, General Rutherford commanding, and marched to the Quaker Meadows, at the head of the Catawba, and thence across the Blue Ridge to the Cherokee country. Having severely chastised the Indians and compelled them to sue for peace, the expedition returned.

In 1779, he volunteered under Captain William Polk, and marched to South Carolina, to subdue the Tories on Wateree River. Soon after this service he was appointed captain of a company to guard the magazine in Charlotte, which, on the approach of Cornwallis, in September, 1780, was removed to a place of safety on the evening before his Lordship's arrival.

After Cornwallis left Charlotte, Captain Alexander raised a company of mounted men to guard the Tuckasege Ford. He occupied this position until it was known Cornwallis had crossed the Catawba River, at Cowan's Ford.

After the death of General Davidson he placed himself under Colonel Lee, of the Continental line, Gen. Pickens commanding, and marched to Hillsboro, near which place they defeated Colonel Pyles, a Tory leader, on Haw River. After this service he volunteered under Colonel Davie, and was with him at the battle of Hanging Rock. After Gates' defeat he was appointed Quarter-master, with orders to attend the hospital in Charlotte.

Major Alexander married Jane, daughter of Neil Morrison, one of the signers of the Mecklenburg Declaration of Independence, and died in 1844, at the age of ninety-two years.

In the "Charlotte Journal," of January 17th, 1845. an obituary notice of this veteran patriot was published, in which it is stated, " he was allied by blood to the two most distinguished families of the period—the Polks and Alexanders, and in his own person blended many of the qualities peculiar to each. He was remarkable for the highest courage and the greatest modesty; for marked dignity of personal deportment, and a disposition the most cheerful, and a heart overflowing with kindness. He crowned all his virtues by a simple, unostentatious and humble piety, and concluded a life, protracted to a period far beyond that allotted to mankind, without a blot, and without reproach, and with the respect, the affection and veneration of all who knew him."

CAPTAIN WILLIAM ALEXANDER.

Captain William Alexander was born in Bucks county, Pennsylvania, in the year 1749. He was long and well known in Mecklenburg county, N. C., among numerous other persons bearing the same name, as "Capt. Black Bill Alexander," from being the reputed leader of a small band of ardent patriots who, in 1771, *blackened their faces*, and destroyed the king's powder, on its way to Hillsboro, to obey the behests of a cruel and tyrannical governor. (For further particulars, see sketch of "Black Boys" of Cabarrus County.)

He first entered the service of the United States as captain of a company, in 1776, under Colonel Adam Alexander, and marched to the head of the Catawba River. The object of this expedition was to protect the valley of the Catawba from the incursions and depredations of the Cherokee Indians during the time the inhabitants were gathering in their harvest. He again entered the service as captain, under Colonel Adam Alexander, General Rutherford commanding, and marched to the head of the Catawba River, and across the Blue Ridge Mountains, against the Cherokee Indians, who were completely routed and their towns destroyed, compelling them to sue for peace.

In 1780 he commanded a company under Col. Francis Locke, and marched from Charlotte for the relief of Charleston, but finding the city closely invested by the

British army, the regiment fell back to Camden, and remained there until their three months' service had expired.

He again served a four months' tour as captain, under General Sumter, and was in the battles of Rocky Mount, Hanging Rock, and in the skirmish at Wahab's (now written Walkup's.)

He also served six weeks as captain under Colonel Thomas Polk, in the winter of 1775-'6, known as the "Snow Campaign," against the Tory leader, Cunningham, in South Carolina.

He again served a three months' tour as captain in the Wilmington expedition, General Rutherford commanding. immediately preceding the battle of Guilford, but was not in that action, on account of an attack of small-pox.

He again marched with General Rutherford's forces against the Tories assembled at Ramsour's Mill, in Lincoln county, but the action having taken place shortly before their arrival, they assisted in taking care of the wounded and in burying the dead.

He again entered the service as captain, for ten months, under General Sumter, in Colonel Wade Hampton's regiment in South Carolina, and was the first captain who arrived with his men at the place of rendezvous.

He was also in the fight at the Quarter House, Monk's Corner, capture of Orangeburg, battle of Eutaw, and in numerous other minor but important services to his country.

Captain William Alexander resided on the public road leading to Concord, six miles east of Charlotte, where he died on the 19th of December, 1836, aged about eighty-seven years.

ELIJAH ALEXANDER.

Elijah Alexander, son of William Alexander, blacksmith, was born in Mecklenburg county, N. C., in 1760.

In 1819, he moved to Maury county, Tenn., where he died at a good old age. In March, 1780, Colonel Thomas Polk called out detachments from the nearest companies of militia to serve as a guard over the public powder placed in the magazine in Charlotte. He then volunteered for three months under Captain Thomas Alexander.

After Cornwallis crossed the Catawba River at Cowan's Ford, on the 1st of February, 1781, at which place General Davidson was killed, a call was made for more men to harass the progress of the British army. For this purpose, a rendezvous was made at the "Big Rock," in Cabarrus county, under Colonel William Polk, Major James Harris and Captain Brownfield. At this time, the small-pox broke out in camp, from the effects of which Moses Alexander, a brother of Governor Nathaniel Alexander, died. After the battle of Guilford, on the 15th of March, 1781, General Greene returned to South Carolina to recover full possession of the State. He then joined his army under Captain James Jack (the bearer of the Mecklenburg Declaration to Congress in 1775), and in Colonel Thomas Polk's regiment. The command marched from Charlotte, along the "Lawyer's Road," to Matthew Stewart's, on Goose Creek, and thence towards Camden, to fall in with General Greene's army. They halted at the noted "Flat Rock," and eat beef butchered on that wide-spread natural table. The command then marched to Rugeley's Mill, where it remained a week or more. After this service he returned home and was honorably discharged.

CAPTAIN CHARLES ALEXANDER.

Captain Charles Alexander was born in Mecklenburg county, N. C., January 4th, 1755. He first entered the service of the United States as a private in July, 1775, in the company of Captain William Alexander, and Colonel Adam Alexander's regiment, General Rutherford commanding, and marched across the Blue Ridge Mountains against the Cherokee Indians. The expedition was completely successful ; the Indians were routed, and their towns destroyed.

He next served as a private for two months, commencing in January, 1776, known as the "Snow Campaign," in Captain William Alexander's company, and Colonel Thomas Polk's regiment, and marched to Rayburn's creek, where the Tories were dispersed. In one of the skirmishes, William Polk was wounded in the shoulder.

In October, 1776, he again served under the same Captain, and in Colonel Caldwell's regiment, but the command of the regiment during this tour of duty, was under Major Thomas Harris, who marched to Camden. S. C.. and remained there about three months.

In 1776, he served in the cavalry company of Captain Charles Polk, who marched to Fort Johnson, near the mouth of Cape Fear river, Colonel Thomas Polk commanding. He again served as a private in 1778, in the company of Captain William Gardner and Lieutenant Stephen Alexander, General Rutherford commanding, who marched to Purysburg, S. C., and there joined the regulars under General Lincoln. at a camp called the "Black Swamp." In 1780, shortly after Gates' defeat, he joined Captain William Alexander's company, and Colonel Thomas Polk's regiment, under General Davie, marched to the Waxhaws, and was in the engagement fought there against the Tories.

He again served under Captain William Alexander, as one of the guard over wagons sent to Fayetteville to procure salt for the army.

In September, 1781, he was elected Captain of a cavalry company, under Major Thomas Harris, and marched against the Tories at Raft Swamp.

Besides the tours herein specified, Captain Alxander performed other important services, of shorter duration, in scouring the surrounding country, and protecting it against the troublesome Tories.

In 1814, Captain Alexander moved to Giles, now Lincoln county, Tenn., and in 1833, to Maury county, where he died at an extreme old age.

The Alexanders, who performed a soldier's duty in the Revolutionary War, residing principally in Mecklenburg county, were very numerous, several of whom can here receive only a passing notice.

John Alexander, son of James Alexander, was in active service for upwards of five years. He was the husband of Mrs. Susanna Alexander, long known and highly esteemed in Mecklenburg county as the ministering angel, who was eminently instrumental in saving the life of Captain Joseph Graham, after he was cut down by the British cavalry, near Sugar Creek Church, and left by them, supposed to be dead. She found him by the road-side, conducted him to her house, dressed his wounds, made by ball and sabre, and tenderly cared for him during the night. On the next day, his symptoms becoming more favorable, she conveyed him to his mother's, about four miles distant, *on her own pony*. Her husband died in 1805. In 1846, when eighty-six years of age, and in needy circumstances, she was granted a pension by the General Government, in behalf of her husband's military services, and lived to be nearly one hundred years old, enjoying the kind regard and veneration of all who knew her.

Dan Alexander, who moved to Hardeman county, Tenn., was born in Mecklenburg county, in March, 1757.

He first entered the service in 1778, for three months, in Captain William Alexander's company, (commonly called "Black Bill Alexander,") and Colonel Irwin's regiment.

In 1780, he served under Captain Thomas Alexander to assist in guarding the public magazine in Charlotte.

In this same year he served in the expedition to Ramsour's Mill, under General Rutherford, and afterward, against Tories assembled in the forks of the Yadkin river: captured several and conveyed them to Salisbury jail.

Soon afterward, he joined the command of Colonel Davie, and marched in the direction of Camden, S. C. Near the South Carolina line, they met Gates' retreating army. He represented Gates as "wearing a *pale blue coat, with epaulettes, velvet breeches, and riding a bay horse.*"

Colonel Davie's command returned, and encamped ten miles north of the Court House.

His last important service was in forming one of the party dispatched by Colonel McCall to surprise a guard of eighteen British grenadiers, stationed at Hart's Mill, near Hillsboro. The movement was successful; several were killed, six made prisoners, and one escaped in the creek.

William Alexander, of Rowan county, entered the service in 1776, and marched under General Rutherford's command against the Cherokee Indians, and in that expedition (Sept. 8th,) was wounded in the foot at the "Seven Mile Mountain."

In 1781, he was elected the Captain of a company of spies, and was in the ten month's service under Colonel Wade Hampton and General Sumter, in South Carolina, acting efficiently in this capacity, until the close of the Revolution.

JOSEPH KERR—"THE CRIPPLE SPY."

Joseph Kerr was born in Chester county, Pa., Nov. 3rd, 1750. At an early age moved with his parents to North Carolina, and settled in Mecklenburg county. He was a *cripple from infancy*, but becoming indignant at the ravages of the British and Tories, and actuated with a true, patriotic spirit, he repaired to the camp of Gen. McDowell and offered his services as *a spy*. In this capacity Gen. McDowell accepted him, and immediately sent him to Blackstock's Ford, on Tiger River, S. C., where the British and Tories were encamped, about fifteen hundred strong. After secreting his horse he proceeded as *a poor cripple, and beggar-like,* made a full examination of the enemy's camp. Furnished with this information, he quietly withdrew, returned quickly as possible to General McDowell, and apprised him and Captain Steen of his discoveries. He was well mounted, and traveled day and night—a distance of ninety miles. General McDowell's forces, upon this intelligence, marched in great haste, attacked the enemy near Blackstock's Ford, and routed them. In this engagement four of Captain Steen's men were killed and seven wounded. He took no prisoners and gave no quarters. Kerr then returned to Mecklenburg county, and soon after joined Colonel Williams' command as *a spy*. Captain Steen informed Colonel Williams that he might safely rely upon Kerr in this kind of service. They then marched to join the *over-mountain boys*, under Sevier, Shelby and other officers. Upon the junction of their forces, a council of war was immediately held, at which Kerr was present. They learned that Ferguson was about twenty miles from them, at Peter Quinn's old place, six miles from King's Mountain. The result of the council of war was that he (Kerr) should go and reconnoiter Ferguson's camp. He did so without delay, and found the British and Tories encamped—arms stacked, and about twelve hundred strong.

As *a poor, innocent cripple,* they informed him they were ready and willing to give "protection" to all who would join them. He soon afterwards withdrew, mounted his fleet charger, and in a brief space of time reported to Colonels Shelby, Sevier and other officers the enemy's strength and situation. Acting upon his report, these officers marched that night a distance of twenty-seven miles, and reached the mountain on the next day, about three o'clock. After a brief consultation as to the plan of the engagement, Ferguson was vigorously attacked on his boasted eminence of security, and, after a fierce conflict of about one hour, was completely conquered. Ferguson and two hundred and twenty-five of his men were killed; one hundred and eighty wounded, and upwards of six hundred made prisoners. The loss of the Whigs was twenty-eight killed and a great many wounded. Colonel Williams was severely wounded in the groin, from the effects of which he died a few hours after the battle. In a few days after this victory, Kerr returned to Mecklenburg county, to the house of his uncle, Joseph Kerr. The brave Captain Steen was afterwards killed by the Tories. He was from Union county, S. C., and not far from " Thicketty Mountain," in the district known as Ninety-six.

At the instance of Captain Barnett, in command of some refugees who returned with him to Mecklenburg, Kerr was sent to York county, S. C., to gain information of the enemy's force and position. His crippled condition readily gained him access to the camp of Colonel Floyd and Major Hook—the latter in charge of the dragoons. He was recognized by some of the Tories, and came very near losing his life. He managed, however, to escape, and traveled all night in order to inform Captain Barnett of the enemy's strength. Captain Barnett immediately set out with thirty-one men, and uniting with Captains Bratton and McLure, completely surprised and routed the enemy, killing ninety-seven, among the number Major Hook and Colonel Ferguson, of the Tory militia. This was Kerr's last service as a spy. After the war he moved to Tennessee, and died in White county, at a good old age.

ROBERT KERR.

Robert Kerr, a soldier of the Revolution, was born in December, 1750, in Chester county, Pennsylvania, and came to North Carolina with his parents when only three years old.

He first entered the service in 1776, in Captain John McKnitt Alexander's company, in the expedition, General Rutherford commanding, against the Cherokee Indians, then severely molesting the frontier settlements.

In 1778, he was drafted into Captain John Brownfield's company, Colonel Francis Locke's regiment, and marched by way of Camden, to the defence of Charleston. After his return, he served under the same officers in the battle of Ramsour's Mill, in Lincoln county.

When Cornwallis was in Charlotte in 1780, he served under Captain James Thompson, the gallant leader of the Spartan band against the foraging party at McIntire's farm, seven miles from Charlotte, on the Beattie's Ford road.

In December, 1780, he joined the company of Captain John Sharpe, at which time, General Davidson, with his accustomed vigilance and activity, announced that all who would then promptly volunteer for six weeks, such service should stand for a three months tour. On this occasion he volunteered, and served under Captain William Henry.

After the death of General Davidson at Cowan's Ford, he was placed in Colonel Locke's regiment, General Pickens commanding, which forces were ordered to harass and impede the march of Cornwallis to Guilford Court House. This was his last important military service.

HENRY HUNTER.

Henry Hunter was born in the county of Derry, Ireland, on the 11th of August, 1751. About the time he became of age, he married Martha Sloan, and, after remaining a little upwards of one year longer in Ireland, he emigrated to America, and landed at Charleston, S. C., after a long and boisterous voyage of thirteen weeks. After reaching the shores of the New World, to which his fond anticipations of superior civil and religious privileges had anxiously turned, on surveying his situation, grim poverty stared him in the face; for, his stock of cash on hand was just "one silver half dollar." Yet, being raised to habits of industry, he did not despair, feeling assured that, 'where there is a *will* there is a *way*" to act in earnest, and battle against the adverse fortunes of life.

Finding in Charleston a wagon from North Carolina, he made suitable arrangements with its owner, and accompanied it on its return to Mecklenburg county, whither his mother and four brothers had emigrated several years before, and settled in the neighborhood of Poplar Tent Church. Here, by strict economy, and persevering industry, he was prospered as a farmer; blest in his "basket and his store," and soon enabled to purchase a comfortable homestead for himself and his rising family.

When the war of the Revolution broke out, being deeply imbued from childhood with the principles of liberty, and the justness of the American cause, he did not hesitate to assist in the great struggle for freedom.

He first entered the service of the United States as a volunteer in Captain William Alexander's company, Colonel George Alexander's regiment, and marched to suppress a large body of Tories assembled under Colonel John Moore at Ramsour's Mill, near the present town of Lincolnton, but failed to reach that place before the battle had been fought and the Tories signally routed by Colonel Locke and his brave associates.

He next entered the service under Captain Thomas Alexander, and was ordered to Charlotte for the purpose of guarding the public magazine in that place. Captain Alexander succeeded in having it removed to a place of safety on the evening before the entrance of the British army into Charlotte on the 26th of September, 1780.

He again entered the service a short time afterward, in Captain William Alexander's comyany, and Colonel George Alexander's regiment. The rendezvous of the regiment was about four miles south of Charlotte. After this service, on account of severe local injury, he was honorably discharged by Colonel Alexander.

Henry Hunter had twelve children, ten sons and two daughters. He was signally blest to see them all attain the age of maturity, and settle on comfortable homes around him. His wife, Martha, the worthy partner of his joys and sorrows, and whose earthly pilgrimage was protracted beyond the usual bounds of life, died on the 30th of September, 1832, in the eightieth year of her age.

He was long a consistent member and ruling Elder of the Associate Reformed Presbyterian Church. Like a sheaf fully ripe in its season, he met his approaching end with peaceful resignation. On his tombstone, in a private cemetery, on the old homestead property, is the following inscription:

"In Memory of

HENRY HUNTER,

Who departed this life on on the 18th of May, 1836, in the eighty-sixth year of his age, leaving a posterity of eleven children, and one hundred grand children, with thirty great-grand children to mourn his loss."

JAMES ORR.

James Orr was born in Pennsylvania in 1750. He early espoused the cause of freedom, and first entered the service in a company of riflemen, commanded by Captain Robert Mebane; marched to Cross Creek (now Fayetteville), and thence to Wilmington, to the assistance of Generals Ashe and Moore. In 1776, he volunteered under Captain Thomas Polk, in Colonel Charles' corps of cavalry, General Rutherford commanding, and marched against a body of Tories assembled at Cross Creek, but they were dispersed before the expedition reached that place. Again, in 1776, he volunteered under Captain Mebane, and marched from Charlotte to the Quaker Meadows, at the head of the Catawba River, against the Cherokee Indians, committing murders and depredations on the frontier settlements. In 1777 he served under Captain Elaby, Colonel Hicks' regiment, in South Carolina.

In 1780 he served under Captain William Alexander, in Colonel William Davidson's battalion, General Rutherford commanding, and marched against the Tories assembled at Ramsour's Mill, in Lincoln county; but the battle had been fought, and the Tories subdued and routed, before the expedition reached that place. This was his last important service.

SKIRMISH AT CHARLOTTE; OR, FIRST ATTACK OF THE "HORNETS."

After the battle of Camden, Cornwallis, believing that he would soon bring the rebels of North Carolina into speedy submission to the British Crown, left the scene of his conquest with as little delay as possible, and designated Charlotte as the most suitable place for his head-quarters. This town had been previously the rallying point, on many occasions, for the American forces, and from which they marched by companies, battalions and regiments, to the front, whenever their services were needed.

Cornwallis entered Charlotte on the 26th of September, 1780. His approach to the town was from the south, on Trade street, and, after taking possession of the place, his army lay encamped eighteen days in the old field, or commons, nearly opposite the residence of the late M. L. Wriston, with the exception of one regiment, which pitched their tents about midway between Charlotte and Colonel Polk's mill (late Bissell's). The head-quarters of his Lordship was in the second house in the rear of the present Springs building, with a front yard facing on Trade street. Many years after the war this building, in which Cornwallis slept *unquietly (per noctem plurima volvens)*, was moved round on Tryon street, and constitutes a part of the house now (1876) occupied by Mr. Taylor, gun-smith, but so changed and remodeled that little of the original structure can be identified to remind us of the past.

The skirmish at Charlotte has been pronounced one of the most "brilliant affairs" of the Revolution; and the correct account of it will be here given in General Davie's own words, taken from his auto-biographical sketches in manuscript, and now on file in the archives of the Historical Society of the State University at Chapel Hill.

He says: "Charlotte, situated on a rising ground, contains about twenty houses, built on two streets, which cross each other at right angles, at the intersection of which stands the court-house. The left of the town, as the enemy advanced, was an open common on the woods, which reached up to the gardens of the village. With this small force, viz., one hundred and fifty cavalry and mounted infantry, and fourteen volunteers, under Major Graham, Davie determined to give his Lordship a foretaste of what he might expect in North Carolina. For this purpose he dismounted one company, and posted it under the court-house, where the men were covered breast high by a stone wall. Two other companies were advanced about eighty yards, and posted behind some houses, and in gardens on each side of the street. While this disposition was making, the Legion (Tarleton's) was forming at the distance of three hundred yards, with a front to fill the street, and the light infantry on their flanks. On sounding the charge, the cavalry advanced at full gallop within sixty yards of the court-house, where they received the American fire, and retreated with great precipitation.

As the infantry continued to advance, notwithstanding the fire of our advanced companies, who were too few to keep them in check, it became necessary to withdraw them from the cross street, and form them in line with the troops under the court-house. The flanks were still engaged with the infantry, but the centre was directed to reserve their fire for the cavalry, who rallied on their former ground, and returned to the charge.

They were again well received by the militia, and galloped off in great confusion, in presence of the whole British army. As the British infantry were now beginning to turn Colonel Davie's right flank, these companies were drawn off in good order, successively covering each other, and formed at the end of the street, about one hundred yards from the court-house, under a galling fire from the British light infantry, who had advanced under cover of the houses and gardens. The British cavalry again appeared, charging in column by the court-house, but upon receiving a fire, which had been reserved for them, they again scampered off. Lord Cornwallis, in his vexation at the repeated miscarriage of his cavalry, openly abused their cowardice. The Legion, reinforced by the infantry, pressed forward on our flanks, and the ground was no longer tenable by this handful of brave men.

A retreat was then ordered on the Salisbury road, and the enemy followed, with great caution and respect, for some miles, when they ventured to charge the rear guards. The guards were of course put to flight, but, on receiving the fire of a single company, they retreated.

Our loss consisted of Lieutenant Locke, and four privates killed, and Major Graham and five privates wounded. The British stated their loss at twelve non-commissioned officers and privates killed, and Major Hanger, Captains Campbell and McDonald, and thirty privates wounded."

This action, although it subjects Colonel Davie to the charge of temerity, only to be excused by the event, and a zeal which we are always ready to applaud, furnishes a striking instance of the bravery and importance of the American militia. Few instances can be shown where any troops, who in one action, changed their position twice in good order, although pressed by superior force, and charged three times by cavalry, thrice their own number, unsupported, in presence of an enemy's whole army, and finally retreating in perfect order.

The graphic account of the skirmish at, and near Charlotte, from Colonel Davie's manuscript sketches, corrects a mistake into which several historians have unintentionally fallen in stating that Colonel Francis Locke was killed in the retreat near Sugar Creek Church, when, on the contrary, it was one of his younger brothers, Lieutenant George Locke, a brave and meritorious officer. This statement is confirmed by the notice of the family of "Hon. Matthew Locke," in Wheeler's "Historical Sketches," by the sworn declaration of William Rankin, of Gaston county, who received his discharge from Colonel Locke in Salisbury, near the time of the battle of Guilford, in March, 1781, and by the declaration of Michael McLeary, of Mecklenburg, who served under Colonel Locke after Cornwallis crossed the Catawba in February, 1781, as will be found published in this work.

The reader may be curious to know the estimate the British officers placed upon this affair—the hornets-like reception his Lordship experienced on his entrance into Charlotte.

Tarleton, in his "History of the Southern Campaign in 1780, and 1781," page 159, says, "Earl Cornwallis moved forward as soon as the Legion under Major Hanger joined him. A party of militia fired at the advanced dragoons and light infantry as they entered the town, and a more considerable body appeared drawn up near the courthouse. The conduct of the Americans created suspicion in the British; an ambuscade was apprehended by the light troops, who moved forward, for some time, with great circumspection; a charge of cavalry, under Major Hanger, dissipated this ill-grounded jealousy, and totally dispersed the militia. The pursuit lasted sometime, and about thirty of the enemy were killed and taken. The King's troops did not come out of this skirmish unhurt; Major Hanger, and Captains Campbell and McDonald were wounded, and twelve non-commissioned officers and men killed or wounded."

Stedman, the English historian who accompanied Cornwallis in his southern campaign, says in his "American War," Vol. II, p. 216, "Charlotte was taken possession of, after a slight resistance from the militia, towards the end of September. At this period, Major Hanger commanded, Colonel Tarleton being ill. In the centre of Charlotte, intersecting the two principal streets, stood a large brick building, the upper part being the court-house, and the under part, the market house. Behind the shambles, a few Americans on horse-back had placed themselves. The Legion was ordered to drive them off; but, upon receiving a fire from behind the stalls, this corps fell back. Lord Cornwallis rode up in person, and made use of these words: 'Legion, remember you have everything to lose, but nothing to gain,' alluding, as was supposed, to the former reputation of this corps. Webster's brigade moved on, and drove the Americans from behind the court-house; the legion then pursued them, but the whole British army was actually kept at bay, for some minutes, by a few mounted Americans, not exceeding twenty in number."

Stedman, who is generally accurate and impartial in his narratives, is mistaken in calling the old court-house a "brick building." It was, as previously stated, a wooden building, placed on brick pillars ten or twelve feet high, and hence the mistake. Some allowance should also be made for Stedman's mistake, as, very near that time, the fierce and buzzing attacks of the "Hornets" greatly obscured the accuracy of his vision. Upon the whole, the account we have of this skirmish, even under British *coloring*, and evasion of the *whole truth*, exemplifies the spirit and bravery of the "handful" of men who actually kept the whole British army in check for some time, and then retreated in good order.

Kendal, in his "Life of Jackson," chapter 4, in speaking of the military school in which the "hero of New

Orleans" was educated, says: "In the chieftains by which he was surrounded, the virtues of patriotism, disinterededness, caution, enterprise and courage exhibited themselves in the highest perfection. As military leaders, Marion was particularly distinguished for enterprise, vigilance and courage; Sumter was his equal in enterprise and courage, but had less circumspection; Davie, who was generally the leader of the Waxhaw settlers, appears to have united the virtues of the two. Perhaps in no instance, where the chief command was in him, did he fail to accomplish the object he undertook. His intelligence was accurate; his plans judicious, and kept profoundly secret; his movements rapid; his blows sudden as the lightning, and his disappearance almost as quick. To pursue him was useless, and it was seldom or never attempted. He frequently dared, with a handful of men, to face an army; and we have seen, by his encounter with the British van at Charlotte, that he knew how to strike terror into an enemy he was not strong enough to conquer."

The situation of Cornwallis in Charlotte was far from being agreeable. The sentinels placed around his encampment were frequently shot down, compelling him to have pits sunk, five or six feet deep, for their protection. He possessed, it is true, a few timid friends and supporters in the adjacent country, but these could not render him any material aid. The panic which had overspread South Carolina, after the British successes in that State, had extended itself, though in a less degree, into North Carolina, and had driven many of the wealthier class to "take protection," and thus save their property. But notwithstanding the terror of arms which preceded his arrival, Cornwallis soon became convinced that his situation was surrounded with humiliating realities which he could not easily remove. The reasons assigned by Tarleton are truthfully set forth, when he says, "Charlotte town afforded some conveniences, blended with great disadvantages. The mills in its neighborhood were supposed of sufficient consequence to render it for the present an eligible position, and in future a necessary post, when the enemy advanced. But the aptness of its intermediate situation between Camden and Salisbury, and the quantity of mills did not counterbalance these defects." And again he says, "It was evident, and had been frequently mentioned to the King's officers, that the counties of Mecklenburg and Rohan (Rowan) were more hostile to England than any others in America. The vigilance and animosity of these surrounding districts checked the exertions of the well-affected, and totally destroyed all communication between the King's troops and loyalists in other parts of the province. No British commander could obtain any information in that position which would facilitate his designs, or guide his future conduct."

No higher encomium of the principles and patriotism of the people of North Carolina could have been well given. It is the testimony of an eye-witness, and he a cruel enemy, with the best means of information before him. Tarleton goes on to say, "The town and its environs abounded with inveterate enemies. The plantations in the neighborhood were small and uncultivated; the roads narrow and crossed in every direction; and the whole face of the country covered with close and thick woods. In addition to these disadvantages, no estimation could be made of the sentiments of half the inhabitants of North Carolina whilst the royal army remained in Charlotte."

And, again, Tarleton informs us, "The foraging parties were every day harassed by the inhabitants, who did not remain at home to receive payment for the product of their plantations, but generally fired from covert places to annoy the British detachments. Ineffectual attempts were made upon convoys coming from Camden, and the intermediate post at Blair's Mill, but individuals with expresses were frequently murdered. An attack was directed against the picket at Polk's Mill, two miles from the town. The Americans were gallantly received by Lieutenant Guyon, of the 23d Regiment; and the fire of his party, from a loop-holed building adjoining the mill, repulsed the assailants. Notwithstanding the different checks and losses sustained by the militia of the district, they continued their hostilities with unwearied perseverance; and the British troops were so effectually blockaded in their present position, that very few, out of a great many messengers, could reach Charlotte in the beginning of October, to give intelligence of Ferguson's situation.

The repulse at McIntyre's, elsewhere noticed in these sketches, is a good illustration of what Tarlton says in these quotations. Truly, the "Hornets" were enraged about that time—more vigilant and out-flying than ever before; but it should be borne in mind they were then fighting the invaders of their own soil, and in defence of the undisturbed enjoyments of "home, sweet home."

Stedman describes, in much the same terms as Tarleton has done, the difficulties encountered by the British in procuring supplies for their army. He says: "In Col. Polk's mill were found 28,000 lbs. of flour and a quantity of wheat. There were several large cultivated farms in the neighborhood of Charlotte. An abundance of cattle, few sheep; the cattle mostly milch cows, or cows with calf, which, at that season of the year, was the best beef. When the army was in Charlotte we killed, upon an average, one hundred head per day. The leanness of the cattle will account for the number killed each day. At this period the royal army was supported by Lord Rawdon's moving with one half of the army one day, and Colonel Webster with the other half the next day, as a covering party to protect the foraging parties and cattle drivers."

The English people had then, as now, the reputation of being great beef-eaters; nor should we blame them, as the florid complexion the Englishman generally wears is mainly owing to the free use of this non-febrile and healthy food, washed down with a few potations of good old London ale.

The surprise at McIntyre's compelled the British to move with greater forces in their foraging expeditions. It is seldom, in the historic annals of any people, that we find it required "one half" of a large army, in a sparsely settled country, to "protect the foraging parties and cattle drivers." It indicated a spirit of determined resistance by the patriots of Mecklenburg and of the State generally, which can only be construed as a faithful maintenance of the principles of freedom proclaimed on the 20th of May, 1775.

After the victory of the Whigs at King's Mountain, and the loss of Ferguson, one of his bravest officers, and his entire command, Cornwallis concluded to leave the rebellious post he then occupied.

William McCafferty, a resident Scotchman, and a man of considerable wealth, was employed as the guide to lead the British army by the nearest road to Winnsboro', S. C. Tradition says, that after so bewildering the army in the swamps that much of their baggage was lost, he contrived to escape, and left them to find their way out, as best they could, by the returning light of day. As the British army progressed, passing through the Steele Creek neighborhood, they encamped about three days on Spratt's plantation, waiting to cross the swollen Catawba, and for the collection of additional supplies. A guard was placed around the encampment, and one of the number assigned to a position between the Charlotte road and a neighboring cane-brake. On the second or third day the sharp crack of a rifle was heard up the Charlotte road, and a small detachment of the British army was immediately dispatched to investigate its meaning. When the detachment arrived at the position of the sentinel, he was found dead, at the foot of a black oak, against which it is supposed he was leaning at the time. Captain William Alexander (better known as "Black Bill,") one of the "terrible Mecklenburg Whigs," fired the fatal shot from the adjoining cane-brake. Many others of the Sugar Creek rebels were with Captain Alexander on this occasion, but he alone ventured within killing distance. Long before Tarleton and his dragoons could reach the scene of action, Alexander and his party were entering the brushy woods of Steele Creek, on their way back to the Whig settlements of Upper Sugar Creek. The associates of Alexander were the Taylors, Barnetts, Walkers, Polks, and other kindred spirits, who shot many of the sentries around the British encampment at Charlotte, and seriously annoyed or cut off the enemy's foraging parties. The last one of the Barnetts, belonging to this "terrible party," died in 1829, at a good old age, within two miles of Cook's mills, on Big Sugar Creek.

A singular incident, occurring at this period, is here deemed worthy of narration. A relative of the Spratts, named Elliott, was living on the plantation at the time the British army arrived there from Charlotte. Believing that they would capture him, if in their power, he broke and ran for the cane-brake, about a half or three-quarters of a mile below the spot where the sentinel was shot. As soon as the alarm was given of his departure, Tarleton's terrible dragoons pursued him, but he succeeded in making good his escape into the densest part of the cane-brake thicket.

While he was listening to the terrible denunciations of Tarleton's dragoons on their arrival at the swampy and imperious thicket, and what they would do if they could only see a bush or a cane move, he felt perfectly safe as long as he could remain motionless in his muddy retreat. But when his fears had somewhat subsided in his place of concealment, still more alarming apprehensions of danger presented themselves, on his espying a venomous moccasin of the largest size, moving slowly along in the water and mud, and directing its course so near that, in all probability, it must strike him. He could not make the least defence against his ugly approaching visitor, for fear of exposing himself to the pistols of the British dragoons. All that he could do in this dreadful predicament was to wave his hand in a gentle manner towards the snake; which caused it to stop its course and throw itself into a coil, preparatory for battle. Fortunately, just at this time, the British dragoons made their welcome departure, and Elliott moved out of the way of his serpentine majesty.

This was the *first* and *last* visit of Lord Cornwallis to "Charlotte town." He came flushed with victory, and firmly anticipated similar success in North Carolina. He departed laboring under vexation and sore disappointment; not without bestowing a characteristic name ("Hornets' Nest") upon the patriotic sons of Mecklenburg around which appellation cluster many thrilling historical and traditional associations, destined to enshrine their memories in the hearts of their countrymen, throughout all coming time.

SURPRISE AT M'INTYRE'S; OR, THE "HORNETS" AT WORK.

After the British army had been in Charlotte about a week, and having, in the meantime, consumed the most of their forage and provisions, Lord Cornwallis was placed under the necessity of procuring a fresh supply. He had already experienced something of the *stinging* propensities of the "hornets" with which he was surrounded, and the fatalities of their attacks upon his sentries near his camp. In order to meet the emergency of his situation, he ordered out on the 3d day of October, 1780, a strong foraging party, under Major Doyle, consisting of four hundred and fifty infantry, sixty cavalry, and about forty wagons, who proceeded up the road leading from Charlotte to Beattie's Ford, on the Catawba river, intending to draw their supplies from the fertile plantations on Long Creek.

Captain James Thompson, and thirteen others who

lived in that neighborhood, anticipating the necessity the British would be under to forage, had early in the morning assembled at Mitchell's, mill, (now Frazier's) three miles from Charlotte, at which farm the corn was pulled—at most other places it was standing in the field. Captain Thompson and his men were expert riflemen, and well acquainted with every place in the vicinity. At this place they lay concealed about an hour, when they heard the wagons and Doyle's party passing by them, and up the main road. As soon as the party had passed about half a mile, Captain Thompson and his brave followers started through the wood, and kept parallel with Doyle's party, and *almost in sight,* reconnoitering the movements of the enemy until they reached McIntyre's farm, seven miles from Charlotte. A boy plowing by the road-side, upon seeing the British soldiers pass by him, quickly mounted his horse, dashed through the nearest by-paths, and barely had time to warn the intervening families of the approach of the "red coats." After the foraging party reached McIntyre's, they left a part of their men and wagons to lay in supplies, while the other part passed on under Doyle with the expectation of proceeding two or three miles further For this reason, Doyle was not *numbered with the slain* in place of his second in command.

Thompson's party, finding some were halted at this place, moved directly towards the thicket down the spring branch, about two hundred yards from the house. The point of a rocky ridge, covered with bushes, passed obliquely from the road to the spring, and within fifty yards of the house which sheltered them from the view or fire of the enemy. They formed into a line about ten feet apart, and advanced silently to their intended positions. The British were soon engaged in their work of plunder; some were at the barn throwing down oats for the wagons, others were running after the chickens, ducks and pigs, while a third party were robbing the dwelling house, the inmates having previously fled out of danger. The soldiery, assisted by the dogs in chasing the poultry, had knocked over some bee-hives ranged along the garden fence. The enraged insects dashed after the men, and at once the scene became one of uproar, confusion and lively excitement. The officer in command, a portly, florid Englishman, laughed heartily at the gestures and outcries of the routed soldiers. The attention of the guard was drawn to this single point, while, at a distance in the fields, the wagons were seen slowly approaching with their cumbrous loads.

The owner of the plantation had cautiously approached, under cover, within gun-shot of his house; the rest of the party, his neighbors, with equal care, advanced sufficiently near for the sure action of their rifles. The distress and anger of the patriots were raised to the highest pitch when they saw the reckless merriment of their enemies, and the fruits of their industry thus suddenly withdrawn. Their feelings could now be no longer restrained while they were anxious to try the effects of their trusty rifles. "Boys," cried one of the sturdy farmers, "I can't stand this any longer—I'll take the captain—each one of you choose his man, and look out for yourselves."

These words were scarcely uttered in a suppressed tone, when the sight of his unerring rifle was drawn upon the expanded breast of the portly Englishman, who suddenly fell prostrate from the doorposts between which he was standing.

In two instances, where two of the patriots were firing at the same man, and seeing him fall, the second one had to quickly change from his *sighted object* and seek another. A sentinel placed near the spot to which they had advanced, appeared to be alarmed, although he had not seen them, probably thinking of the fate of others in his situation around the camp of Cornwallis in Charlotte. Nor were his fears unduly excited

Captain Thompson, at the distance of seventy or seventy-five yards, killed him instantly, when his companions, with a precision of aim equally fatal, laid low on the earth his respective foe. To Captain Thompson is also ascribed the honor of mortally wounding the commanding officer, when he was standing near the barn door. He was conveyed to Charlotte, with several others in similar condition, in one of the foraging wagons, and died of the wound received, at the house of Samuel McCombs, two days after. When the smoke rose, after the first discharge of the rifles, the commander, nine men and two horses lay dead or wounded on the ground. The trumpets immediately sounded a recall. But by the time the scattered dragoons had collected and formed, a straggling fire from a different direction, into which the patriots had extended, showed the unerring aim of each American marksman, and greatly increased the confusion of the surprise. Perfectly acquainted with every foot of the grounds, the patriots constantly changed their position, giving in their fire as they loaded, so that it appeared to the British they were surrounded by a large force. When that portion of Doyle's command who had proceeded forward to forage upon other farms heard the firing, they immediately returned to the assistance of his party at McIntyre's branch. Every preparation for defence, attack and retreat was made by the Americans The alternate hilly and swampy grounds and thickets, with woods on both sides of the public road, baffled the efficient action of the British dragoons. Some dismounted, while others called out to "set on the hounds" against a foe scarcely visible, except from their deadly effects. The dogs, at first, seemed to take the track, and were followed by the soldiers. The foremost hound approached very near one of the patriots who had just discharged his rifle, and was in full retreat after his companions; but as soon as the hound came near with open mouth, he was shot dead by a pistol drawn from the breast of the rifleman. The next hound stopped at the dead body, and, after smelling it, gave a whining howl, and the whole pack retreated from the contest.

A considerable number of the dragoons were killed. The leading horses in the wagons were killed before they could ascend the hill, thus blocking up the road. Many of the soldiers in charge of the wagons cut loose some of the uninjured animals, and galloped after their retreating comrades. The precise loss of the British is not known. It is believed, however, from reliable tradition, that they had at least twenty killed and *a few* wounded.

That a British detachment of four hundred and fifty infantry and sixty cavalry should be compelled to desist from a foraging expedition and return to Charlotte with only a small amount of provisions and a considerable loss of their number by a handful of patriots, well exemplifies the vigilance, pertinacity and courage of the "hornets" of Mecklenburg in endeavoring to protect their homes, and repel the invaders of their soil.

The country people, early advised of the advance of the foraging party, mounted their horses, rifle in hand, from every direction; and, occupying well protected positions along the main road, also faithfully endeavored to diminish the number of his Majesty's forces, and hastened the retreat of the British into Charlotte, the survivors swearing after their arrival that "every bush along the road concealed a rebel."

The names of this gallant band of patriots, of "Hornets' Nest" notoriety, were: 1. James Thompson, captain; 2. Francis Bradley; 3. George Graham; 4. James Henry; 5. Thomas Dickson; 6. John Dickson; 7. George Houston; 8. Hugh Houston; 9. Thomas McLure; 10. John Long; 11. John Robinson; 12. George Shipley; 13. Edward Shipley.

REMARKS.—Tradition says Francis Bradley was a large and very strong man, and a "terror" to the British as well as the Tories. The British officers were extremely anxious to take him as a prisoner, for his activity in harassing their scouts and foraging parties, and more particularly for the fatal aim of his rifle in *picking off* their sentries while their army was encamped at Charlotte. The rifle he carried for six years during the Revolution, and which did such *telling* execution, was the property of Major John Davidson (now in possession of one of his grandsons,) who, being a staff officer, could not make it perform, as it should, its death-dealing mission upon the enemies of his country. About three weeks after the gallant affair at McIntyre's Branch, Bradley was attacked, overpowered and killed by four lurking and base-hearted Tories (said not to be natives of the county). His mortal remains now repose in the graveyard at Hopewell Church, where also sleep many of his illustrious compatriots in arms. On his gravestone are sculptured two drawn and crossed swords, and beneath them the motto, *Arma Libertatis* The inscription reads thus:

"In memory of
FRANCIS BRADLEY,
A friend of his country, and privately slain by the enemies of his country,
November 14th, 1780, aged 37 years."

The two Dicksons moved to Tennessee; the two Houstons and McLure moved to Kentucky; Robinson settled on Crowder's Creek, Gaston county.

Doyle, the British commander, before the close of the war was made a Colonel, and afterward a Brigadier-General. In 1816 he was styled Sir John Doyle, and Governor of the Islands of Guernsey, Jersey, Alderney and Sark, on the coast of France. Surely, it could not have been for his gallant behavior at McIntyre's he acquired such honor and promotion!

JUDGE SAMUEL LOWRIE.

Judge Lowrie was born in New Castle county, Del., on the 12th of May, 1756. His parents moved, when he was a child, to North Carolina, and settled in Rowan county. He was educated at Clio Academy (now in Iredell county) under the Rev. James Hall, an eminent Presbyterian minister of the gospel, and Captain of a company during the Revolutionary War. He studied law in Camden, S. C., and, soon gaining eminence in his profession, was elected to the House of Commons from Mecklenburg county in 1804,–'5 and '6. In the last named year he was elected a Judge of the Superior Court, which position he held until his death on the 22d of December, 1818, in the sixty-third year of his age.

In 1788, he married Margaret, eldest daughter of Captain Robert Alexander, of Lincoln county. His wife died, leaving him with several children. In 1811, he again married, Mary, daughter of Marmaduke Norfleet, of Bertie county, N. C. He was a man of fine talents, and dignified the responsible position he held. He resided in Mecklenburg county, about three miles north from the Tuckasege Ford, on the Salisbury road, (now owned by Robert S. McGee, Esq.)

His mortal remains, with those of his first wife and three infant children, and other relatives, repose in the graveyard of Goshen Church, Gaston county, N. C.

THE LADIES OF THE REVOLUTIONARY PERIOD.

It has been well said that "patriotic mothers nursed the infancy of the Republic." During the progress of British encroachment and arbitrary power, producing great colonial discontent, every sagacious politician could discern in the distant future the portentous shadow of the approaching conflict. In the domestic circle was then nurtured and imparted that love of civil liberty which afterwards kindled into a flame, and shed its genial and transforming light upon the world. The conversation of matrons in their homes, or among their neighbors, was of the people's wrongs and of the tyranny that oppressed them. Under such early training their sons, when grown to manhood, deeply imbued with proper notions of their just rights, stood up in the hour of trial prepared to defend them to the last. The counsels and the prayers of mothers mingled with their deliberations, and added sanctity to all their patriotic efforts for American independence. They animated the courage, confirmed the self-devotion, and shared in the sacrifices of those who, in the common defence, "pledged their lives, their fortunes and their sacred honor."

Among the widowed mothers who early instilled into their rising generation a deep love of their country, and a manful determination to defend their firesides and their homes, might be named Mrs. Steele, Mrs. Flinn, Mrs. Sharpe, Mrs. Graham, Mrs. Hunter, Mrs. Jackson and many others, as bright examples in Mecklenburg, Rowan and adjoining counties. In the hour of deepest gloom they frowned upon apathy in the common cause, materially assisted by their benefactions, and urged on the desponding in the path of patriotic duty.

General Moultrie, in his "Memoirs of the American Revolution," pays a handsome compliment to the ladies of that section of country in which his military services were performed. He says: "Before I conclude my memoirs I must make my last tribute of thanks to the patriotic fair of South Carolina and Georgia for their heroism and virtue in those dreadful and dangerous times whilst we were struggling for our liberties. Their conduct deserves the highest applause, and a pillar ought to be raised to their memory. Their conduct was such as gave examples even to the men to stand firm; and they despised those who were not enthusiasts in their country's cause. The hardships and difficulties they experienced were too much for their delicate frames to bear; yet they submitted to them with a heroism and virtue that has never been excelled by the ladies of any country; and I can with safety say that their conduct during the war contributed much to the independence of America."

Nor were the young ladies of that period less patriotic

than their venerable mothers. Their kind sympathies and voluntary contributions were exhibited on every occasion, calling for prompt and beneficent action for the gallant soldier. With fair and willing hands they embroidered colors for military companies, and presented them with the animating charge, *never to desert them.* They formed themselves into associations throughout the colonies, renouncing the use of teas and other imported luxuries, and engaged to card, spin and weave their own clothing. And still further, to arouse a patriotic spirit in every hesitating or laggard bosom, we find in the "South Carolina and American General Gazette," of February 9th, 1776, the following paragraph, illustrative of female patriotism under a manly and *singular* incentive:

"The young ladies of the best families of Mecklenburg county, North Carolina, have entered into a voluntary association that they will not receive the addresses of any young gentlemen of that place, except the brave volunteers who served in the expedition to South Carolina, and assisted in subduing the Scovilite insurgents. The ladies being of opinion that such persons as stay loitering at home, when the important calls of their country demand their military services abroad, must certainly be destitute of that nobleness of sentiment, that brave, manly spirit, which would qualify them to be the defenders and guardians of the fair sex. The ladies of the adjoining county of Rowan have desired the plan of a similar association to be drawn up and prepared for signature."

Accordingly, at a meeting of the Committee of Safety, held in Salisbury, May 8th, 1776, we find the following entry in their minutes: "A letter from a number of young ladies in the county, directed to the chairman, requesting the approbation of the committee to a number of resolutions enclosed, entered into, and signed by the same young ladies being read,

Resolved, That this committee present their cordial thanks to the said young ladies for so spirited a performance; look upon these resolutions to be sensible and polite; that they merit the honor, and are worthy the imitation of every young lady in America."

And who were the young ladies of Mecklenburg and Rowan counties then prepared to sign such an association, and willing to bestow their fair hands, and pledge their loving hearts *only to those brave soldiers*, who, on the calls of duty, fought the battles of their country? Imagination carries us back to that eventful period, and pictures to our admiring view, among others, the following daughters of Western Carolina, as actuated by such patriotic motives:

Miss Elizabeth Alexander, daughter of Abraham Alexander, Chairman of the Mecklenburg Convention of the 20th of May, 1775, who married William Alexander, son of Hezekiah Alexander, one of the signers of the Mecklenburg Declaration.

Miss Mary Wilson, daughter of Samuel Wilson, Sen., who married Ezekiel Polk, grandfather of James K. Polk, one of our best Presidents, who consented to serve *only for one term*.

Miss Violet Wilson, sister of the above, who married Major John Davidson, one of the signers of the Mecklenburg Declaration.

Miss Jane Morrison, daughter of Neill Morrison, one of the signers of the Mecklenburg Declaration, who married Major Thomas Alexander.

Miss Polk, daughter of Colonel Thomas Polk, who married Dr. Ephraim Brevard, one of the secretaries and signers of the Mecklenburg Declaration.

Miss Margaret Polk, sister of the above, who married Nathaniel Alexander, Representative to Congress from 1803 to 1805, and in the latter year, elected Governor of the State.

Miss Jane Brevard, daughter of John Brevard, and sister of the "seven brothers in the rebel army," who married General Ephraim Davidson.

Miss Mary Brevard, sister of the above, who married General William Davidson, killed at Cowan's Ford, on February 1st, 1781.

Miss Charity Jack, sister of Captain James Jack, the bearer of the Mecklenburg Declaration to Philadelphia, who married Dr. Cornelius Dysart, a distinguished surgeon of the Revolutionary army.

Miss Lillis Wilson, daughter of Samuel Wilson, Sen., by the third wife (Margaret Jack), who married James Connor, a native of Ireland, who came to America when 21 years old, volunteered in the army, and fought all through the Revolutionary war.

Miss Hannah Knox, daughter of Captain Patrick Knox, killed at the battle of Ramsour's Mill, who married Samuel Wilson, a soldier of the Revolution.

These are the names of a few of the patriotic young ladies, then on the theater of action, who would be willing to sign such an association, stimulate the "loitering young men" to a proper sense of their duty, and promote the cause of freedom by all *fair means*.

MRS. ELEANOR WILSON.

The wives and mothers of Mecklenburg county bore a large share of the trials and dangers of the Revolution. Among these, and as a fair type of many others that might be mentioned, was Eleanor, wife of Robert Wilson, of Steele Creek—a woman of singular energy of mind, and warmly devoted to the American cause. Her husband, with three brothers and and other kinsmen, settled in Mecklenburg about 1760, having moved from the colony of Pennsylvania. These brothers were Scotch Presbyterians, and arrayed by early religious education against tyranny in every form. At the Convention in Charlotte on the 20th of May, 1775, Zaccheus Wilson, representing all his kinsmen, signed that declaration, pledging himself, and his extensive connections, to its support and maintenance. At this crisis of our history there were a considerable number of timid persons, who shook their heads and characterized the actors in this opening scene of the bloody drama of the Revolution, as *madmen, rebels and traitors*. From the first to the last, Mrs. Wilson espoused the cause of liberty, and exulted in every patriotic success.

Animated by her enthusiasm, her husband and sons entered warmly into the contest. At the surrender of Charleston, her sons, Robert and Joseph, were made prisoners, but having given their parols, were allowed to return home. But they had scarcely reached their home in Mecklenburg when the British general issued his proclamation declaring the country subdued, and requiring every able-bodied militiaman to join the royal standard. Refusing to fight against their country, and being no longer bound as they believed, by their parols, they immediately repaired to the standard of General Sumter, and were with him in several battles. In the battle of the Hanging Rock, Captain David Reid, one of their kinsmen, was mortally wounded, and being in great agony, called for water, when Robert Wilson brought him some in his hat. In the same action, Joseph, a little in advance, was assaulted by a Tory, a powerful man, whom he knew; after a severe struggle, he killed him, and bore off his sword, now in possession of his son, David Wilson, of Maine county, Tennessee.

The elder Robert Wilson and his son John, having collected a supply of provisions and forage for General Sumter's corps, from the neighborhood of Steele Creek, were hastening to meet them at Fishing Creek, and reached that vicinity a short time after the surprise. While engaged in this employment, the two Wilsons and the supplies were captured. The prisoners were hurried to the rear, after having been brutally threatened with hanging on the nearest tree, and by a forced march reached Camden next day, where they were added to a crowd of honorable captives, such as Andrew Jackson, Colonel Isaacs, General Rutherford and others.

In the meantime, Cornwallis, leaving Rawdon at Camden, marched with the larger portion of his army to "rebellious" Charlotte, to forage upon its farms, and to punish its inhabitants for their well-known resistance to royal authority. He reached Charlotte on the 26th of September, 1780, and during his stay of eighteen days, many scenes of rapine, house burnings and plunderings took place in and around that place. But the bold Whigs of Mecklenburg—the "hornets" of that section—although unable to keep the open field, were vigilant and at work, constantly popping the sentinels, and insolent dragoons of Tarleton, sent out as scouts and on foraging excursions Becoming uneasy by these bold attacks of the rebels, frequently driving his foraging parties within sight of his camp, Cornwallis, when he heard of the defeat of Ferguson at King's Mountain, concentrated his army, and, on the 14th of October, commenced his retrograde march towards Winnsboro, S C. During this march, the British army halted for the night at Wilson's plantation, near Steele Creek. Cornwallis and Tarleton occupied the house of Mrs. Wilson, requiring her to prepare a meal for them as though they had been her friends. Cornwallis, in the meantime, finding out that her husband and one of her sons were his prisoners in the Camden jail, artfully attempted to enlist her in the King's cause.

"Madam, said he, your husband and son, are my prisoners; the fortune of war may soon place others of your sons—perhaps all your kinsmen, in my power. Your sons are young, aspiring, and brave. In a good cause, fighting for a generous and powerful king, such as George III., they might hope for rank, honor and wealth. If you could but induce your husband and sons to leave the rebels, and take up arms for their lawful sovereign, I would almost pledge myself that they shall have rank and consideration in the British army. If you, madam, will pledge yourself to induce them to do so, I will immediately order their discharge."

To this artful appeal, Mrs. Wilson replied that "her husband and children were indeed dear to her, and that she was willing to do anything she thought right to promote their real and permanent welfare; but, in this instance, they had embarked in the holy cause of liberty; had fought and struggled for it during five years, never faltering for a moment, while others had fled from the contest, and yielded up their hopes at the first obstacle. I have," she continued, "seven sons who are now, or have been, bearing arms—indeed, my seventh son, Zaccheus, who is only fifteen years old, I yesterday assisted to get ready to go and join his brothers in Sumter's army. Now, sooner than see one of my family turn back from the glorious enterprise, I would take these boys (pointing to three or four small sons) and would myself enlist under Sumter's standard, and show my husband and sons how to fight, and, if necessary, to die for their country."

"Ah General," interrupted the cold-hearted Tarleton, "I think you've got into a hornet's nest! Never mind, when we get to Camden, I'll take good care that old Robin Wilson never comes back."

On the next day's march, a party of scouts captured Zaccheus, who was found on the flank of the British army with his gun, endeavoring to diminish the number of His Majesty's forces. He was immediately conducted to Cornwallis, who, finding out his name, took him along as a guide to the best ford on the Catawba. Arriving at the river, the head of the army entered at the point designated by the lad, but the soldiers soon found themselves in deep water, and drawn by a rapid current down the stream. Cornwallis, believing that the boy had purposely led him into deep water in order to embarras his march, drew his sword, and swore he would cut off his head for his treachery. Zaccheus replied that he had the power to do so, as he had no arms, and was his prisoner;

"but, sir," said this resolute boy, "don't you think it would be a cowardly act for you to strike an unarmed boy with your sword. If I had but the half of your weapon, it would not be so cowardly, but then you know, it would not be so safe."

Cornwallis, struck by the boy's cool courage, calmed down, told him he was a fine fellow, and that he would not hurt a hair of his head. Having discovered that the ford was shallow enough by bearing up the stream, the British army crossed over it safely, and proceeded to Winnsboro.

On this march, Cornwallis dismissed Zaccheus, telling him to go home and take care of his mother, and to tell her to keep her boys at home. After he reached Winnsboro, he dispatched an order to Rawdon, at Camden, to send Robin Wilson and his son John, with several others, to Charleston, carefully guarded. Accordingly, about the 20th of November, Wilson, his son, and ten others, set off under the escort of an officer and fifteen or twenty men. Wilson formed several plans of making his escape, but owing to the presence of large parties of the enemy, they could not be executed. At length, being near Fort Watson, they encamped before night, the prisoners being placed in the yard, and the guard in the house and in the portico. In a short time the arms of the guard were ordered to be stacked in the portico, a sentinel placed over them, and all others were soon busily engaged in preparing their evening meal. The prisoners, in the meantime, having bribed a soldier to buy some whiskey, as it was a rainy day, *pretended* to drink freely of it themselves, and one of them seemingly more intoxicated than the rest, insisted upon treating the sentinel. Wilson followed him, as if to prevent him from treating the sentinel, it being a breach of military order. Watching a favorable opportunity, he seized the sentinel's musket, and the drunken man suddenly becoming sober, seized the sentinel. At this signal, the prisoners—like vigilant hornets, rushed to the stacked arms in the portico, when the guard, taking the alarm, rushed out of the house. But it was too late; the prisoners secured the arms, drove the soldiers into the house at the point of the bayonet, and the whole guard surrendered at discretion. Unable to take off their prisoners, Wilson made them all hold up their right hands and swear never again to bear arms against the "cause of liberty, and the Continental Congress," and then told them they might go to Charleston on parole; but if he ever found "a single mother's son of them in arms again, he would hang him up to a tree like a dog."

Wilson had scarcely disposed of his prisoners before a party of British dragoons came in sight. As the only means of escape, they separated into several small companies, and took to the woods. Some of them reached Marion's camp at Snow Island, and Wilson, with two or three others, arrived safely in Mecklenburg, over two hundred miles distant, and through a country overrun with British troops.

Mrs. Wilson was the mother of eleven sons. She and her husband lived to a good old age, were worthy and consistent members of the Presbyterian Church, died near the same time, in 1810, and are buried in Steele Creek grave-yard.

About 1792, all the sons moved to Tennessee, where at the present time, and in other portions of the West, their descendants may be counted by the hundreds. Robert Wilson, who was said to be the first man that crossed the Cumberland mountains with a wagon, married Jane, a daughter of William and Ellen McDowell, of York county, S. C. Both Jane and her mother went to King's Mountain after the battle, and remained several days in ministering to the wants of the wounded soldiers. It was mainly on the account of Robert Wilson's distinguished bravery at King's Mountain that William McDowell gave him his daughter Jane in marriage—a worthy gift, and worthily bestowed on a gallant soldier.

QUEEN'S MUSEUM.

One of the most useful institutions of the Revolutionary period, and around which cluster many patriotic associations, was the College in Charlotte, known as Queen's Museum. As the early fount of educational training in Mecklenburg, and the *nursery of freemen*, as well as of scholars, it should ever claim our warmest regard and veneration. A brief notice of its origin, progress and termination may be acceptable to the general reader.

The counties of Mecklenburg, Rowan and other portions of the State, lying in the track of the southern tide of emigration from more northern colonies, were principally settled by the Scotch-Irish, who, inheriting an independence of character and free thought from their earliest training, soon became the controlling element of society, and directed its leading religious and political movements. They were not only the friends of a liberal education, but the early and unflinching advocates of civil and religious liberty. The "school-master was abroad in the land," and as duly encouraged as in our own day. Wherever a preacher was established among them, to proclaim the gospel of salvation, there, with rare exceptions, soon sprang up into lively existence a good school, both of a common and classical order. Prominently among these seminaries of learning may be named Sugar Creek, Poplar Tent, Center, Bethany, Thyatira, Rocky River, and Providence, all located in Mecklenburg and Rowan counties. Of all these, Sugar Creek was probably the oldest. The time of its commencement is not certainly known.

After the death of the Rev. Alexander Craighead, in 1766, the first settled pastor of Sugar Creek, the Rev. Joseph Alexander (a nephew of John McKnitt Alexander) became his successor for a short time, previous to his removal to Bullock's Creek, S. C., where he ended his days. Mr. Alexander was a fine scholar, having graduated at

Princeton College, and through his influence, confirmed by that of the Alexanders and Polks, Waightstill Avery, Dr. Ephraim Brevard and others, residing in or near Charlotte, vigorous efforts were made to elevate the Sugar Creek school to the rank and usefulness of a college; nor were their efforts in vain. The Colonial Legislature which met at Newbern, in December, 1770, passed an Act entitled "An Act for founding, establishing and endowing of Queen's College, in the town of Charlotte." This charter, not suiting the intolerant notions of royalty, was set aside by the King and council; afterward amended; a second time granted by the Colonial Legislature, in 1771, and a second time repealed by royal proclamation.

"And," enquires a writer in the "University Magazine," of North Carolina, "why was this?" An easy answer is found in the third section of the act for incorporating the school at Newbern, and afterward engrafted upon the act incorporating the Edenton Academy (which were the only two schools incorporated before Queen's College), compared with the character of the leading men of Mecklenburg, and the fact that several of the Trustees of the new College were Presbyterian ministers. No compliments to his queen could render *Whigs* in politics, and *Presbyterians* in religion, acceptable to George III.

A College, under such auspices, was too well calculated to insure the growth of the "*numerous democracy.*"

The section referred to in the charter of the Newbern school, is in these words: "Provided always, that no person shall be permitted to be master of said school, but who is of the Established Church of England, and who, at the recommendation of the trustees or directors, or a majority of them, shall be duly licensed by the Governor! or Commander-in-Chief for the time being."

"The Presbyterians," says Lossing, "who were very numerous, resolved to have a seminary of their own, and applied for an unrestricted charter for a college. It was granted; but notwithstanding it was called Queen's College, in compliment to the consort of the King, and was located in a town called by her name, and in a county of the same name as her birth-place, the charter was repealed in 1771 by royal decree. The triple compliment was of no avail."*

But Queen's Museum, or College, flourished without a charter for several years, in spite of the intolerance of the King and Council. Its hall became the general meeting-place of literary societies and political clubs preceding the Revolution. The King's fears that the College would prove to be a fountain of Republicanism, and calculated to ensure the growth of the "numerous Democracy," were happily, for the cause of freedom, realized in the characters of its instructors and pupils. The debates, preceding the adoption of the Mecklenburg Declaration, were held in its hall, and every reader can judge of the patriotic sentiments which pervade that famous document. After the Revolution commenced, the Legislature of North Carolina granted a charter, in 1777, to this insritution, under the name of "Liberty Hall Academy." The following persons were named as trustees, viz.: Isaac Alexander, M. D., president; Thomas Polk, Abraham Alexander, Thomas Neal, Waightstill Avery, Ephraim Brevard, John Simpson, John McKnitt Alexander, Adlai Osborn, and the Rev. Messrs. David Caldwell, James Edmonds, Thomas Reese, Samuel E. McCorkle, Thomas H. McCaule and James Hall.

The Academy received no funds or endowment from the State, and no further patronage than this charter. At the time the charter was obtained the institution was under the care of Dr. Isaac V. Alexander, who continued to preside until some time in the year 1778. From a manuscript in the University of North Carolina, drawn up

---

* Lossing's "Pictorial Field Book of the Revolution," vol. II, p. 393.

by Adlai Osborne, one of the trustees, it appears, the first meeting of the board of trustees was held in Charlotte, on the 3rd day of January, 1778. At this meeting Isaac Alexander, M. D., Ephraim Brevard, M. D., and the Rev. Thomas H. McCaule, were appointed a committee to frame a system of laws for the government of the Academy. They were also empowered to purchase the lots and improvements belonging to Colonel Thomas Polk, for which they were to pay him £920. The salary of the president was fixed at £195, to be occasionally increased, according to the prices of provisions, then greatly fluctuating in consequence of the war.

In the month of April, 1778, the system of laws, drawn up by the committee, was adopted without any material alteration. The course of studies marked out was similar to that prescribed for the University of North Carolina, though more limited. Shortly before these transactions, overtures were made to the Rev. Alexander McWhorter, of New Jersey, so favorably known to the churches by his missionary visit in 1764 and 1765,' with the Rev. Elihu Spencer; and also by a more recent visit to the Southern country, to encourage the inhabitants in the cause of independence, soliciting him to succeed Dr. Alexander in the presidency of the Academy.

Dr. McWhorter having declined accepting the presidency on account of the deranged state of his affairs at that time, Mr. Robert Brownfield, a good scholar, and belonging to a patriotic family of Mecklenburg, agreed to assume the duties of the office for one year. During the next year, the invitation to Dr. McWhorter was renewed, and a committee consisting of the Rev. Samuel E. McCorkle, and Dr. Ephraim Brevard was sent to New Jersey to wait upon him; and in the event of his still declining, to consult Dr. Witherspoon and Professor Houston, of Princeton College (the latter, a distinguished son of old Mecklenburg,) respecting some other fit person to whom the presidency should be offered. In compliance with this second invitation, Dr. McWhorter removed to Charlotte and immediately entered upon the duties of his office with flattering evidences of success. Many youths from Mecklenburg and adjoining counties, yet too young to engage in the battles of their country, and others of older years, whose services were not imperiously needed on the tented field, flocked to an institution where a useful and thorough education could be imparted.

But, owing to the invasion of the Carolinas by Cornwallis in the fall of 1780, the operations of the Academy were suspended and not resumed during the remainder of the war. After a short service in the Presidency of the Academy, Dr. McWhorter, to the great regret of the patrons of learning in the South, returned to New Jersey.

During the occupation of Charlotte by the British army under Lord Cornwallis, Liberty Hall Academy, which stood upon the lot now owned by A. B. Davidson, Esq., was used as a hospital, and greatly defaced and injured. The numerous graves in the rear of the Academy, visible upon the departure of the British army, after a stay of eighteen days, bore ample evidence of their great loss in this "rebellious county"—the "Hornet's Nest" of America.

After the close of the war, Dr. Thomas Henderson, who had been educated at the Academy, and who frequently represented Mecklenburg in the Legislature near the beginning of the present century, set up a High School, and carried it on with great reputation for a number of years. Classical schools of a high order were numerous after the Revolutionary war, principally under the direction of Presbyterian clergymen. These early efforts in the cause of a sound and liberal education, constantly mingled with patriotic teachings, made a telling impress upon the Revolutionary period, and greatly assisted in achieving our independence.

CHAPTER II.

CABARRUS COUNTY.

Cabarrus county was formed in 1792, from Mecklenburg county, and was named in honor of Stephen Cabarrus, a native of France, a man of active mind, liberal sentiments, and high standing in society. He entered public life in 1784, and was frequently elected a member from Chowan county, and, on several occasions, Speaker of the House of Commons.

The Colonial and Revolutionary history of Cabarrus is closely connected with that of Mecklenburg county. No portion of the State was more fixed and forward in the cause of liberty than this immediate section. In the Convention at Charlotte, on the 20th of May, 1775, this part of Mecklenburg was strongly represented, and her delegates joined heartily in pledging "their lives, their fortunes and most sacred honor" to maintain and defend their liberty and independence.

The proceedings of that celebrated Convention, its principal actors, and attendant circumstances, will be found properly noticed under the head of Mecklenburg County. But there is one bold transaction connected with the early history of Cabarrus, showing that the germs of liberty, at and before the battle of Alamance, in 1771, were ready to burst forth, at any moment, under the warmth of patriotic excitement, is here deemed worthy of conspicuous record.

THE "BLACK BOYS" OF CABARRUS.

Previous to the battle of Alamance, on the 16th of May, 1771, the first blood shed in the American Revolution, there were many discreet persons, the advocates of law and order, throughout the province, who sympathized with the justness of the principles which actuated the 'Regulators," and their stern opposition to official corruption and extortion, but did not approve of their hasty conduct and occasional violent proceedings. Accordingly, a short time preceding that unfortunate conflict, which only smothered for a time the embers of freedom, difficulties arose between Governor Tryon and the Regulators, when that royal official, in order to coerce them into his measures of submission, procured from Charleston, S. C., three wagon loads of the munitions of war, consisting of powder, flints, blankets, &c. These articles were brought to Charlotte, but from some suspicions arising in the minds of the Whigs as to their true destination and use, wagons could not be hired in the neighborhood for their transportation. At length, Colonel Moses Alexander, a magistrate under the Colonial Government, succeeded in getting wagons by *impressment*, to convey the munitions to Hillsboro, to obey the behests of a tyrannical governor. The vigilance of the jealous Whigs was ever on the lookout for the suppression of all such infringements upon the growing spirit of freedom, then quietly but surely planting itself in the hearts of the people.

The following individuals, viz.: James, William and John White, brothers, and William White, a cousin, all born and raised on Rocky River, and one mile from Rocky River Church, Robert Caruthers, Robert Davis, Benjamin Cockrane, James and Joshua Hadley, bound themselves by a most solemn oath not to divulge the secret object of their contemplated mission, and, in order more effertually to prevent detection, *blackened their faces* preparatory to their intended work of destruction.

They were joined and led in this and other expeditions by William Alexander, of Sugar Creek congregation, a brave soldier, and afterward known and distinguished from others bearing the same name as " Captain Black Bill Alexander," and whose sword now hangs in the Library Hall of Davidson College, presented in behalf of his descendants by the late worthy, intelligent and Christian citizen, W. Shakespeare Harris, Esq.

These determined spirits set out in the evening, while the father of the Whites was absent from home with two horses, each carrying a bag of grain. The White boys were on foot, and wishing to move rapidly with their comrades, all mounted, in pursuit of the wagons loaded with the munitions of war, fortunately, for their feet, met their father returning home with his burdens, and immediately demanded the use of his horses. The old gentleman, not knowing who they were (*as black as Satan himself*) pleaded heartily for the horses until he could carry home his bags of meal; but his petitions were in vain. The boys (*his sons*) ordered him to dismount, removed the bags from the horses, and placed them by the side of the road. They then immediately mounted the disburdened horses, joined their comrades, and in a short space of time came up with the wagons encamped on "Phifer's Hill," three miles west of the present town of Concord, on the road leading from Charlotte to Salisbury. They immediately unloaded the wagons, stove in the heads of the kegs, threw the powder into a pile, tore the blankets into strips, made a train of powder a considerable distance from the pile, and then Major James White fired a pistol into the train, which produced a tremendous explosion. A stave from the pile struck White on the forehead, and cut him severely. As soon as this bold exploit became known to Colonel Moses Alexander, he put his whole ingenuity to work to find out the perpetrators of so foul a deed against his Majesty. The transaction remained a mystery for some time. Great threats were made, and, in order to induce some one to turn traitor, a pardon was offered to any one who would turn King's evidence against the rest. Ashmore and Hadley, being half brothers, and composed of the same rotten materials, set out unknown to each other, to avail themselves of the offered pardon, and accidently met each other on the treshold of Moses Alexander's house. When they made known their business, Alexander remarked, "that, by virtue of the Governor's proclamation, they were pardoned, but they were the first that ought to be hanged." The rest of the "Black Boys" had to flee from their country. They fled to the State of Geogia, where they remained for some time.

The Governor, finding he could not get them into his grasp, held out insinuations that if they would return and confess their fault, they should be pardoned. In a short time, the boys returned from Georgia to their homes. As soon as it became known to Moses Alexander, he raised a guard, consisting of himself, his two brothers, John and Jake, and a few others, and surrounded the house of the old man White, the father of the boys. Caruthers, the son-in-law of White, happened to be at his (White's) house at the same time. To make the capture doubly sure, Alexander placed a guard at each door. One of the guard, wishing to favor the escape of Caruthers, struck up a quarrel with Moses Alexander at one door, while his brother, Daniel Alexander, whispered to Mrs. White, if there were any of them within, they might pass out and he would not notice it; in the meantime, out goes Caruthers, and in a few jumps was in the river, which opportunely flowed near the besieged mansion. The alarm was immediately given, but pursuit was fruitless.

At another time, the royalists heard of some of the boys being in a harvest field and set out to take them; but always having some one in their company to favor their escape, as they rode up in sight of the reapers, one of them, duly instructed, waved his hand, which the boys understood as a signal to make their departure. On that occasion they pursued Robert Dairs so closely that it is said he jumped his horse thirty feet down a bank into the river, and dared them to follow him.

And thus the "Black Boys" fled from covert to covert to save their necks from the blood-thirsty loyalists, who were constantly hunting them like wild beasts. They would lie concealed for weeks at a time, and the neighbors would carry them food until they fairly wearied out their pursuers. The oath by which they bound themselves was an imprecation of the strongest kind, and the greater part of the imprecation was literally fulfilled in the sad ends of Hadley and Ashmore. The latter fled from his country, but he lived a miserable life, and died as wretchedly as he had lived. Hadley still remained in the country, and was known for many years to the people of Rocky River. He was very intemperate, and in his fits of intoxication was very harsh to his family in driving them from his house in the dead hours of the night. His neighbors, in order to chastise him for the abuse of his family, (among whom were some of the "Black Boys"), dressed themselves in female attire, went to his house by night, pulled him from his bed, drew his shirt over his head and gave him a severe whipping. The castigation, it is said, greatly improved the future treatment of his family. He continued, however, through life, the same miserable wretch, and died without any friendly hand to sustain him or eye to pity his deplorable end.

Frequently, when the royalists ranged the country in pursuit of the "Black Boys," the Whigs would collect in bodies consisting of twenty-five or thirty men, ready to pounce upon the pursuers, if they had captured any of the boys. From the allurements held out to the Boys to give themselves up, they went, at one time, nearly to Hillsboro to beg the pardon of the Governor, (Tryon), but finding out it was his intention, if he could get them into his hands, to have hanged every one of them, they returned, and kept themselves concealed until patriotic sentiment grew so rapidly from that time (1771) to the Mecklenburg Declaration, (20th of May, 1775), that concealment was no longer necessary. When the drama of the Revolution opened, these same "Black Boys" stood up manfully for the cause of American freedom, and nobly assisted in achieving, on many a hard-fought battle-field, the independence of our country.

DR. CHARLES HARRIS.

Dr. Charles Harris was born in the eastern part of Mecklenburg county, (now Cabarrus), on the 23d of November, 1762. He was distinguished as a patriot, a soldier, and a physician. While pursuing his studies in Charlotte, the invasion of the town by the British army, under Lord Cornwallis, caused him to exchange the gown for the sword. Accordingly, when a call was made for troops to resist and hold in check the invaders of his country, he joined the corps of cavalry under Col. William R. Davie, and was with that brave and chivalric officer in much of his daring career.

After the war was ended he resumed his studies at Clio Academy, in Iredell county, (then a part of Rowan), under the control of the Rev. James Hall. Soon after this classical preparation he commenced the study of medicine under Dr. Isaac Alexander, at Camden, S. C., and graduated at Philadelphia. On his return home, he settled in Salisbury, and practiced there for some length of time with encouraging success. He then removed to Favoni, his family seat in Cabarrus county, where he ended his days.

Devoted to his profession he soon became unrivaled as a physician and surgeon. In a short time his reputation was widely extended over the surrounding country, and his skill and success justified this celebrity. He kept up for many years, a medical school, and instructed *ninety-three* young men in the healing art. In his day and generation, good physicians and surgeons (especially the latter) were remarkably scarce—something like angels' visits, "few and far between." He was frequently called upon to perform surgical operations from fifty to one hundred miles from home.

He possessed a cheerful temper, and suavity of manner which gained for him a ready admittance into the confidence and cordial friendship of all classes of society. But, before he had reached his "three-score years and ten," the infirmities of old age were rapidly stealing upon him, and admonishing him of his early departure from the scenes of earth. He died on the 21st of September, 1825, leaving several children. One of his sons, the late William Shakspeare Harris, Esq., widely known as a worthy and intelligent citizen, represented Cabarrus county in the House of Commons in 1836. Another son, Charles J. Harris, Esq., resides at present about one mile from Poplar Tent Church, and is a gentleman of great moral worth and christian integrity.

On the tombstone of Dr. Harris is the following inscription: "This monument is erected to perpetuate the memory of Charles Harris, M. D., born 23d of November, 1762; died 21st of September, 1825, aged sixty-three years. Dr. Harris was engaged in the practice of medicine and surgery for forty years; eminent in the former, in the latter pre-eminent. He was a man of extensive reading, of an acute, inquisitive mind, friendly to all, and beloved by all. His heart entered deeply into the sufferings of his patients, mingling the medicine he administered with the feelings of a friend. He lived usefully, and died resignedly; and we humbly trust, through the sovereign virtue of the all-healing medicine of the Great Physician, he was prepared to rest in this tomb, 'where the wicked cease from troubling, and the weary are at rest.'"

Dr. Charles Harris was one of five brothers who emigrated from Pennsylvania to North Carolina, viz: Robert, James, Richard, Thomas, and Charles, the subject of this sketch His father married the widow Baker, a daughter of the Rev. John Thompson, who is buried in Baker's Grave-yard, five Miles east of Beattie's Ford, in Iredell county.

CAPT. THOMAS CALDWELL.

Capt. Thomas Caldwell, of Irish parentage, was born in the eastern part of Mecklenburg county, (now Cabarrus), in 1753. He early espoused the cause of liberty, and entered the service in 1775, in Capt. John Springs' company as a private, and marched to the protection of the frontier settlements from the murderous and plundering incursions of the Cherokee Indians.

He again joined the service in Capt. Ezekiel Polk's company and marched against the Tories in South Carolina, near the post of Ninety-Six. In 1776, he volunteered under Captain William Alexander, Colonels Adam Alexander and Robert Irwin, General Rutherford commanding; marched to the Quaker Meadows, at the head of the Catawba River, and thence to the Cherokee country, beyond the mountains. After severely chastising the Indians, killing a few, and laying waste their country, causing them to sue for peace, the expedition returned.

In 1870, he was appointed Captain by General Thomas Polk to assist in opposing the advance of Lord Cornwallis.

After Cornwallis left Charlotte, in October, 1780, he raised a company, placed himself under Colonel Williams, of South Carolina, and fought under him and Colonel Lee, at Pyles' defeat, on Haw River. He also acted for some time as Quartermaster, at the Hospital, in Charlotte.

In 1781 he volunteered under Colonel Davie, and was with him at the battle of Hanging Rock.

This was Captain Caldwell's last important service.

The distinguished physician, Dr. Charles Caldwell, also of Irish parentage, and nearly related to Captain Thomas Caldwell, was born in the immediate vicinity of Poplar Tent Church, in Cabarrus county, on land now owned by Colonel Thomas H. Robinson, a worthy son of Dr. John Robinson, D.D., who so long and faithfully proclaimed the gospel of salvation to this congregation. No vestige of the family mansion now remains, but its site is easily recognized at the present time by a large fig bush, growing at or near where the chimney formerly stood, as a lingering memento of the past, and producing annually its delicious fruit.

Although this eminent physician, in his ardent pursuit of material Philosophy, wandered for many years "after strange gods," until much learning made him mad; yet, it is pleasing to know, in his maturer age, and under calm reflection, the early gospel precepts so impressingly instilled into his youthful mind by his pious parents, yielded at length their happiest results, and that he died at the Medical College of Louisville, in Kentucky, in 1853, full of years and of honors, and in the faith of his fathers, many of whom sleep in the grave-yard of Poplar Tent Church.

CHAPTER III.

ROWAN COUNTY.

Rowan county was formed in 1753 from Anson county. In 1770 Surry, and in 1777 Burke counties were severally taken off, previous to which separations Anson county comprehended most of the western portion of North Carolina and Tennessee. Like a venerable mother, Rowan beholds with parental complacency and delight her prosperous children comfortably settled around her. Salisbury, her capital, derives its name from a handsome town in England, situated on the banks of the classic Avon, and near the noted Salisbury Plain, a dry, *chalky surface*, which accounts for the origin of its Saxon name, which means a *dry town*.

Rowan was first settled by Protestants, about 1720-25, from Moravia, fleeing from the persecutions of Ferdinand, the Second, by the Scotch, after the unsuccessful attempts of Charles Edward (commonly called the "Pretender") to ascend the English throne, and by the Irish, after the rebellion of the Earls of Tyrone and Tyrconnell, who were offered their pardon on condition of their emigrating to America and in assisting to colonize the English possessions there. The staid prudence of the German, the keen sagacity of the Scotch, and fiery ardor of the Irish commingled on American soil, and were fit materials to form the elemental foundations of an *industrious, progressive* and *independent* nation.

The early history of Rowan, and of her distinguished sons, affords of itself ample materials to fill an instructive volume. Within her borders resided such venerable patriots as Matthew Locke, Moses Winslow, Griffith Rutherford, John Brevard, William Sharpe, Samuel Young, William Kennon, Adlai Osborne, Francis McCorkle, James Brandon, James McCay, and many others, all true and constant friends of liberty; but alas! how little of their eminent services has been preserved. Even yet, it is believed, some one of her gifted sons might do much in collecting from traditional sources, and from her musty records a rich store of historical facts, hitherto unwritten, illustrative of the fair name and fame of her Revolutionary career.

In the struggles of the Regulators against the extortions of Governor Tryon and the crown officers, the spirit of the people of Rowan was plainly manifested. In March, 1770, Maurice Moore, one of the Colonial Judges, attended Salisbury to hold the Superior Court. He reported to Governor Tryon at Newbern that "from the opposition of the people to the taxes, no process of the law could be executed among them."

Upon this information Governor Tryon repaired in person to Salisbury. In his original journal, procured from the archives of the State Paper office in London by the Honorable George Bancroft, late our envoy at that Court, we can see his actions, and admire the spirit of a Captain Knox, who refused to join him with his troops. Violent as were the acts of the Regulators, the subsequent oppressive measures of the crown officers justified their conduct. The Clerk of Rowan county (Thomas Frohock) was allowed to charge *fifteen dollars* for a marriage license. The effect of this official extortion was such as to constrain some of the inhabitants on the head-waters of the Yadkin river to "*take a short cut,*" as it was termed in uniting their conjugal ties for "better or for worse," as man and wife.

The indignation of the people of Rowan, Guilford, Orange, and other counties, was aroused against such official misconduct. On the 7th of March, 1771, a public meeting was held in Salisbury, when a large and influential committee was appointed, who, armed with the authority of the people, met the clerk, sheriff, and other officers of the crown, and compelled them to disgorge their unlawful extortions. By a writing signed by these officers, they agreed to settle and pay back all moneys received over and above their lawful fees.

This was indemnity for the past. The security for the future was, that when any doubt should arise as to fees, they should not be paid to the officers themselves, but to such other persons as were appointed by the people.

Matthew Locke and Herman Husbands were among those selected to receive these lawful fees. An instance, says Wheeler, of more determined resistance, or of purer democracy, is not to be found in the annals of any people."

Most of the histories of the day have done the Regulators great injustice, and denounced this whole body of men as composed of a factious and turbulent mob, who, without proper cause, disturbed the public tranquility. Nothing could be more untrue or unjust. Their assemblages were orderly, and some evidence of the temper and characters of the principal actors may be gathered from the fact that from these meetings, by a law of their own, they vigorously excluded all intoxicating drinks. But they had been oppressed and exasperated by the impositions of corrupt officers until forbearance, with them, had ceased to be a a virtue. On their side was the spirit of liberty, animating the discordant multitude, but, unfortunately, without trained leaders, or a sufficiency of arms, going forth to make its first essay at battle on American soil. Redress of grievances was sought at first by the Regulators in a quiet way, by resorting to the courts of law. The officers were indicted and found guilty, but the punishment was the mere nominal one of "a penny and costs." In short, all resorts to the tribunals of justice ended in a perfect mockery, and hastened the "War of the Regulation" in North Carolina.

The public press of that day was used by the Regulators in a peaceable way to set forth their grievances. Their productions, circulated in manuscript, or in print, display no proofs of high scholarship, or of polished writing, but there is a truthful earnestness in some of them, and cogency of reasoning more effective than the skill of the mere rhetorician. Sometimes they appeared in ballad form, and sometimes as simple narrative. The rough poet of the period (the American Revolution can boast of many) was Rednap Howell, who taught the very children to sing, in doggerel verse, the infamy of the proud officials who were trampling on their rights. A short selection from the many similar ones will be here presented for the amusement of the reader·

"Says Frohock to Fanning, to tell the plain truth,
When I came to this country, I was but a youth;
My father sent for me; I wasn't worth a cross,
And then my first study was stealing a horse,
I quickly got credit, and then ran away,
And havn't paid for him to this very day.
Says Fanning to Frohock, 'tis folly to lie,
I rode an old mare that was blind of one eye;
Five shillings in money I had in my purse,
My coat was all patched, but not much the worse;
But *now* we've got rich, and its very well known,
That we'll do very well, *if they'll let us alone*."

The truthful sentiment conveyed in the last line will find many fit illustrations in our own times.

The power of the Royal government was called into requisition to put down this "Regulation" movement. The military spirit of Tryon resolved to appeal to the sword. On the 24th of April, 1771, he left Newbern at the head of three hundred men, a small train of artillery, and with a considerable number of his adherents. General Waddell was sent forward to Salisbury to raise troops, munitions of war having been previously ordered from Charleston.

While he was in Salisbury waiting for the arrival of this supply of warlike munitions, the "Black Boys" of what is now Cabarrus county, under the lead of "Black Bill Alexander," seized the convoy of wagons, and completely destroyed the "King's powder," well knowing it was intended to obey the behest of a tyrannical Governor. When Waddell advanced his troops from Salisbury to join Tryon, the bold sons of Rowan rose in arms and ordered him back. On the 10th of May, 1771, at Potts' Creek, he held a council of his officers, and they, believing "prudence to be the better part of valor," fell back, and recrossed the Yadkin. Waddell soon found that many of his own men sympathised with the cause of the Regulators. He promptly sent a message to Tryon, then encamped on Eno, informing him of his critical situation. Tryon hastened on with his forces, crossed Haw river on the 13th of May, and, on the next evening, pitched his camp on the bank of the Alamance. On the 16th of May, 1771, the unfortunate battle of Alamance was fought in which was shed the *first blood* of the American Revolution. After that disastrous event, in which, for want of skilful leaders, and concert among their men, the Regulators were subdued, the bloody "Wolf of North Carolina," as Tryon was called by the Cherokee Indians, advanced in all "the pomp and circumstance" of official station, and joined Waddell on the 4th of June, near Salisbury, about eight miles east of the Yadkin river. He then marched by a circuitous route to Hillsboro, where he had court held to try the Regulators, by his pliant tool, Judge Howard. On the 20th he left Hillsboro, and reached Newbern on the 24th; and on the 30th left North Carolina for the colony of New York, over which he had just been appointed Governor. Thus was our State rid of one who had acted the part of an oppressive ruler and a blood-thirsty tyrant.

The efforts of Tryon had been too successful in enlisting under his banners, before the designs of the British government were openly discovered, many of the bravest and best officers of his day. Caswell, Ashe, Waddell, Rutherford, and other distinguished persons who gave in their adhesion to Governor Tryon in 1771, only three years later, at the first Provincial Congress, directly from the people, held at Newbern on the 25th of August, 1774, were found to be true patriots, when it became apparent the entire subjugation of the country was the object of the British crown. To the first assemblage of patriots, adverse to the oppressions of the British government, held at Newbern in August, 1774, the delegates from Rowan were William Kennon, Moses Winslow and Samuel Young.

To the same place, in April, 1775, the delegates were Griffith Rutherford, William Sharpe and William Kennon.

To Hillsboro, on the 21st of August, 1775, the delegates were Matthew Locke, William Sharpe, Moses Winslow, William Kennon, Samuel Young and James Smith, This Provincial Congress appointed as Field Officers and Minute Men, for Salisbury District, Thomas Wade, of Anson, Colonel; Adlai Osborne, of Rowan, Lieutenant Colonel; Joseph Harben, Major.

To Halifax, on the 22d of April, 1776, Rowan sent Rutherford Griffith and Matthew Locke as delegates.

At this assembly Griffith Rutherford was appointed Brigadier General of the Salisbury District; Francis Locke, Colonel of Rowan; Alexander Dobbins, Lieutenant Colonel; James Brandon, 1st Major; James Smith, 2d Major.

To the Congress at Halifax, November 12th, 1776, which formed the first Constitution, the delegates were Griffith Rutherford, Matthew Locke, William Sharpe, James Smith and John Brevard.

In 1775 the Royal government ceased in North Carolina by the retreat of Governor Martin.

The Civil Government, vested in: 1. A Provincial Council for the whole State, composed of two members from each Judicial District, and one for the State at large, who was chairman and *de facto* Governor. 2. Committees of Safety for the towns; and 3. County Committees of Safety, a part of whose duty it was to arrest suspicious persons, and take especial care that the public interest suffered no detriment.

The journal of the Committee of Safety for Rowan county, from the 8th of August, 1774, to the 17th of May, 1776, has been preserved, and throws much light on the patriotic transactions of that exciting period in our Revolutionary history. The journal in full may be seen in Wheeler's "Historical Sketches."

ROUTE OF THE BRITISH ARMY THROUGH MECKLENBURG AND ROWAN COUNTIES.

After Cornwallis effected his passage over the Catawba river, at Cowan's Ford, on the 1st of February, 1781, he only remained about three hours in attending to the burial of his dead. Tarleton was dispatched in advance to pursue the Whigs retreating in the direction of Torrence's Tavern. Early in the morning of the same day a simultaneous movement was made by Colonel Webster, with his own brigade, the artillery, and a small supporting detachment to Beattie's Ford, six miles above Cowan's Ford, where a small guard had been placed on the eastern bank. Colonel Webster, with a view of dispersing the guard, fired several shots (six pounders) across the river, which had its intended effect, and thus enabled him to pass over without meeting with serious opposition. This was a mere feint, intended to create the impression that the whole British army would cross there.

The two British forces pressing forward with as little delay as possible, united at Torrence's, ten miles from

Cowan's Ford, where a considerable body of the Whig militia had hastily assembled; but having no one to assume command, and greatly discouraged by the death of General Davidson on the approach of Tarleton's cavalry, poured in one effective fire, killed seven of the British horsemen, wounded others, and then dispersed in all directions with a small loss. This skirmish, occurring soon after Tarleton's defeat at the Cowpens, led him to boast of it in his journal as a brilliant victory!

Lord Cornwallis, in his general orders on the 2d of February, returns his "thanks to the Brigade of Guards for their cool and determined bravery in the passage of the Catawba, while rushing through that long and difficult ford under a galling fire."

Another order, issued from his camp on the evening of the preceding day, does credit to his head as well as his heart, and shows that he was sometimes governed by the noble principles of moral rectitude. The order is in the following words:

"HEADQUARTERS, CROSS ROADS TO SALISBURY,
February 1st, 1781.

Lord Cornwallis is highly displeased that several houses were set on fire during the march this day—a disgrace to the army. He will punish, with the utmost severity, any person or persons who shall be found guilty of committing so disgraceful an outrage. His Lordship requests the commanding officers of corps to find out the persons who set fire to the houses this day."

It is presumable his Lordship never received the desired information. The order, no doubt, has reference to the burning of the houses of John Brevard, who had "seven sons at one time in the rebel army," and of Adam Torrence, a staunch Whig, where the skirmish had taken place.

General Greene, having been apprised of the battle of the Cowpens, and the result, on the same day when Cornwallis commenced his pursuit of General Morgan, ordered General Stevens to march with his Virginia militia (whose term of service was almost expired) by way of Charlotte, N. C., to take charge of Morgan's prisoners, and conduct them to Charlottesville, in Virginia.

General Greene being anxious to confer with Morgan, personally, left his camp on the Pee Dee, under the command of General Huger and Colonel O. H. Williams, and started with one aid, and two or three mounted militia, for the Catawba. On the route, he was informed of Cornwallis' pursuit. General Morgan had previously crossed the Catawba at the Island Ford. On the 31st of January, General Greene reached Sherrill's Ford, a few miles below the Island Ford, where he had an interview with Morgan, and directed his future movements.

The British army reached Salisbury on that night, and on the next morning started in pursuit of Green and Morgan. These officers did not await the dawn, but crossed the Yadkin river at the Trading Ford, six miles beyond Salisbury, while his Lordship was quietly slumbering, and dreaming, perhaps, of future conquest and glory! When Cornwallis awoke on the morning of the third, he hastened to strike a fatal blow on the banks of the Yadkin, but the Americans were beyond his reach, and Providence had again placed an impassable barrier of water between them. Copious rains in the mountains had swollen the Yadkin to a mighty river. The horses of Morgan had forded the stream at midnight, and the infantry passed over in boats at dawn. These vessels were fastened on the eastern shore of the Yadkin, and Cornwallis was obliged to wait for the waters to subside before he could attempt to cross. Again he had the Americans *almost within his grasp.* A corps of riflemen were yet on the Western side when O'Hara, with the vanguard of the British army, approached, but these escaped across the river, after a slight skirmish. Nothing was lost but a few wagons belonging to Whig families, who, with their effects, were fleeing with the American army.

Lord Cornwallis, after an ineffectual cannonade over the river, returned to Salisbury, and, on the 7th, marched up the western bank of the Yadkin, and crossed at the Shallow Ford, near the village of Huntsville.

Dr. Read, the surgeon of the American army, has left this record of the cannonading scene: "At a little distance from the river was a small cabin, in which General Greene had taken up his quarters. At this building the enemy directed their fire, and the balls rebounded from the rocks in the rear of it. But little of the roof was visible to the enemy. The General was preparing his orders for the army, and his dispatches to the Congress. In a short time the balls began to strike the roof, and clap-boards were flying in all directions. But the General's pen never stopped, only when a new visitor arrived, or some officer for orders; and then the answer was given with calmness and precision, and Greene resumed his pen."

It is related as a truthful tradition that, after the British army reached Salisbury, Lord Cornwallis, Tarleton, and other royal officers, were hospitably entertained by Dr. Anthony Newman, although he was a true Whig. There, in presence of Tarleton, and other spectators, Dr. Newman's two little sons were engaged in playing the game of the "battle of the Cowpens," with grains of corn; red grains representing the British officers, and white grains the Americans.

Washington and Tarleton were particularly represented, and as one pursued the other, as in a real battle, the little fellows shouted, "Hurrah for Washington, Tarleton runs! Hurrah for Washington." Colonel William A. Wasnington, it will be recollected, commanded the American cavalry. Tarleton looked on for a while, but soon becoming irritated at the playful but truthful scene, he exclaimed: "See these cursed little rebels!"

The pursuit of Morgan by Cornwallis was the most exciting and prolonged military chase of the American Revolution. Under various tangible interpositions of Providence, the retreat, as we have seen, proved finally successful, and Morgan's forces saved for the future service of his country.

GENERAL GRIFFITH RUTHERFORD.

General Griffith Rutherford was an Irishman by birth, brave and patriotic, but uncultivated in mind and manners. He resided west of Salisbury, in the Locke settlement, and actively participated in the internal government of the county, associated with such early and distinguished patriots as Moses Winslow, Alexander Osborn, Samuel Young, John Brevard, James Brandon, William Sharpe, Francis McCorkle, and others. He represented Rowan county in the Provincial Congress which met at Halifax on the 4th of April, 1776, and during this session he received the appointment of Brigadier General of the "Salisbury District." Near the close of the summer of 1776, he raised and commanded an army of two thousand four hundred men against the Cherokee Indians. After being reinforced by the Guilford Regiment, under Colonel James Martin, and by the Surry Regiment under Colonel Martin Armstrong, at Fort McGahey, General Rutherford crossed the "Blue Ridge," or Alleghany mountains, at Swannanoa Gap, near the western base of which the beautiful Swannanoa river ("nymph of beauty") takes its rise. After reaching the French Broad he passed down and over that stream at a crossing-place which to this day bears the name of the "War Ford." He then passed up the valley of "Hominy Creek," leaving Pisgah Mountain on the left, and crossed Pigeon River a little below the mouth of East Fork. He then passed through the mountains to Richland Creek, above the present town of Waynesville; ascended the creek and crossed the Tuckaseegee River at an Indian town. Pursuing his course, he crossed the Cowee Mountain, where he had a small engagement with the enemy, in which one of his men was wounded. As the Indians carried off their dead and wounded, their loss could not be ascertained. Thence he marched to the "Middle Towns," on the Tennessee river, where, on the 14th of September, he met General Williamson with troops from South Carolina on the same mission of subduing the Indians.

In skirmishes at Valley Town, Ellajay, and near Franklin, General Rutherford lost three men, but he completely subdued the Indians. He then returned home by the same route, since known as "Rutherford's Trace." The Rev. James Hall, of Iredell county, accompanied this expedition as chaplain.

The uniforms of the officers and men was a hunting-shirt of domestic, trimmed with cotton : their arms were rifles, and *none knew better how to use them.* Many of the hardy sons of the west there experienced their first essay in arms, and their bravery was nobly maintained afterwards at King's Mountain, the Cowpens, and elsewhere in the South.

General Rutherford commanded a brigade in the battle of Camden, (16th of August, 1780), and was there made a prisoner. After he was exchanged he again took the field, and commanded the expedition which marched by way of Cross Creek (now Fayetteville) to Wilmington, when that place, on his approach, was evacuated by the British, near the close of the war.

He frequently represented Rowan county in the Senate during and subsequent to the war, showing the high appreciation in which his services were held by the people.

Shortly after his last service in 1786, he joined the strong tide of emigration to Tennessee, where his well-earned fame and experience in governmental matters had preceded him. The Knoxville *Gazette* of the 6th of September, 1794, contains the following announcement:

"On Monday last the General Assembly of this territory commenced their session in this town. General Rutherford, long distinguished for his services in the Legislature of North Carolina, is appointed President of the Legislative Council."

General Rutherford died in Tennessee near the beginning of the present century, at a good old age, and it is to be regretted more has not been preserved of his life and services.

LOCKE FAMILY.

Matthew Locke, one of the first settlers of Rowan county, and the patriarchal head of a large family, was born in 1730. He was an early and devoted friend of liberty and the rights of the people. His stability of character and maturity of judgment caused him to be held in high esteem in all controversial matters among his fellow-citizens. In 1771, during the "Regulation" troubles, he was selected by the people, with Herman Husbands, to receive the lawful fees of the sheriffs, and other crown officers, whose exorbitant exactions and oppressive conduct were then everywhere disturbing the peace and welfare of society. In 1775, he was a member of the Colonial Assembly, and in 1776 member of the Provincial Congress, which met on the 12th of November of that year, and formed the first Constitution. From 1793 to 1799 he was a member of Congress, and was succeeded by the Hon. Archibald Henderson. He married a daughter of Richard Brandon, an early patriot of the same county. He died in 1801, aged seventy-one years.

Matthew Locke had at one time four sons in the Revolutionary war. Francis Locke, his eldest son, was appointed by the Provincial Congress which met at Halifax on the 4th of April, 1776, Colonel of the 1st Rowan Regiment, with Alexander Dobbins as Lieutenant Colonel; James Brandon, 1st Major, and James Smith, 2d Major. He was attached to General Lincoln's army when General Ashe was defeated at Brier Creek, and composed one of the members of the court-martial to inquire into that unfortunate affair. Colonel Locke commanded the forces which attacked and signally defeated a large body of Tories assembled at Ramsour's Mill, under Col. John Moore. (For particulars, see "Lincoln county"). Another son, Lieutenant George Locke, a brave young officer, was killed by the British in the skirmish near Charlotte, in September, 1780.

Hon. Francis Locke, son of Francis Locke, the "hero of Ramsour's Mill," was born on the 31st of October, 1766. He was elected Judge of the Superior Court in 1803, and resigned in 1814, at which time he was elected a Senator in Congress in 1814–'15. He never married, and died in January, 1823, in the forty-fourth year of his age. His mortal remains, with those of his father, Colonel Francis Locke, repose in the grave-yard of Thyatira Church, Rowan county, N. C.

HON. ARCHIBALD HENDERSON.

(Condensed from Wheeler's "Historical Sketches.")

Hon. Archibald Henderson was born in Granville county, N. C., on the 7th of August, 1768; studied law with Judge Williams, his relative, and was pronounced by the late Judge Murphy, who knew him long and well, to be "the most perfect model of a lawyer that our bar has produced." * * * No man could look upon him without pronouncing him one of the great men of the age. The impress of greatness was upon his countenance; not that greatness which is the offspring of any single talent or moral quality, but a greatness which is made up by blending the faculties of a fine intellect with exalted moral feelings. Although he was at all times accessible and entirely free from austerity, he seemed to live and move in an atmosphere of dignity. He exacted nothing by his manner, yet all approached him with reverence and left him with respect. His was the region of high sentiment; and here he occupied a standing that was pre-eminent in North Carolina. He contributed more than any man, since the time of General Davie and Alfred Moore, to give character to the bar of the State. His career at the bar has become identified with the history of North Carolina: and his life and his example furnish themes for instruction to gentlemen of the bench and to his brethren of the bar. May they study his life and profit by his example!

He represented his district in Congress from 1799 to 1803, and the town of Salisbury frequently in the State Legislature. He married Sarah, daughter of William Alexander, and sister of William Alexander and Nathaniel Alexander, afterward Governor of the State. He left two children, the late Archibald Henderson, Esq., of Salisbury, and Mrs. Boyden, wife of the late Hon. Nathaniel Boyden.

He died on the 21st of October, 1822, in the fifty-fourth year of his age.

RICHMOND PEARSON.

(Condensed from Wheeler's "Historical Sketches.")

Richmond Pearson, late of Davie county when a part of Rowan, was born in Dinwiddie county, Va., in 1770, and at the age of nineteen years came to North Carolina and settled in the forks of the Yadkin river.

When the war of the Revolution broke out he was a Lieutenant in Captain Bryan's company (afterward the celebrated Colonel Bryan, of Tory memory). After the Declaration of Independence, at the first muster which occurred, he requested some on whom he could rely to load their guns. When Captain Bryan came on the ground he ordered all the men into ranks. Pearson refused, and tendered his commission to Bryan, whereupon he ordered him under arrest. This was resisted, and he was told that the men had their guns loaded. They then came to a parley, and it was agreed by the crowd, as matters stood, that Bryan and Pearson, on a fixed day, should settle this national affair by a fair *fist fight*, and whichever whipped, the company should belong to the side of the conqueror, whether Whig or Tory. At the appointed time and place the parties met, and the Lieutenant proved to be the victor. From this time the Fork company was for liberty, and Bryan's crowd, on Dutchman's creek, were Loyalists. The anecdote illustrates by what slight circumstances events of this period were affected. When Cornwallis came south, Pearson, with his company, endeavored to harass his advance. He was present at Cowan's Ford on the 1st of February, 1781, where General Davidson fell in attempting to resist the passage of the British. Captain Pearson was a successful merchant and an enterprising planter. He died in 1819, leaving three sons and one daughter: 1st, Jesse A.; 2d, Joseph; 3d, Richmond; and 4th, Elizabeth Pearson. Jesse A. Pearson was frequently a member of the General Assembly from Rowan county. In 1814 he marched as Colonel of a Regiment to the Creek Nation, under General Joseph Graham, and was afterward elected Major General of the State Militia. He died in 1823, without issue.

Hon. Joseph Pearson was a member of the General Assembly in the House of Commons from Rowan county in 1804 and 1805, and a member of Congress from 1809 to 1815. He died at Salisbury on the 27th of October, 1834. He was thrice married. By his first wife, Miss McLinn, he had no issue; by the second, Miss Ellen Brent, he had two daughters—one, the wife of Robert Walsh, Esqr., of Philadelphia—the other, the wife of Lieutenant Farley, of the U. S. Navy; and by the third wife (Miss Worthington, of Georgetown), he left four children.

Richmond Pearson married Miss McLinn. He was never in public life, but was an active, enterprising man. He left the following children: 1st. Sarah, who married Isaac Croom, of Alabama; 2d. Eliza, who married W. G. Bently, of Bladen county, N. C.; 3d. Charles, who died without issue; 4th. Hon. Richmond M. Pearson was born in June, 1805, educated at Statesville by John Mushat, and graduated at Chapel Hill in 1823. He studied law under Judge Henderson, and was licensed in 1826. He entered public life in 1829 as a member to the State Legislature from Rowan county, and continued as such until 1832. In 1836 he was elected one of the Judges of the Superior Court, and in 1848 was transferred to the Supreme Court, which elevated position he now occupies; 5th. Giles N. Pearson married Miss Ellis, and was a lawyer by profession. He died in 1847, leaving a wife and five children; 6th. John Stokes Pearson married Miss Beattie, of Bladen county. He died in 1848, leaving four children.

The reader may be curious to know something of the fate of Colonel Samuel Bryan, who commanded the Tory regiment in the forks of the Yadkin, which was so roughly handled and cut to pieces by Colonel Davie and his brave associates, at the battle of the hanging Rock. About the time Major Craig evacuated Wilmington in 1781, Colonel Bryan, Lieutenant Colonel John Hampton and Captain Nicholas White, of the same regiment, returned to the forks of the Yadkin, were arrested and tried for high treason, under the act of 1777, entitled "An Act for declaring what Crimes and Practices against the State shall be Treason," &c.

Judges Spencer and Williams presided. The prosecution was ably conducted by the Attorney General, Alfred Moore, and the defence by Richard Henderson, John Penn, John Kinchen and William R. Davie, truly a fine array of legal talent.

Public indignation was so greatly excited that Governor Burke found it necessary, after the trial, to protect the prisoners from violence by a military guard.

Colonel Davie's defence of Colonel Bryan, in the argument made to the jury upon the occasion, was said to have been a brilliant exhibition of his forensic ability. For many years afterwards his services were required in all capital cases, and as a criminal lawyer he had no rival in the State. They were all convicted, had sentence of death passed upon them, were pardoned, and subsequently exchanged for officers of equal rank, who were at the time confined within the British lines.

MRS. ELIZABETH STEELE.

The long, arduous and eventful retreat of General Morgan through the Carolinas, after the battle of the Cowpens, and the eager pursuit of Cornwallis to overtake him, encumbered with more than five hundred prisoners, on his way to a place of safety in Virginia, affords many interesting incidents. General Greene having met Morgan on the eastern banks of the Catawba river, at Sherrill's Ford, and directed his forward movements, proceeded to Salisbury, a little in advance of his forces. It had been slightly raining during the day, and his wet garments, appearance of exhaustion and dejection of spirits at the loss of General Davidson at Cowan's Ford, as he dismounted at the door of the principal hotel in Salisbury, indicated too clearly that he was suffering under harassing anxiety of mind. Dr. Reed, who had charge of the sick and wounded prisoners, while he waited for the General's arrival, was engaged in writing the necessary paroles for such officers as could not go on. General Greene's aids having been dispatched to different parts of the retreating army, he was alone when he rode up to the hotel. Dr. Reed, noticing his dispirited looks, remarked that he appeared to be fatigued; to which the wearied officer replied: "Yes, fatigued, hungry, alone, and penniless!" General Greene had hardly taken his seat at the well-spread table, when Mrs. Steele, the landlady of the hotel, entered the room and carefully shut the door behind her. Approaching her distinguished guest, she reminded him of the despondent words he had uttered in her hearing, implying, as she thought, a distrust of the devotion of his friends to the cause of freedom. She declared money he should have, and immediately drew from under her apron two small bags full of specie, probably the earnings of several years. "Take these, General," said she, "you need them and I can do without them." This offering of a benevolent heart, accompanied with words of kindness and encouragement, General Greene accepted with thankfulness. "Never," says his biographer, "did relief come at a more propitious moment; nor would it be straining conjecture to suppose that he resumed his journey with his spirits cheered and lightened by this touching proof of woman's devotion to the cause of her country."

General Greene did not remain long in Salisbury; but before his departure from the house of Mrs. Steele, he left a memorial of his visit. Seeing a picture of George III. hanging against the wall, sent as a present to a connection of Mrs. Steele from England, he took it down and wrote with chalk on the back, "O George, hide thy face, and mourn," and replaced it with the face to the wall. The picture, with the writing uneffaced, is still in possession of a grand daughter. Mrs. Steele was twice married; her first husband was a Gillespie, by whom she had a daughter, Margaret, who married the Rev. Samuel E. McCorkle, a distinguished Presbyterian minister; and Richard Gillespie, who was a Captain in the Revolution, and died unmarried. By her second husband, William Steele, she had only one child, the Hon. John Steele, who died in Salisbury on the 14th of August, 1815. He was a conspicuous actor in the councils of the State and Nation, and one whose services offer materials for an interesting and instructive biography.

Mrs. Steele died in Salisbury on the 22d of November, 1790. She was distinguished not only for her strong attachment to the cause of freedom, but for the piety which shone forth brightly in her pilgrimage upon earth. Among her papers was found, after her death, a written dedication of herself to her Creator, and a prayer for support in the practice of christian duty; with a letter, left as a legacy to her children, enjoining it upon them to make religion the great work of life.

CHAPTER IV.

IREDELL COUNTY.

Iredell county was formed in 1788 from Rowan county, and named in honor of James Iredell, one of the Associate Judges of the Supreme Court of the United States.

At the time of the war of the Revolution the county of Rowan embraced all that beautiful and agricultural region extending from the foot of the Blue Ridge Mountains, eastwardly, to where the Yadkin river loses its name in the great Peedee; comprising a territory equal in extent to several of the States of the American Union, and presenting a varied topography, unsurpassed for bold mountain scenery and lovely landscapes spreading over the charming champaign country lying between the Yadkin and Catawba rivers. Within this territory are now organized many counties, with attractive features, one of which is the county of Iredell.

COLONEL ALEXANDER OSBORN.

Alexander Osborn was born in New Jersey in 1709, and emigrated to the western part of Rowan county (now Iredell) about 1755. He was a Colonel in the Colonial government, and as such marched with a regiment of Rowan troops to Hillsboro' in 1768 to assist Governor Tryon in suppressing the "Regulation" movement.

He married Agnes McWhorter, a sister of Dr. Alexander McWhorter, president of Queen's Museum College in

Charlotte. His residence (called Belmont) was one of the earliest worshiping places of the Presbyterians of Rowan county before the present " Center Church " was erected, and became by compromise the *central* meeting-house of worship for a large extent of surrounding country. Colonel Osborn was a man of fine character and wielded a strong influence in his day and generation.

In the grave yard of Center Church, on a double headstone, are the following records:

"Here lys the body of Col. Alexander Osborn, who deceased July y* 11th, 1776, aged 67 years;" and, separated by a dividing upright line, this record appears:

"Here lys the body of Agnes Osborn, who deceased July y* 9th, 1776." From these records it would appear that this worthy couple left the scenes of earth for a brighter world only two days apart, and not on the same day, as stated by some authorities. They left one son, Adlai Osborn, who graduated at Princeton College in 1768. He was Clerk of the Court for Rowan county under the Royal gavernment, and continued in that office until 1809. He was a man of fine literary attainments, the warm friend of education, and one of the first Trustees of the State University. He died in 1815, leaving a large family, among whom were Spruce McCay Osborn, who graduated at Chapel Hill in 1806; studied medicine, entered the army as surgeon, and was killed at the massacre of Fort Mimms in the war of 1812; and Edwin Jay Osborn, who was distinguished as a lawyer of eloquence and learning, and was the father of the late Judge James W. Osborn, of Charlotte, one of Mecklenburg's most worthy, gited and lamented sons.

CAPTAIN WILLIAM SHARPE.

Captain William Sharpe was born on the 13th of December, 1742, and was the eldest son of Thomas Sharpe, of

Cecil county, Maryland. At the age of twenty-one he came to North Carolina and settled in Mecklenburg county, where he married a daughter of David Reese, one of the signers of the Mecklenburg Declaration of Independence. He was a lawyer by profession and had a large practice. Soon after his marriage he moved to the western part of Rowan county (now Iredell) and took an active and decided stand for liberty. The Journal of the "Committee of Safety" for Rowan county, from 1774 to 1776, presents a noble record of his activity and influence.

He was a member from Rowan county to the Provincial Congress which met at Newbern in April, 1775; and also of the Congress at Hillsboro, in August, 1775. In November, 1776, he was a member of the Convention at Halifax which formed our first State Constitution. He acted as aid to General Rutherford in his campaign against the Cherokee Indians in 1776. In 1777 he was appointed with Waightstill Avery, Joseph Winston and Robert Laneer to form a treaty with the same tribe of Indians.

In 1779 he was appointed a member of the Continental Congress at Philadelphia, and served until 1782. He died in July, 1818, in the 77th year of his age, leaving a widow and twelve children. Two of his sons, William and Thomas, were in the battle at Ramsour's Mill,—the former commanding a company with distinguished bravery, and, near the close of the action, shot down one of the Tory captains which speedily terminated the fortunes of the day in favor of the American arms.

His eldest daughter, Matilda, married William W. Erwin, of Burke county, who, for more than forty years, was Clerk of the Superior Court for that county, and in November, 1789, was the delegate to the Convention at Fayetteville which ratified the Federal Constitution. Like a faithful vine she raised fifteen children who have held honorable positions in society. His second daughter, Ruth, married ol. Andrew Caldwell, of Iredell county, who was often a member of the State Legislature. He was the father of the late Judge David F. Caldwell, the Hon. Joseph P. Caldwell, Dr. Elam Caldwell, of Lincolnton, and others.

MAJOR WILLIAM GILL, CAPTAIN ANDREW CARSON, AND OTHERS.

Many interesting events which transpired within the territory of "old Rowan" during the war of the Revolution, have unfortunately been buried from our view by those who have passed away. A few traditions still linger in the memory of the descendants of those who were actors in those scenes relating more particularly to the north-eastern portion of Iredell, and of some of the families who resided there. And although such traditions can only be now presented as detached and fragmentary items of history, yet they are worthy of being preserved and placed on permanent record.

The facts given in this sketch relate to that part of Iredell lying between Statesville, its county seat, and Yadkinville, the county seat of Yadkin county, and mostly near to the dividing line of these two counties.

The numerous creeks and small streams which water this portion of Iredell, empty into three large streams of about the same size, flowing through it, named South Yadkin, Rocky Creek, and Hunting Creek. These streams mingle their waters in a common channel before their confluence with the Great Yadkin, in the county of Davie.

In the year 1778, Thomas Young removed from Mecklenburg, Virginia, to North Carolina, and settled on Hunting Creek, within three miles of the place where the counties of Yadkin, Davie, and Iredell now form a common corner. He was then passed the age for military service, but had furnished three sons-in-law and two sons to the army of General Washington, and a third son, at sixteen years of age, to the army at Norfolk, Va.

One of his sons-in-law, Major William Gill, entered the service at the beginning of the war, and became connected with the staff of General Washington. He served in the capacity of aid to the Commander-in-chief through the war, and was with him at the surrender of Cornwallis, at Yorktown. From this point he returned to his family, in Mecklenburg, Va., who had not heard from him in two years.

Soon after the establishment of peace, Major Gill, with his family, and the other two sons-in-law of Mr. Young, viz: Major Daniel Wright and Dr. Thomas Moody, and his sons, William, Henry, and Thomas Young, removed to North Carolina and settled near him. Major Gill settled on Rocky Creek, near to the site of the present village of Olin, and, at his death, was interred in the family burying ground on the lands of his father-in-law. The record on his tombstone states that he died on the 4th of September, 1797, in the 47th year of his age. His commission is now in possession of his descendants, in Iredell county.

The part which Major Gill bore in the great struggle for independence, was once familiar in the traditions of his family, and must have been satisfactory to General Washington, from the fact that he continued with him to the end of the war, and bore with him into retirement the commission which made him one of the military family of the father of his country.

A single incident will show the spirit with which Maj. Gill bore himself on the battle-field. At the battle of Brandywine, while discharging his duty, he became separated from his command, and, in the dense smoke of the conflict, rode into the ranks of the enemy. Upon discovering his situation, the only means of escape which presented itself, was to leap his horse over a high rail fence, which was being scattered by the artillery of the enemy. This feat he accomplished successfully, and afterward received the congratulations of his General for the spirited adventure and escape.

It has not been recorded in history that the mortal remains of a member of the staff of General Washington repose on the banks of Hunting Creek, in the county of Iredell, N. C. The tradition here given of the fact, can be yet fully attested by surviving members of the family of Major Gill, as well as by his commission.

Captain Andrew Carson was a younger son-in-law of Mr. Young, having married after the family removed to North Carolina. He and his brother, Lindsay Carson, both joined the service in the southern army. And let it be recorded, in passing, that Lindsay Carson was the father of Christopher Houston Carson, now widely known as "Kit Carson," the great Indian scout, and that "Kit" was born on Hunting Creek, within half a mile of the residence of Mr. Thomas Young.

Andrew Carson, like his nephew, "Kit," was of an adventurous disposition, and was the bearer of dispatches from the commanding officers in the up-country to those in South Carolina. This duty made him acquainted with the command of General Francis Marion, which suited his taste, and he connected himself with it. He was with the "Swamp Fox," so greatly dreaded by the British and the Tories, in many of his stealthy marches and daring surprises, the recital of which would send the blood careering through the veins of his juvenile listeners, half a century ago. The memory of them now awakens a dim recollection of the thrill and absorbing interest then experienced.

Captain Carson was connected with the command of Baron DeKalb, at the battle of Camden, and was by the side of that noble officer when he was shot down while crossing a branch, and bore him out in his own arms. Captain Carson also sleeps in the same family cemetery with Major Gill.

With a family thus engaged in the defence of their country, it will be readily understood that their parental home was no ordinary rendezvous for sympathisers in its vicinity. When Mr. Young settled in an almost unbroken forest on the banks of Hunting Creek, he located and constructed his improvements with the view of defence in cases of emergency. He built two substantial log houses, about forty feet apart, fronting each other, and closed the end openings with strong stockades. Port holes were provided to be used for observation, or otherwise, as occasion might demand. The buildings are yet standing, in a good state of preservation. This was headquarters for the Whigs for many miles around. It was the point for receiving and distributing information, as well as for concerting measures for the aid of the cause of freedom, and for depositing supplies for friends in the field. The Brushy Mountains were but a few miles distant, and were infested with Tories, who made predatory incursions into this part of Iredell, carrying off stock, devastating farms, and ambuscading and shooting Whigs, who were especially obnoxious to them.

Mr. Young's fortifications presented a rallying point for defence against such invasions, as Fort Dobbs did four miles north of Statesville.

He was himself a member of an association of eight neighbors, who were engaged in manufacturing powder in a rude way for the use of their home department. Against this association the Tories were extremely bitter, and conspired to kill them. They succeeded in murdering seven of them, and detailed one of their number to way-lay and shoot Mr. Young. The man assigned to this duty was named Aldrich, who concealed himself in the woods near the dwelling of his intended victim, and watched for an opportunity to perpetrate the murderous deed. The habitual circumspection of Mr. Young foiled him in his purpose until he was discovered by a member of the family, and became so frightened as to induce him to abandon the effort.

After peace had been proclaimed, Captain Andrew Caldwell, who resided on Rocky Creek, and was the father of Judge David F. and Hon. Joseph P. Caldwell, and other sons well known in the public offices of Iredell, was appointed the Commissioner to administer the oath of allegiance in that part of the county. Aldrich presented himself among them, but the recollection of his seven murders, still fresh in the memory of all, so aroused the indignation of Captain Caldwell and Captain Andrew Carson, who was present, that instead of making him a loyal citizen of the United States, they went to work and forthwith hung him on one of the joists of the barn, in which they were transacting their lawful business.

In many places, Whigs who were past the age for service in the field, organized themselves into vigilance associations for the welfare of the country and their own protection. The duties devolving upon them rendered them familiar with events as they really transpired, and often caused them to pass through thrilling and adventurous scenes. They learned to know and how to trust each other. Attachments thus formed by heads of families were strengthened, and more strongly united in ties of friendship after the restoration of peace. The descendants of these associated friends were educated to revere the memories of the fathers, and to cultivate the society and friendship of their children. The traditions of the "dark days" of the war were always topics of family and fireside conversation with the "old folks," and they always found attentive listeners in their posterity, upon whose youthful minds impressions then made were as enduring as time.

CAPTAIN ALEXANDER DAVIDSON.

Captain Alexander Davidson was one of the earliest settlers of the western part of Rowan county (now Iredell.) He took an active part in the Revolutionary struggle for independence. When Cornwallis was moving from Charleston toward North Carolina, and General Gates was ordered to meet him, Governor Caswell, of North Carolina, ordered a draft of men to strengthen Gates' army. In response to this order the people in that part of Iredell county bordering on the Catawba river below the Island Ford, assembled at a central point, afterward known as Brown's Muster Ground, when a company was formed under the draft and Alexander Davidson was elected its captain. Soon afterward Captain Davidson marched his company to Gates' rendezvous, when that officer moved his army to the unfortunate and sanguinary field of Camden, S. C.

In that disastrous engagement Captain Davidson's company took an active part, and the greater portion of them was cut to pieces. Captain John Davidson, a grand son of Captain Alexander Davidson, now (1876) resides near Statesville, in Iredell county. He well remembers that the commission of his grand father, as captain of this company, and a diary of his services during the war of the Revolution, were in the possession of his father's family until 1851 when they were taken to Washington City by the late Hon. J. P. Caldwell and were not returned.

Captain John Davidson is one of the most prominent and public-spirited citizens of Iredell county, and implicit reliance may be placed in his statements.

CAPTAIN JAMES HOUSTON.

Captain James Houston was born in 1747, and was an early and devoted friend of liberty. In the battle of

Ramsour's Mill, near the present town of Lincolnton, he took an active part, and by his undaunted courage greatly contributed to the defeat of the Tories on that occasion. During the engagement Captain Houston was severely wounded in the thigh, from the effects of which he never fully recovered. Seeing the man who inflicted the severe and painful wound he shot him in the back and killed him as he ran. When it was ascertained that Cornwallis had crossed the Catawba river at Cowan's Ford, and was approaching with his army, the family of Captain Houston conveyed him to the "big swamp" in the immediate vicinity, known as "Purgatory," and there concealed him until the British had marched quite through the country.

When the British army passed the residence of Captain Houston some of them entered the yard and house, and threatened Mrs. Houston with death if she did not quickly inform them where her husband was, and also where her gold and silver and China-ware were kept, using, at the same time, very course and vulgar language. Mrs. Houston, knowing something of "woman's rights" in every civilized community, immediately asked the protection of an officer, who, obeying the better impulses of human nature, ordered the men into line and marched them off.

Mrs. Houston and "Aunt Dinah" had taken the timely precaution to hide the China ware in the *tan vats* and the *pewter-ware* in the mud immediately beneath the pole over which it was necessary to walk in conveying provisions to Captain Houston in his place of concealment. The pole was put under the water and mud every time by aunt Dinah when she returned, so that no track or trace could be discovered of her pathway into the swamp.

Captain James Houston was the father of the late Dr. Joel B. Houston, of Catawba, and the grandfather of R. B. B. Houston, Esq., who now wares the gold sleeve buttons of his patriotic ancestor with his initials, J. H. engraved upon them. Dr. J. H. G. Houston, of Alabama, who married Mary Jane Simonton, is another grandson.

The following is

CAPTAIN JAMES HOUSTON'S MUSTER ROLL.

Captain, James Houston ; Lieutenant, William Davidson ; David Evins, David Byers, Robert Byers, Nat. Ewing, Alexander Work, William Creswell, William Erwin, John Hovis, John Thompson, John Beard, John Poston, Robert Poston, Paul Cunningham, John M. Connell, Moses White, Angus McCauley, Robert Brevard, Adam Torrence, Sr., Adam Torrence, Jr., Charles Quigley, James Gulick, Benjamin Brevard, Thomas Templeton, John Caldwell, Joseph McCawn, James Young James Gray, Philip Logan (Irish), William Vint, Daniel Bryson, John Singleton.

Many of these have descendants in Iredell at the present time, and they can refer with veneration to the names of their patriotic ancestors.

Captain James Houston died on the 2d of August, 1819, in the 73d year of his age, and is buried in Center Church graveyard.

REV. JAMES HALL, D. D.

Rev. James Hall, a distinguished soldier of the Revolution—the Captain of a company and Chaplain of a Regiment at the same time—was born at Carlisle, Pennsylvania, on the 22d of August, 1744. When he was about eight years old his parents, who were Scotch-Irish, removed to North Carolina and settled in the upper part of Rowan county, (now Iredell), in the bounds of the congregation to which he afterward gave thirty-eight years of his ministerial life.

Secluded in the forests of Rowan, and removed to a great extent from the follies of the great world, James Hall grew up under the watchful care of pious parents, receiving such early instruction as the country schools then afforded.

In his twenty-sixth year he commenced the study of the classics, and made rapid progress, as his mind was matured and his application close and unremitting. When duly prepared he entered Princeton College, under the direction of President Witherspoon, one of the signers of the National Declaration of Independence. He graduated in 1774, in his thirty-first year. The Theological reading of Mr. Hall was pursued under the direction of Dr. Witherspoon, that eminent minister and patriot, whose views in religion and politics were thoroughly imbibed by his student. In the spring of 1776 he was licensed by the Presbytery of Orange to preach the Gospel of everlasting Peace. During the exciting scenes of the Revolution, in which he had been licensed and ordained, Mr. Hall held the office of pastor over the three congregations of Fourth Creek, Concord and Bethany, which extended from the South Yadkin river to the Catawba. After the Revolution he served these three congregations until 1790, when, wishing to devote more time to the cause of domestic missions, he was released from his connection with Fourth Creek and Concord His connection with Bethany continued until his death, in July, 1826.

A full account of Mr. Hall's patriotic services during the Revolution would far transcend the prescribed limits of this sketch. The principles of civil and religious freedom which he received in his parental, as well as in his collegiate training, would not allow him to remain neuter or indifferent, when a cruel, invading foe was trampling on the just and dearest rights of his country.

Accordingly, in response to the warm, patriotic impulses of his nature, when General Rutherford called out an army of over two thousand men from the surrounding counties to subdue the Cherokee Indians, who were committing numerous murders and depredations on the frontier settlements, Mr. Hall promptly volunteered his services, and was gladly accepted by the commanding officers as their Chaplain.

In the brief, diary notes of Captain Charles Polk, (now before the author), who commanded a company in this expedition, he says: "On Thursday, the 12th of September, we marched down the river three miles, to Cowee Town, and encamped. On this day there was a party of men sent down this river (*Nuckessey*) ten miles, to cut down the corn; the Indians fired on them as they were cutting the corn and killed Hancock Polk, of Colonel Beekman's Regiment." On Friday, the 13th, they remained encamped in Cowee Town. On Saturday, the 14th, "we marched to Nuckessey Town, six miles higher up the river, and encamped. On Sunday, the 15th, one of Captain Irwin's men was buried in *Nuckessey* Town. On Monday, the 16th, we marched five miles—this day with a detachment of twelve hundred men—for the Valley Towns, and encamped on the waters of Tennessee river. Mr. Hall preached a sermon last Sunday; in time of sermon the express we sent to the South army returned home. On Tuesday, the 17th, we marched six miles, and arrived at a town called *Nowee*, about 12 o'clock; three guns were fired at Robert Harris, of Mecklenburg, by the Indians, said Harris being in the rear of the army. We marched one mile from *Nowee* and encamped on the side of a steep mountain, without any fire."

These extracts show that Mr. Hall was then at his post of duty, and ready to deliver religious instruction to the American army. The sermon was directly prompted by the death of a fellow soldier. Who can tell how many hearts were touched and benefitted by the gospel truths proclaimed by the youthful preacher on that solemn occasion? The counsels of Eternity can alone answer the question.

In 1779, when South Carolina was overrun by the British and Tories, Mr. Hall's spirit was stirred within him on receiving intelligence of the massacres and plunderings experienced by the inhabitants of the upper part of that State. Under this state of feeling he assembled his congregation and addressed them in strong, patriotic language on what he believed to be their present duty. He pictured to their view, in a most thrilling manner, the wrongs and sufferings of their afflicted countrymen. The appeal to their patriotism was not made in vain. With as little delay as possible a company of cavalry, composed of choice young men from his congregation, was promptly raised. On its organization, Mr. Hall was unanimously chosen for their Captain; all his excuses were overruled, and, in order to encourage his countrymen *to act* rather than *to talk*, he accepted the command. "Heart within, and God o'erhead." During this tour of service two of his men were taken prisoners. As he could not recover them by force of arms, their case was made the subject of prayer, both in his private devotions and in public with his company. In a few days afterward the prisoners made their escape and rejoined their fellow soldiers.

They stated that, as their captors lay encamped one night on Broad River, in South Carolina, the sentinel placed at the door of the guard-house was observed to be drowsy; they remaining quiet, he soon fell asleep. When the prisoners discovered he was truly reposing in " balmy sleep," they quietly stepped over him as he lay with his gun folded in his bosom, and quickly ran for the river. The noise of their plunge into the water, aroused the attention of another more wakeful sentry; the alarm was given, and boats were manned for the pursuit, but the active swimmers reached the opposite bank in safety and thus effected their escape, to the great joy of the praying Captain and his faithful company.

In the winter of 1781, when Lord Cornwallis was approaching the Catawba river with his army, General Davidson, who was in command of the Whigs on the opposite or Mecklenburg side of that stream, concentrated his forces, stationed at different points on the river, to resist him at Cowan's Ford. In order to strengthen himself as much as possible, he sent couriers to the adjoining counties, calling on the Whigs to rally to his assistance. One of these couriers, sent to Fourth Creek Church, (now Statesville), in Iredell county, arrived on the Sabbath, while the pastor, the Rev. James Hall, was preaching. The urgency of his business did not permit him to delay in making known the nature of his mission, and, as the best course of doing so, he walked up to the pulpit and handed Davidson's call to the pastor, the Rev. James Hall, whose patriotic record was well known. Mr. Hall glanced over the document, and understanding its purport, brought his discourse to a speedy close, descended from the pulpit, and read it to his congregation.

After reading it he made a patriotic appeal to his audience to respond to this call of their country. Whereupon, a member of the congregation moved that they organize by calling Mr. Hall, the pastor, to preside, and proceed to take such action as the circumstances demanded. The pastor accepted the position of President of the meeting, renewed his appeal to the patriotism of his people, and demonstrated his sincerity in calling for volunteers by placing his own name at the head of the list. His example was quickly followed by a sufficient number of his congregation to form a company. It was then decided to adjourn, and meet again at the church at 10 o'clock next morning, mounted, with arms and supplied with ammunition, and five days rations, at which time they would elect officers and proceed to the scene of conflict.

Accordingly, on the following morning the pastor and the greater part of the male members of his congregation responded to roll call under the noble oaks, where then, and now, stands Fourth Creek Presbyterian Church, in the corporate limits of the town of Statesville, the county seat of Iredell.

The assemblage proceeded immediately to the election of officers, when the Rev. James Hall, their pastor, was unanimously chosen Captain.

In accordance with the choice of his beloved congregation, so cordially given, Mr. Hall instantly assumed command, put his men in rapid motion, and, in due time, reported to General Davidson and took his position in line, to resist the invaders of his country.

This was the sort of patriotism that burned in the bosoms of the Scotch-Irish Presbyterians between the Yadkin and Catawba rivers; which was enkindled by the pastors of the seven churches of Mecklenburg, and burst forth into a flame upon the classic site of Charlotte, on the 20th of May, 1775.

When the war of the revolution had ended, Mr. Hall devoted himself, with undivided energies, to his beloved work, the gospel ministry. The effects of the long and harassing war upon the churches in Carolina were deplorable; the regular ordinances of the gospel had been broken up, and the preached word had become less valued. His efforts in promoting vital godliness met with the Divine approbation, were attended with His blessing, and resulted in a revival of religion.

One sphere of usefulness in which Mr. Hall excelled, was the education of young men. Near the commencement of the war he conducted for a time a classical

school, called Clio's Nursery, on Snow Creek, in Iredell
county. This he superintended with care, and through
its agency brought out many distinguished men that
might not otherwise have obtained an education.

This eminent minister of the gospel died on the 25th
of July, 1826, in the eighty-second year of his age, and is
buried in the graveyard of Bethany Church, in Iredell
county.

HUGH LAWSON WHITE.

Hugh Lawson White was born in Iredell county in
1773, on the plantation now owned by Thomas Caldwell,
Esq., about two miles west of Center Church, and five
miles east of Beattie's Ford, on the Catawba river. The
old family mansion has long since disappeared, and the
plow now runs smoothly over its site. His grandfather,
Moses White, emigrated to America from Ireland about
1742, and married a daughter of Hugh Lawson, one of
the patriarchal settlers of the country. He had six sons,
James, Moses, John, William, David and Andrew; many
of whose descendants now reside in Iredell county.
James White, the father of Hugh, was a soldier of the
Revolution. About 1786 he moved to Knox county,
East Tennessee, and was one of the original founders of
the present flourishing city of Knoxville. When the
Creek (Indian) war broke out he entered the army, was
soon made a Brigadier General, and was distinguished
for his bravery, energy and talents.

Hugh L. White's education was conducted under the
care of Rev. Samuel Carrick, Judge Roane, and Dr. Patterson, of Philadelphia. After completing his studies he
returned home and commenced the practice of his profession. By close attention to business he soon acquired
eminence, numerous friends, and a handsome competency. At the early age of twenty-eight he was elected

one of the Judges of the Superior Court. In 1807 he resigned his Judgship and retired to his farm.

There appears, says a writer on biography, always to be a congeniality between the pursuits of agriculture and all great and good minds. We do not pretend to analyze the *rationale* of this, or why it is that patriotism exists with more elevation and fervency in the retirement of a farm than in the busy mart of crowded cities. The history of man proves this fact, that the noblest instances of self-sacrificing patriotism which have adorned the drama of human life, have been presented by those who are devoted to agricultural pursuits. It is the only pursuit that man followed in his state of primal innocence, and surviving his fall, allows the mind

"To look through nature, up to nature's God."

But his well-known abilities were too highly appreciated by his fellow-citizens to grant him a long retirement. Soon after his resignation of the judicial robes he was elected a Senator to the State Legislature.

In 1809, when Tennessee remodeled her judiciary department, and created the Supreme Court, Judge White was unanimously chosen to preside over this important tribunal of justice. He could not with propriety refuse to accept a position so cordially tendered, and highly honorable in its character. For six years he presided over its deliberations with such fidelity and strict integrity as to win universal esteem and unfading honors for his reputation. At the same time he was elected President of the State Bank. Under his able management its character acquired stability and public confidence.

The State of Tennessee was then severely suffering from the hostile incursions and savage depredations of the Creek Indians. At the darkest period of the campaign, when General Jackson was in the midst of a wild territory, and surrounded, not only by cruel savages, but enduring famine, disaffection and complaints, Judge

White left the Supreme Court Bench, and with a single companion, sought and found, after days and nights of peril, the camp of the veteran Jackson. He immediately volunteered their services, and they were gladly accepted. While Judge White was absent on this campaign he lost several terms of his court; and as the Judges were only paid for services actually rendered, the Legislature resolved that there should be no deduction in his annual salary as Judge. This continuance of salary, so gratefully offered, he declined to receive.

In 1822 he was appointed, with Governor Tazewell of Virginia, and Governor King, of Alabama, a commissioner under the convention with Spain, which position he accepted and held until its term expired in 1824.

In 1825, General Jackson having resigned his seat as a Senator in Congress, Judge White was unanimously elected to fill out his term. In 1827 he was unanimously elected for a full term; and in 1832 was chosen President of the Senate. In 1836 he was voted for as President of the United States.

He died, with the consciousness of a well spent life, at his adopted home in Tennessee, on the 10th of April, 1840, aged sixty-seven years.

CHAPTER V.

LINCOLN COUNTY.

Lincoln county was formed in 1768, from Mecklenburg county, and named Tryon, in honor of William Tryon, at that time the Royal Governor, but his oppressive administration, terminating with cold-blooded murders at the battle of Alamance in 1771, caused the General Assembly in 1779 to blot out his odious name and divide the territory into Lincoln and Rutherford counties. These names were imposed during the Revolution when both of the honored heroes were fighting the battles of their country.

Lincoln county, separated from Mecklenburg by the noble Catawba river, has a Revolutionary record of peculiar interest. In June, 1780, the battle of Ramsour's Mill was fought, which greatly enlivened the Whigs, and, in a corresponding degree, weakened the Tory influence throughout the surrounding country. In January, 1781, Lord Cornwallis, with a large invading army, passed through the county and camped for three days on the Ramsour battte-ground. General O'Hara, one of his chief officers, camped at the "Reep place," about two miles and a half west of Ramsour's Mill. Tarleton, with his cavalry, crossed the South Fork, in "Cobb's bottom," and passed over the ridge on which Lincolton now stands (before the place had a "local habitation and a name,") in approaching his lordship's headquarters.

Although Lincoln county contained many who were misled through the artful influence of designing men, and fought on the *wrong side*, yet, within her borders were found a gallant band of unflinching patriots, both of German and Scotch-Irish descent, who acted nobly throughout the struggle for independence, and " made their mark " victoriously at Ramsour's Mill, King's Mountain, the Cowpens, and at other places in North and South Carolina.

Lincoln county, as Tryon, sent to the first popular Convention, which met at Newbern, on the 25th of August, 1774, Robert Alexander and David Jenkins. To Hillsboro, August 21st, 1775, John Walker, Robert Alexander, Joseph Hardin, William Graham, Frederick Hambright and William Alston. To Halifax, April 4th, 1776, James Johnston and Charles McLean. To the same place, November 12th, 1776, (which body formed the first State Constitution,) Joseph Hardin, William Graham, Robert Abernathy, William Alston and John Barber. Several of these names will be noticed in the subsequent sketches.

BATTLE OF RAMSOUR'S MILL.

The unsuccessful attempt made by General Lincoln to take Savannah, and the subsequent capture of the army under his command at Charleston, induced Sir Henry Clinton to regard the States of South Carolina and Georgia as subdued and restored to the British Crown. The South was then left, for a time, without any regular force to defend her territory. Soon after the surrender of Charleston, detachments of the British army occupied the principal military posts of Georgia and South Carolina. Col. Brown re-occupied Augusta; Col. Balfour took possession of Ninety-Six, on the Wateree, and Lord Cornwallis pressed forward to Camden. Sir Henry Clinton then embarked with the main army for New York, leaving four thousand troops for the further subjugation of the South. After his departure the chief command devolved on Lord Cornwalls, who immediately repaired to Charleston to establish commercial regulations and organize the civil administration of the State, leaving Lord Rawdon in command at Camden. North Carolina had not yet been invaded, and the hopes of the patriots in the South now seemed mainly to rest on this earliest pioneer State in the cause of liberty.

Charleston surrendered on the 12th of May, 1780. On the 29th of the same month Tarleton defeated Col. Buford in the Waxhaw settlement, upwards of thirty miles south of Charlotte, on his way to the relief of Charleston. Just before the surrender, a well organized force from Mecklenburg, Rowan and Lincoln counties, left Charlotte with the same object in view, but arrived too late, as Charleston was then completely invested by the British army. And yet this force, after its return, proved of great service in protecting the intervening country, and prevented the invasion of North Carolina until a few weeks after the battle of Camden.

At this critical period General Rutherford ordered out the whole militia, and by the 3d of June about nine hundred men assembled near Charlotte. On the next day the militia were addressed by the Rev. Alexander McWhorter, the patriotic President of "Liberty Hall Academy," (formerly Queen's Museum"), after which General Rutherford dismissed them, with orders to hold themselves in readiness for another call. Major, afterward General, Davie having recovered from his wounds received at Stono, near Charleston, again took the field, and part of his cavalry were ordered to reconnoiter between Charlotte and Camden. Having heard that Lord Rawdon had retired with his army to Hanging Rock, General Rutherford moved from his rendezvous to Rea's plantation, eighteen miles north-east of Charlotte, to Mallard Creek. On the 14th of June the troops under his command were properly organized. The cavalry, sixty-five in number under Major Davie, were equipped as dragoons, and formed into two companies under Captains Lemmonds and Martin. A battalion of three hundred light infantry were placed under the command of General William Davidson, a regular officer, who could not join his Regiment in Charleston after that place was invested. About five hundred men remained under the immediate command of General Rutherford. On the evening of the 14th of June he received intelligence that the Tories, under Col. John Moore, had embodied themselves in strong force at Ramsour's Mill, near the present town of Lincolnton. He immediately issued orders to Colonel Francis Locke, of Rowan; Major David Wilson, of Mecklenburg; also to Captains Falls, Knox, Brandon, and other officers, to raise men to disperse the Tories, deeming it unwise to weaken his own force until the object of Lord Rawdon, still encamped at Waxhaws, should become better known.

On the 15th General Rutherford advanced to a position two miles south of Charlotte. On the 17th he was informed Lord Rawdon had retired towards Camden. On the 18th he broke up his camp south of Charlotte, and marched twelve miles to Tuckaseege Ford, on the Catawba river. On the evening of that day he dispatched an express to Col. Locke, advising him of his movements, and ordering him to unite with him (Rutherford) at Col. Dickson's plantation, three miles northwest of Tuckaseegee Ford, on the evening of the 19th or on the morning of the 20th of June. The express miscarried, in some unaccountable way, and never reached Colonel Locke.

When General Rutherford crossed the river on the evening of the 19th, it was believed he would march in the night, and attack the Tories next morning; but still supposing his express had reached Colonel Locke, he waited for the arrival of that officer at his present encampment in Lincoln county, where he was joined by

Col. Graham's regiment. At ten o'clock at night of the 19th, Col. James Johnston, a brave officer, and well acquainted with the intervening country, arrived at Gen. Rutherford's camp. He had been dispatched by Colonel Locke from Mountain Creek, sixteen miles from Ramsour's Mill, to inform Gen. Rutherford of his intention of attacking the Tories next morning at sunrise, and requested his co-operation. Gen. Rutherford, still expecting his express would certainly reach Col. Locke soon after Col. Johnston left his encampment on Mountain Creek, made no movement until early next morning.

In pursuance of the orders given to Col. Locke and other officers from headquarters at Mallard Creek, on the 14th of June, they quickly collected as many men as they could, and on the 18th Major Wilson, with sixty-five men, crossed the Catawba at Toole's Ford and joined Major McDowell, from Burke, with twenty-five horsemen. They passed up the river at a right angle with the position of the Tories, for the purpose of meeting other Whig forces. At McEwen's Ford, being joined by Captain Falls with forty men, they continued their march up the east side of Mountain Creek, and on Monday, the 19th, they united with Col. Locke, Captain Brandon and other officers, with two hundred and seventy men. The whole force now amounted to nearly four hundred men. They encamped on Mountain Creek at a place called the *glades*. The officers met in council and unanimously agreed it would be unsafe to remain long in their present position, and, notwithstanding the disparity of the opposing forces, it was determined that they should march during the night and attack the Tories in their camp at an early hour next morning. It was said that the Tories being ignorant of their inferior force, and being suddenly attacked would be easily routed. At this time, Col. Johnston, as previously stated, was dispatched from Mountain Creek to apprise General Rutherford of their determination. Late in the evening they commenced their march from Mountain Creek, and passing down the south side of the mountain they halted at the west end of it in the night when they again consulted on the plan of attack. It was determined that the companies under Captains Falls, McDowell and Brandon should act on horseback and march in front. No other arrangement was made, and it was left to the officers to be governed by circumstances after they reached the enemy. They accordingly resumed their march and by day light arrived within a mile of the Tories, assembled in strong force, about two hundred and fifty yards east of Ramsour's Mill, and half a mile north of the present town of Lincolnton. The Tories occupied an excellent position on the summit of the ridge, which has a gentle slope, and was then covered with a scattered growth of trees. The foot of the hill on the south and east was bounded by a glade, and its western base by Ramsour's mill pond. The position was so well chosen that nothing but the most determined bravery enabled the Whigs, with a greatly inferior force to drive the Tories from it, and claim the victory of one of the most severely contested battles of the Revolution.

The forces of Colonel Locke approached the battle ground from the east, a part of his command, at least, having taken "refreshments" at Dellinger's Taven, which stood near the present residence of B. S. Johnson, Esq., of Lincolnton. The companies of Captains Falls, McDowell and Brandon were mounted, and the other troops under Col. Locke were arranged in the road, two deep, behind them. Under this organization they marched to the battle-field. The mounted companies led the attack. When they came within sight of the picket, stationed in the road a considerable distance from the encampment, they perceived that their approach had not been anticipated. The picket fired and fled to their camp. The cavalry pursued, and turning to the right out of the road, they rode up within thirty steps of the line and fired at the Tories. This bold movement of the cavalry threw them into confusion, but seeing only a few men assailing them they quickly recovered from their panic and poured in such a destructive fire upon the horsemen as to compel them to retreat. Soon the infantry hurried up to their assistance, the cavalry rallied, and the fight became general on both sides. It was in this first attack of the cavalry that the brave Captain Gilbraith Falls was mortally wounded in the breast, rode about one hundred and fifty yards east of the battle ground, and fell dead from his horse. The Tories, seeing the effect of their fire, came a short distance down the hill, and thus brought themselves in fair view of the Whig infantry. Here the action was renewed and the contest fiercely maintained for a considerable length of time. In about an hour the Tories began to fall back to their original position on the ridge, and a little beyond its summit, to shield a part of their bodies from the destructive and unceasing fire of the Whigs. From this strong and elevated position the Tories, during the action, were enabled at one time to drive the Whigs nearly back to the glade.

At this moment Captain Hardin led a small force of Whigs into the field, and, under cover of the fence, kept up a galling fire on the right flank of the Tories. This movement gave their lines the proper extension, and the contest being well maintained in the center, the Tories began to retreat up the ridge. Before they reached its summit they found a part of their former position in possession of the Whigs. In this quarter the action became close, and the opposing parties in two instances mixed together, and having no bayonets they struck at each other with the butts of their guns. In this strange contest several of the Tories were made prisoners, and others, divesting themselves of their mark of distinction, (a twig of green pine-top stuck in their hats), intermixed with the Whigs, and all being in their common dress, escaped without being detected.

The Tories finding the left of their position in possession of the Whigs, and their center closely pressed, retreated down the ridge toward the pond, still exposed to the incessant fire of the Whig forces. The Whigs pursued their advantages until they got entire possession of the ridge, when they discovered, to their astonishment, that the Tories had collected in strong force on the other side of the creek, beyond the mill. They expected the fight would be renewed, and attempted to form a line, but only eighty-six men could be paraded. Some were scattered during the action, others were attending to their wounded friends, and, after repeated efforts, not more than one hundred and ten men could be collected.

In this situation of affairs, it was resolved by Colonel Locke and other officers, that Major David Wilson of Mecklenburg, and Captain William Alexander of Rowan, should hasten to General Rutherford, and urge him to press forward to their assistance. General Rutherford had marched early in the morning from Colonel Dickson's plantation, and about six or seven miles from Ramsour's, was met by Wilson and Alexander.

Major Davie's cavalry was started off at full gallop, and Colonel Davidson's battalion of infantry were ordered to hasten on with all possible speed. After progressing about two miles they were met by others from the battle, who informed them the Tories had retreated. The march was continued, and the troops arrived at the battleground two hours after the action had closed. The dead and most of the wounded were still lying where they fell.

In this action the Tories fought and maintained their ground for a considerable length of time with persistent bravery. Very near the present brick structure on the battle-ground, containing within its walls the mortal remains of six gallant Whig captains, the severest fighting took place. They here sealed with their life's blood their devotion to their country's struggle for independence.

In addition to those from their own neighborhoods, the Tories were reinforced two days before the battle by two hundred well-armed men from Lower Creek, in Burke county, under Captains Whiston and Murray. Colonel John Moore, son of Moses Moore, who resided six or seven miles west of Lincolnton, took an active part in arousing and increasing the Tory element throughout the county. He had joined the enemy the preceding winter in South Carolina, and having recently returned, dressed in a tattered suit of British uniform and with a sword dangling at his side, announced himself as Lieutenant Colonel in the regiment of North Carolina loyalists, commanded by Colonel John Hamilton, of Halifax. Soon thereafter, Nicholas Welch, of the same vicinity, who had been in the British service for eighteen months, and bore a Major's commission in the same regiment, also returned, in a splendid uniform, and with a purse of gold, which was ostensibly displayed to his admiring associates, accompanied with artful speeches in aid of the cause he had embraced. Under these leaders there was collected in a few weeks a force of thirteen hundred men, who encamped on the elevated position east of Ramsour's Mill, previously described.

The Tories, believing that they were completely beaten, formed a stratagem to secure their retreat. About the time that Wilson and Alexander were dispatched to General Rutherford, they sent a flag under the pretense of proposing a suspension of hostilities for the purpose of burying the dead, and taking care of the wounded. To prevent the flag officer from seeing their small number, Major James Rutherford and another officer were ordered to meet him a short distance from the line. The proposition being made, Major Rutherford demanded that the Tories should surrender in ten minutes, and then the arrangements as requested could be effected. In the meantime Moore and Welch gave orders that such of their own men as were on foot, or had inferior horses, should move off singly as fast as they could; so that, when the flag returned, not more than fifty men remained. These very brave officers, *before the battle,* and who misled so many of their countrymen, were among the first to take their departure from the scene of conflict, and seek elsewhere, by rapid flight, *more healthy quarters.* Col. Moore, with thirty of his followers, succeeded in reaching the British army at Camden, where he was threatened with a trial by court-martial for disobedience of orders in attempting to embody the Loyalists before the time appointed by Lord Cornwallis.

As there was no perfect organization by either party, nor regular returns made after the action, the loss could not be accurately ascertained. Fifty-six men lay dead on the side of the ridge, and near the present brick enclosure, where the hottest part of the fight occurred. Many of the dead were found on the flanks and over the ridge toward the Mill. It is believed that about seventy were killed altogether, and that the loss on either side was nearly equal. About one hundred were wounded, and fifty tories made prisoners. The men had no uniform, and it could not be told to which party many of the dead belonged. Most of the Whigs wore a white piece of paper on their hats in front, which served as a mark at which the Tories frequently aimed, and consequently, several of the Whigs, after the battle, were found to be shot in the head. 'In this battle, neighbors, near relatives and personal friends were engaged in hostile array against each other. After the action commenced, scarcely any orders were given by the commanding officers. They all fought like common soldiers, and animated each other by their example, as in the battle of King's Mountain, a little over three months after. In no battle of the Revolution, where a band of patriots, less than four hundred in number, engaged against an enemy, at least twelve hundred strong, was there an equal loss of officers, showing the leading part they performed, and the severity of the conflict. They were all

> "Patriots, who perished for their country's right,
> Or nobly triumphed on the field of fight."

Of the Whig officers, Captains Falls, Knox, Dobson, Smith, Bowman, Sloan, and Armstrong were killed. Captain William Falls, who commanded one of the cavalry companies, was shot in the breast in the first spirited charge, as previously stated, and riding a short distance in the rear, fell dead from his horse. His body, after the battle was over, was wrapped in a blanket procured from Mrs. Reinhardt and conveyed to Iredell (then a part of Rowan) for burial. Captain Falls lived in Iredell county, not far from Sherrill's Ford, on the Catawba. There is a reliable tradition which states that when Captain Falls was killed a Tory ran up to rob the body, and had taken his watch, when a young son of Falls, though only fourteen years old, ran up suddenly behind the Tory, drew his father's sword and killed him. Captain Falls was the maternal grandfather of the late Robert Falls Simonton, who had the sword in his possession at the time of his death, in February, 1876.

Captain Patrick Knox was mortally wounded in the thigh; an artery being severed, he very soon died from the resulting hemorrhage. Captain James Houston was severely wounded in the thigh, from the effects of which he never fully recovered. Captain Daniel McKissick was also severely wounded, but recovered, and represented Lincoln county in the Commons from 1783 to 1787. Captains Hugh Torrence, David Caldwell, John Reid, all of Rowan county, and Captain Smith, of Mecklenburg, came out of the conflict unhurt. William Wilson had a horse shot down under him, and was wounded in the second fire. Several of the inferior officers were killed. Thirteen men from the vicinity of Fourth Creek (Statesville) lay dead on the ground after the battle, and many of the wounded died a few days afterward. Joseph Wasson, from Snow Creek, received five balls, one of which it is said he carried *forty years to a day*, when it came out of itself. Being unable to stand up he lay on the ground, loaded his musket, and fired several times.

The brick monumental structure on the southern brow of the rising battle-ground, about fifty or sixty yards from the present public road, contains the mortal remains of six Whig Captains; also those of Wallace Alexander, and his wife, who was a daughter of Captain Dobson, one of the fallen heroes on this hotly-contested field of strife.

The loss of the Tories was greater in privates, but less in officers, than the Whigs. Captains Cumberland, Warlick and Murray were killed, and Captain Carpenter wounded. Captains Keener, Williams and others, including Lieutenant-Colonel John Moore and Major Welch, escaped with their lives, but not " to fight another day."

On the highest prominence of the battle-ground, in a thinly-wooded forest, is a single headstone pointing out the graves of three Tories, probably subordinate officers, with the initials of their names inscribed in parentheses, thus: "(I. S.): (N. W.): (P. W.): "—with three dots after each name, as here presented. A little below are two parallel lines extending across the face of the coarse soap stone, enclosing three hearts with crosses between, as much as to say, *here lie three loving hearts.*

Near a pine tree now standing on the battle-ground, reliable tradition says a long trench was dug, in which was buried nearly all of the killed belonging to both of the contending forces, laid side by side, as the high and the low are perfectly equal in the narrow confines of the grave.

INCIDENTS OF THE BATTLE.

Early on the morning of the 20th of June, 1780, when the Tories were forming their forces in martial array near the residence of Christian Reinhardt, situated on the south-western brow of the battle-ground, he conducted his wife, with two little children in his arms, and several small negroes, across the creek to a dense cane-brake extending along and up the western bank of the mill pond as a place of safety. He then returned to his residence, and in a very short time the battle commenced. As the contest raged, and peal after peal of musketry reverberated over the surrounding hills and dales, his dwelling-house, smoke-house, and even his empty stables were successively filled with the dead, the dying and the wounded. When the battle was nearly over, and victory about to result in favor of the Whigs, many of the Tories swam the mill pond at its upper end, and thus made their escape. Two of these fleeing Tories, with green pine tops in their hats, (their badge of distinction), rushed through the cane-brake very near to Mrs. Reinhardt and her tender objects of care, exclaiming as they passed: "We are whipped! we are whipped!!" and were soon out of sight. During the unusual commotion and terrific conflict of arms, even the deer were aroused from their quiet retreat. One of these denizens of the cane-brake, with sprangling horns, dashed up near to Mrs. Reinhardt, and after viewing for a moment, with astonishment, the new occupants of their rightful solitude, darted off with a celebrity little surpassing that of the fleeing Tories. As soon as the firing ceased, Mrs. Reinhardt came out of her covert with her little ones, and, on reaching the bridge, at the mill, found it had been torn up by the retreating Tories, but, being met there by her husband, she was enabled to cross over, reach her home, and witness the mournful scene which presented itself. The tender sympathy of woman's heart, ever ready to minister to the wants of suffering humanity, was then called into requisition, and kindly extended. In a short time her house was stripped of every disposable blanket and sheet to wrap around the dead, or be employed in some other useful way. Neighbors and relatives, a few hours before bitter enemies, were now seen freely mingling together and giving every kind attention to the sufferers, whether Whig or Tory, within their power.

ROUTE OF THE BRITISH ARMY THROUGH LINCOLN COUNTY.

After the battle of the Cowpens, on the 17th of January, 1781, Lord Cornwallis left his headquarters at Winnsboro, S. C., being reinforced by General Leslie, and marched rapidly to overtake General Morgan, encumbered with more than five hundred prisoners, and necessary baggage, on his way to a place of safety in Virginia. His Lordship was now smarting under two signal defeats (King's Mountain and the Cowpens) occurring a little more than three months apart. But the race is not always to the swift nor the battle to the strong. "Man proposes, but God disposes."

The original manuscript journal of Lord Cornwallis, now on file in the archives of the Historical Society of the State University at Chapel Hill, discloses, with great accuracy, the movements of the British army through Lincoln, Mecklenburg and Rowan counties.

On the 17th of January, 1781, the headquarters of General Leslie were at Sandy Run, Chester county, S. C. On the 18th, at Hillhouse's plantation, in York county, he returns his thanks to the troops under his command, and informs them that all orders in future will issue from Lord Cornwallis and the Adjutant General. At eight o'clock at night, Lord Cornwallis issues his orders to the army to march at eight o'clock on the ensuing morning in the following order: 1. Yagers; 2. Corps of Pioneers; 3. two three pounders; 4. Brigade Guards; 5. Regiment of Bose; 6. North Carolina Volunteers; 7. two six pounders; 8. Lieutenant Colonel Webster's Brigade; 9. Wagons of the General; 10. Field Officers' wagons; 11. Ammunition wagons; 12. Hospital wagons; 13. Regimental wagons; 14. Provision train; 15. Bat. horses; a captain, two subalterns, and one hundred men from Col. Webster's Brigade, to form a rear guard. On the 19th the army camped at Smith's house, near the Cherokee Iron Works, on Broad river. On the 20th the army camped at Saunder's plantation, on Buffalo creek. On the 23d the army crossed the North Carolina line, and camped at Tryon old Court House, in the western part of the present county of Gaston. On the 24th the army arrived at Ramsour's Mill, near the present town of Lincolnton. Here Cornwallis was compelled to remain three days to lay in a supply of provisions for his large army. To accomplish this, foraging parties were sent out in different directions to purchase all the grain, of every kind, that could be procured. Ramsour's Mill, surrounded with a guard of eight or ten men, was set to work, running *day and night*, converting the grain into meal or flour.

General O'Hara camped at the "Reep place," two miles and a half northwest of Ramsour's Mill. His forces crossed the South Fork, about a mile above the bridge, on the public road leading to Rutherfordton. Tarleton's cavalry crossed the same stream in "Cobb's bottom," passing over the present site of Lincolnton, to form a junction with Cornwallis. This small divergence from the direct line of travel, and subsequent concentration at some designated point, was frequently made by sections of the British army for the purpose of procuring supplies.

Lord Cornwallis, during his transitory stay, made his headquarters nearly on the summit of the rising ground, two hundred and fifty yards east of the Mill, on which had been fought the severe battle between the Whigs, under Colonel Francis Locke, and the Tories, under Lieutenant Colonel John Moore (son of Moses Moore), in which the former were victorious.

Christian Reinhardt, one of the first German settlers of the county, then lived near the base of the rising battle ground, and carried on a tan-yard. He owned a valuable servant, named Fess, (contraction of Festus,) whose whole *soul* was exerted in making good *sole* leather, and upper too, for the surrounding country. This servant, greatly attached to his kind master, was forced off, very much rgainst his will, by some of the British soldiery on their departure; but his whereabouts having been found out, Adam Reep, and one or two other noted Whigs, adroitly managed to recover him from the British camp, a few days afterward, and restored him to his rightful owner.

The Marquee of Lord Cornwallis was placed near a a pine tree, still standing on the battle ground, left there by the present owner of the property, (W. M. Reinhardt, Esq., grand son of Christian Reinhardt,) in clearing the land, as a memento of the past—where Royalty, for a brief season, held undisputed sway, and feasted on the fat of the land.

Reliable tradition says that some of the British soldiery, while encamped on the Ramsour battle-ground, evinced a notable propensity for depredating upon the savory poultry of the good old house-wife, Mrs. Barbara Reinhardt—in other words, they showed a fondness for procuring *fowl meat* by *foul means*, in opposition to the principles of honesty and good morals. As soon as the depredations were discovered by Mrs. Reinhardt she immediately laid in her complaints at head-quarters. Whereupon his lordship, placing greater stress upon the sanctity of the eighth commandment than his loyal soldiers, promptly replied, "Madam, you shall be protected," and accordingly had a guard placed over her property until his departure.

Another incident relating to the advance of the British army is to the following effect. As Tarleton's cavalry passed through the southern part of Lincoln county (now Gaston) they rode up to the residence of Bejamin Ormand, on the head-waters of Long Creek, and tied one of the horses, which they had taken, to the top of a small white oak, growing in his yard. This little Revolutionary *sapling* is still living in the serenity of a robust old age, and now measures, two feet from the ground, *twenty-seven feet in comcumference!* Its branches extend all around in different directions from forty to fifty feet, and the tree is supposed to contain at least ten cords of wood.

When Tarleton's cavalry were on the point of leaving, they took the blanket from the cradle in which James Ormand, the baby, was lying, and used it as a saddle-blanket, and the large family Bible of Benjamin Ormand was converted into a *saddle!!*

The Bible was afterward found near Beattie's Ford, on the Catawba river, in the line of the British march, and restored to its proper owner. Mr. Z. S. Ormand, a grandson of Benjamin Ormond, and a worthy citizen of Gaston county, now lives at the old homestead, where the Bible, considerably injured, can be seen at any time, as an abused relic of the past, and invested with a most singular history. Tarleton's cavalry also seized and carried off the bedding and blankets in the house, and some of the cooking utensils in the kitchen.

Mr. Ormand also informs the author that he frequently heard his grandmother, who then lived near Steele Creek Church, say that she was present at the great meeting at Charlotte, on the 20th of May, 1775, and that she exhibited, on that occasion, *a quilt of her own manufacture.* She said it was a large turn out of people from all parts of the county, and was considered a suitable time for the *fair sex* to exhibit productions of their own hands.

Having replenished his commissary department as much as possible while encamped on the Ramsour battle-ground, and having experienced too much delay in his late march in consequence of the encumbrance of his baggage, Cornwallis destroyed, before moving, all such as could be regarded as superfluous. The baggage at head-quarters was first thrown into the flames, thus converting the greater portion of his army into light troops, with a view of renewing more rapidly the pursuit of Morgan, or of forcing General Greene into an early action.

It is said "pewter plates" were freely distributed among some "loyal" friends in the immediate vicinity, or thrown into the mill-pond; and large numbers of very strong glass bottles, originally filled with English ale, or *something stronger*, were broken to pieces on the rocks, fragments of which may be seen scattered around at the present time.

Thus disencumbered, Cornwallis, early on the morning of the 28th of January, broke up camp and marched to the Catawba river, but finding it much swollen, and rendered impassable in consequence of heavy rains at its sources, he fell back to Forney's plantation, five miles from the river. Jacob Forney was a thrifty, well-to-do farmer, and a well-known Whig. The plantation is now (1876) owned by Willis E. Hall, Esq. Here the British army lay encamped for three days, waiting for the sudsidence of the waters, and consumed, during that time, Forney's entire stock of cattle, hogs, sheep and poultry, with all of which he was well supplied. (For further particulars, see sketch of "Jacob Forney, Sen.")

Having dried their powder, and laid in an additional supply of provisions and forage, the British army was now prepared to renew more actively the pursuit of Morgan. On the evening before the marching of the main army, Colonel Webster moved forward with the artillery, and a small detachment as a rear guard, and took position at Beattie's Ford. This was a mere feint, intended to create the impression that the whole British army would cross there, as it was the most eligible pass, and thus elude the vigilance of the Whigs.

At half-past two o'clock, on the morning of the 1st of February, 1781, Cornwallis broke up his camp at Forney's plantation, and marched to a private crossing-place known as Cowan's Ford, six miles below Beattie's Ford. As he approached the river, a little before the dawn of a cloudy, misty morning, numerous camp fires on the eastern bank assured him his passage would be resisted; but General Davidson had neglected to place his entire force, about three hundred and fifty in number, near the ford, so as to present an imposing appearance. As it was, only the companies of Captain Joseph Graham, and of two or three other officers, probably not more than one third of the whole force on duty, actually participated in the skirmish which immediately took place; otherwise, the result might have been far more disastrous to the British army.

The river at Cowan's Ford, for most of the distance across, has a very rugged bottom, abounding with numerous rocks, of considerable size, barely visible at the low water of summer-time. With judicious forethought, Cornwallis had hired the services of Frederick Hager, a Tory, on the western bank, and, under his guidance, the bold Br.t-ons plunged into the water, with the firm determination of encountering the small band of Americans on the eastern bank.

Stedman, the English commissary and historian, who accompanied Cornwallis in his Southern campaigns, thus speaks of the passage of the river at Cowan's Ford:

"The light infantry of the guards, led by Colonel Hall,

first entered the water. They were followed by the grenadiers, and the grenadiers by the battalions, the men marching in platoons, to support one another against the rapidity of the stream. When the light infantry had nearly reached the middle of the river, they were challenged by one of the enemy's sentinels. The sentinel having challenged thrice, and receiving no answer, immediately gave the alarm by discharging his musket; and the enemy's pickets were turned out. No sooner did the guide (a Tory) who attended the light infantry to show them the ford, hear the report of the sentinel's musket than he turned around and left them. This, which at first, seemed to portend much mischief, in the end, proved a fortunate incident. Colonel Hall, being forsaken by his guide, and not knowing the true direction of the ford, led the column directly across the river to the nearest part of the opposite bank."

This direct course carried the British army to a new landing-place on the eastern, or Mecklenburg side, so that they did not encounter a full and concentrated fire from the Whigs. Upon hearing the firing, General Davidson, who was stationed about half a mile from the ford, (in the Lucas house, still standing,) with the greater portion of the militia, hastened to the scene of conflict, evincing his well-established bravery, but it was too late to change the issue of the contest, and array any more effectual resistance. At this moment, General Davidson arrived near the river, and in attempting to rally the Whig forces for renewed action, received a fatal shot in the breast, fell from his horse, and almost instantly expired. The few patriots on the bank of the river nobly performed their duty, but had soon to retreat before vastly superior numbers.

The British infantry waded the river, preceded by their Tory guide, staff in hand, to show them the proper ford, and the statement made by some historians that General

Davidson was killed by this guide is not corroborated by Stedman, the English historian; but, on the contrary, he leaves us to infer that the American General met his death at the hands of one of their own troops. The same authority states their own loss to be Colonel Hall and three privates killed, and thirty-six wounded. The horse of Lord Cornwallis was fatally shot and fell dead just as he ascended the bank. The horse of General O'Hara, after tumbling over the slippery rocks several times, producing a partial submersion of his rider, finally reached the bank in safety. The British reserved their fire until they reached the eastern shore, and then pouring in two or three volleys into the ranks of the opposing Whig forces, now considerably disconcerted, soon compelled them to retreat with small loss.

Colonel Hall was buried on the edge of the alluvial land a short distance below the crossing-place, with a head and foot stone of rock from the adjoining hill, which were long visible and could be pointed out by the nearest neighbors; but these were finally concealed from view by successive overflows of sand from the swollen river. The privates of both contending forces were buried on the rising ground, near the scene of conflict, and with such haste on the part of the British interring party as to leave one of their mattocks behind them at the graves of their fallen comrades, eager to overtake the vigilant Morgan.

GEN. JOSEPH GRAHAM.

(Condensed from Wheeler's "Historical Sketches.")

General Joseph Graham was born in Pennsylvania on the 13th of October, 1759. His mother being left a widow with five small children, and slender means of support, removed to North Carolina when he was about seven years of age, and settled in the neighborhood of Charlotte. He received the principal part of his education at "Queen's Museum" in Charlotte, (afterward called "Liberty Hall Academy,") and was distinguished for his talents, industry and manly deportment. His thirst for knowledge led him at an early period to become well acquainted with all those interesting and exciting events which preceded our Revolutionary struggle. He was present in Charlotte on the 20th of May, 1775, when the first Declaration of Independence was formally and publicly made. The deep impression made upon his mind by the solemn and illustrious decisions of that day gave good evidence that he was then preparing for the noble stand which he took during the war.

He enlisted in the army of the United States in May, 1778, at the age of nineteen years. He served in the Fourth Regiment of North Carolina regular troops, under Col. Archibald Lytle, acting as an officer in Captain Gooden's company. The troops to which he was attached were ordered to rendezvous at Bladensburg, Md. Having marched as far as Caswell county they received intelligence of the battle of Monmouth, when he returned home on a furlough.

He again entered the service on the 5th of November, 1778, and marched under General Rutherford to Purysburg, on the Savannah river, soon after the defeat of Gen. Ashe at Brier Creek. He was with the troops under Gen. Lincoln, and fought in the battle of Stono, against Gen. Prevost, on the 20th of June, 1779, which lasted one hour and twenty minutes. During nearly the whole of this campaign he acted as quartermaster. In July, 1779, he was taken with the fever, and after two months' severe illness was discharged near Dorchester, and returned home.

After the surrender of Charleston, and defeat of Col. Bufort at the Waxhaw, he again entered the service as adjutant of the Mecklenburg Regiment, and spent the summer in opposing the advance of Lord Rawdon into

North Carolina, and assailing his troops, then within forty miles of Charlotte.

When it was understood that the British were marching to Charlotte he was ordered by General Davidson to repair to that place, and take command of such a force as he could readily collect, and join Col. Davie. *About midnight* of the 25th of September, 1780, Col. Davie reached Charlotte. On the next day the British army entered Charlotte, and received such a *stinging* reception as to cause Lord Cornwallis to designate the place as the "Hornets' Nest of America." After a well-directed fire upon the British from the Court House to the gum tree, Gen. Graham, with the troops assigned to his command, retreated, opposing Tarleton's cavalry and a regiment of infantry for four miles on the Salisbury road. On the plantation formerly owned by Joseph McConnaughey, he again formed his men, and attacked the advancing British infantry. After again retreating, he formed on the hill above where Sugar Creek Church now stands. There, owing to the imprudent but honest zeal of Major White, they were detained too long, for by the time they had reached the cross-roads a party of British dragoons were in sight, and, after close pursuit for nearly two miles, overtook them. It was at this time that Lieut. George Locke, a brother of Col. Francis Locke, of Rowan county, was killed at the margin of a small pond, now to be seen at the end of Alexander Kennedy's lane. Between that spot and where James A. Houston now lives, Gen. Graham was cut down and severely wounded. He received nine wounds, six with the saber and three from musket balls. His life was narrowly and mercifully preserved by a large stock buckle which broke the violence of the stroke. He received four deep gashes of the saber over his head and one in his side; and three balls were afterward removed from his body. After being much exhausted by loss of blood, he reached the house of the late

Mrs. Susannah Alexander, where he was kindly nursed and watched during the night, and his wounds dressed as well as circumstances would permit. On the next day he reached his mother's residence, where the late Major Bostwick resided, and from that place transferred to the hospital in Charlotte.

Thus, at the tender age of twenty-one years, we see this gallant young officer leading a band of as brave men as ever faced a foe, to guard the ground first consecrated by the Mecklenburg Decleration of Independence, leaving his blood as the best memorial of a righteous cause, and of true heroism in its defence.

As soon as he recovered from his wounds, he again entered the service of his country. Gen. Davidson, who had command of all the militia in the western counties of the State, applied to him to raise one or more companies, promising him such rank as the number of men raised would justify. Through his great energy, perseverance and influence he succeeded in raising a company of fifty-five men in two weeks. These were mounted riflemen, armed also with swords, and some with pistols.

They supplied themselves with their own horses and necessary equipments, and entered the field without commissary or quartermaster, and with every prospect of hard fighting, and little compensation. After Tarleton's signal defeat at the Cowpens, Cornwallis resolved to pursue Gen. Morgan, encumbered with upwards of five hundred prisoners. At that time Gen. Greene had assumed command of the southern army, and stationed himself with a portion of it at Hicks' Creek, near to Cheraw. After Gen. Morgan's successful retreat, Gen. Greene left his main army with Gen. Huger, and rode one hundred and fiffty miles to join Gen. Morgan's detachment near the Catawba river. The plan of opposing Lord Cornwallis in crossing the Catawba was arranged by Gen. Greene, and its execution assigned to Gen. Davidson.

Lieutenant Col. Webster moved forward and crossed the Catawba in advance with a detachment of cavalry to create the impression that the whole British army would cross there, but the real intention of Cornwallis was to make the attempt at Cowan's Ford. Soon after the action commenced, Gen. Davidson was killed, greatly lamented by all who knew him as a brave and generous officer. The company commanded by Gen. Graham commenced the attack upon the British as they advanced through the river, and resolutely kept it up until they ascended the bank. The British then poured in a heavy fire upon Graham's men, two of whom were killed. Col. William Polk and Rev. T. H. McCaule were near Gen. Davidson when he fell. Col. Hall and three or four of the British were killed and upwards of thirty wounded. The British were detained here about three hours in burying their dead and then resumed their march in pursuit of Gen. Morgan.

The body of General Davidson was secured by David Wilson and Richard Barry, conveyed to the house of Samuel Wilson, Sen., there dressed for burial, and interred that night in the grave-yard of Hopewell Church.

The North Carolina militia were then placed under the command of General Pickens, of South Carolina, and continued to harass the British as they advanced toward Virginia. General Graham with his company, and some troops from Rowan county, surprised and captured a guard at Hart's Mill, one mile and a-half from Hillsboro, where the British army then lay, and the same day joined Colonel Lee's forces. On the next day, under General Pickens, he was in the action against Colonel Pyles, who commanded about three hundred and fifty Tories on their way to join Tarleton. These Tories supposed the Whigs to be a company of British troops sent for their protection, and commenced crying, "God save the King." Tarleton was about a mile from this place, and retreated to Hillsboro. Shortly afterward General Graham was in an engagement under Colonel Lee, at Clapp's Mill, on the Alamance, and had two of his company killed, three wounded and two made prisoners. Again, a few days afterward, he was in the action at Whitsell's Mill, under Colonel Washington. As the term of service of his men had expired, and the country was annoyed with Tories, General Greene directed him to return with his company and keep them in a compact body until they crossed the Yadkin, which they did on the 14th of March, 1781.

After the battle of Guilford the British retired to Wilmington, and but little military service was performed in North Carolina during the summer of 1781. About the 1st of September Fannin surprised Hillsboro and took Governor Burke prisoner. General Rutherford, who had been taken prisoner at Gates' defeat, was set at liberty, and returned home about this time. He immediately gave orders to General Graham, in whose military prowess and influence he placed great confidence, to raise a troop of cavalry in Mecklenburg county. These troops of dragoons, and about two hundred mounted infantry, were raised and formed into a legion, over which Robert Smith was made Colonel and General Graham Major. They immediately commenced their march toward Wilmington. South of Fayetteville, with ninety-six dragoons and forty mounted infantry, made a gallant and successful attack against a body of Tories commanded by the noted Tory Colonels, McNeil, Ray, Graham and McDougal. This action took place near McFalls' Mill, on the Raft swamp, in which the Tories where signally defeated, their leaders dispersed, and their cause greatly damaged. In this spirited engagement one hundred and thirty-six Whigs opposed and vanquished six hundred Tories, reflecting great credit upon the bravery and military sagacity of General Graham.

A short time afterward he commanded one troop of

dragoons and two of mounted infantry, and defeated a band of Tories on Alfred Moore's plantation, opposite Wilmington. On the next day he led the troops in person, and attacked the British garrison near the same place. Shortly afterward he commanded three companies in defeating Colonel Gagny, near Waccamaw lake. This campaign closed General Graham's services in the Revolutionary war, having commanded in fifteen engagements with a degree of courage, wisdom, calmness and success, surpassed, perhaps, by no officer of the same rank.

Hundreds who served under him have delighted in testifying to the upright, faithful, and undaunted manner in which he discharged the duties of his trying and responsible station. Never was he known to shrink from any toil, however painful, or quail before any danger, however threatening, or stand back from any privations or sacrifices which might serve his country. After the close of the war he was elected the first Sheriff of Mecklenburg county, and gave great satisfaction by the faithful performance of the duties of that office. From 1788 to 1794 he was elected to the Senate from the same county. About the year 1787 he was married to Isabella, the second daughter of Major John Davidson. By this marriage he had twelve children. Not long after his marriage he removed to Lincoln county and engaged in the manufacture of iron. For more than forty years before his death he conducted a large establishment of iron works with great energy and success.

In 1814 General Graham commanded a Regiment of North Carolina Volunteers against the Creek Indians, and arrived about the time the last stroke of punishment was inflicted upon this hostile tribe by General Jackson, at the battle of the Horse Shoe. For many years after the war he was Major General of the 5th Division of the North Carolina Militia. By a life of temperance and regular exercise, with the blessing of God, he enjoyed remarkable health and vigor of constitution.

On the 13th of October, 1836, he made the following minute in his day-book: "This day I am seventy-seven years of age, *Dei Gratia.*" He rode from Lincolnton on the 10th of November, soon thereafter was struck with apoplexy, and on the evening of the 12th closed his eyes upon the cares and trials of a long, useful and honorable life.

General Joseph Graham was the father of the late Ex-Governor William A. Graham, one of North Carolina's most worthy, honorable, and illustrious sons.

BREVARD FAMILY.

(Condensed from Wheeler's "Historical Sketches.")

The Brevard family acted a very conspicuous part during our Revolutionary war. The first one of the name of whom anything is known was a Huguenot who fled from France on the revocation of the edict of Nantes in 1685, and settled among the Scotch-Irish in the northern part of Ireland. He there formed the acquaintance of a family of McKnitts, and with them set sail for the American shores. One of this family was a young and blooming lassie, "very fair to look upon." Brevard and herself soon discovered in each other kindred spirits, and a mutual attachment sprung up between them. They joined their fortunes, determined to share the hardships and trials incident to a settlement in a new country, then filled with wild beasts and savages. They settled on Elk river, in Maryland. The issue of this marriage were five sons and one daughter; John, Robert, Zebulon, Benjamin, Adam, and Elizabeth. The three elder brothers, with their sister and her husband, came to North Carolina between 1740 and 1750. The three brothers were all Whigs during the Revolution. John Brevard, whose family is the immediate subject of this sketch, married a sister of Dr. Alexander McWhorter, a distinguished Presbyterian minister from New Jersey, who had for a time the control of Queen's Museum in Charlotte. Soon after his marriage, Brevard also emigrated to North Carolina, and settled about two miles from Center Church, in Iredell county. Dr. McWhorter was a very zealous Whig, and it is said the British were anxious to seize him on account of his independent addresses, both in and out of the pulpit. But they failed in their endeavors, and, after the invasion of Charlotte by Cornwallis in 1780, he returned to the North.

At the commencement of the Revolutionary war, John Brevard, then an old and infirm man, had eight sons and four daughters, Mary, Ephraim, John, Hugh, Adam, Alexander, Robert, Benjamin, Nancy, Joseph, Jane and Rebecca. He was a well known and influential Whig, and early instilled his patriotic principles into the minds of his children. When the British army under Cornwallis passed near his residence a squad of soldiers went to his house and burned every building on the premises to the ground. No one was at home at the time except his wife, then quite old and infirm, the daughters having been sent to a neighboring house across a swamp to preserve them from any indignities that might be offered to them by a base soldiery. When the soldiers came up a self-authorized officer drew a paper from his pocket, and after looking at it for a moment said, " these houses must be burned." They were accordingly set on fire. Mrs. Brevard attempted to save some articles of furniture from the flames, but the soldiers would throw them back as fast as she could take them out Everything in the house was consumed. The reason assigned by the soldiery for this incendiary act was she then had " eight sons in the rebel army."

Mary, the eldest daughter of John Brevard, married

Gen. Davidson who was killed at Cowan's Ford on the Catawba river.

Nancy married John Davidson. They were both killed by the Indians at the head of the Catawba river.

Jane married Ephraim, a brother of John Davidson. Though very young, he was sent by Gen. Davidson, on the night before the skirmish at Cowan's Ford, with an express to Col. Morgan, warning him of the approach of the British forces.

Rebecca married a Jones and moved to Tennessee.

Ephraim Brevard, the eldest son, married a daughter of Col. Thomas Polk. After a course of preparatory studies he went to Princeton College. Having graduated, he pursued a course of medical studies and settled as a physician in Charlotte. Being highly educated, and possessed of a superior mind, and agreeable manner, he exerted a commanding influence over the youthful patriots of that day. In the language of Dr. Foote, "he thought clearly; felt deeply; wrote well; resisted bravely, and died a martyr to that liberty none loved better, and few understood so well." (For further particulars respecting Dr. Brevard, see Sketches of the Signers of the Mecklenburg Declaration.)

John Brevard, Jr., served in the Continental Army with the commission of Lieutenant, displaying, on all occasions, unflinching bravery and a warm devotion to the cause of American freedom.

Hugh Brevard, with several brothers, was at the battle of Ramsour's Mill. Early in the war he was appointed a Colonel of the militia, and was present at the defeat of General Ashe at Brier Creek. He settled in Burke county, and was elected a member of the Legislature in 1780 and 1781, was held in high esteem by his fellow-citizens, and died about the close of the war.

Adam Brevard first served one year in the Northern Army under General Washington. He then came South, and was present at the battle of Ramsour's Mill. He there had a button shot from his pantaloons, but escaped unharmed. He was a blacksmith by trade, and, after the war followed this occupation for a considerable length of time. Being fond of reading he studied law in his shop, when not much pressed with business, and found a greater delight in the law-telling *strokes* of a Blackstone than in the hard-ringing strokes of a blacksmith's hammer. He finally abandoned his trade and engaged in the practice of the law, in which he was successful. He was a man of strong intellect, sound judgment, and keen observation. He wrote a piece called the "Mecklenburg Censor," abounding with sarcastic wit and well-timed humor, making him truly the "learned blacksmith" of Mecklenburg county.

Alexander Brevard first joined the army as a cadet. He then received the commission of Lieutenant, and soon afward that of Captain in the Continental Army. He was engaged in the battles of White Plains, Trenton, Princeton, Brandywine, Monmouth, and Germanton, and remained in the Northern Army under General Washington until some time in the year 1779, when, his health failing, he was sent into the country. After a short absence he reported himself for service to Gen. Washington. This illustrious and humane commander, seeing his slender figure and delicate appearance, remarked that he was unfit for hard service, and enquired of him where his parents lived. The reply was, in North Carolina. Gen. Washington then advised him to return home. With this advice he complied, and his health, in the meantime, having improved in the genial climate of Western North Carolina, he immediately joined the Southern Army under General Gates. Being a Captain in the regular service, and removed from his command, he was appointed quartermaster, and acted as such at the battle of Camden. After the defeat of Gen. Gates, the Southern Army was placed under the command of Gen.

Greene. Alexander Brevard was with this gallant commander in all his battles; so that, with little interruption, he was in active service *from the beginning to the end of the war.* He thought his hardest fighting was at the Eutaw Springs. He was there in command of his company, and in the hottest part of the fignt, losing eighteen of his brave men. At one time he and his company were in a very critical situation. A division of the British army came very unexpectedly upon their rear while they were closely engaged in front; but, just at that moment, Col. Washington, perceiving their imminent danger, made an impetuous charge with his cavalry upon this division of the enemy. A portion of his men broke through, and formed again with the intention of renewing the charge. This was prevented by the retreat of the British into a position where it was impossible for the cavalry to pursue them.

Colonel Washington was unhorsed and made a prisoner, but succeeded with his brave men in preventing the meditated attack in the rear. Brevard had not observed this division of the enemy, and the first thing he saw was the flying caps and tumbling horses of the cavalry as they made their dashing charge upon them. This was the last important battle in which Capt. Brevard was engaged, fought on the 8th of September, 1781, and near the close of the war. On all occasions he maintained an unflagging zeal and promptitude of action in achieving the independence of his country, and evincing a persistent bravery unsurpassed in the annals of the American Revolution.

After the war Captain Brevard married Rebecca, a daughter of Major John Davidson, one of the signers of the Mecklenburg Declaration. Major Davidson suggested to himself and General Joseph Graham, another son-in-law, the propriety of entering into the manufacture of iron. They readily approved of the suggestion and went over into Lincoln county. There they found General Peter Forney in possession of a valuable iron ore bank. With him they formed a copartnership and erected Vesuvius Furnace on the public road from Beattie's Ford to Lincolnton—at present known as Smith's Furnace. After operating for a time altogether, Forney withdrew. Davidson and Brevard then left Graham in the management of Vesuvius Furnace, and built Mount Tirzah Forge, now known as Brevard's Forge. The sons-in-law shortly afterward bought out Davidson, and finally they dissolved. Brevard then built a furnace on Leeper's Creek, above Mount Tirzah Forge, and continued in the iron business until his death.

Captain Brevard, being of a retiring disposition, never sought political favor, but preferred to discharge his obligations to his country rather by obeying than by making her laws. His manners were frank and candid, and the more intimately he was known the better was he beloved. The dishonest met his searching eye with dread, but the industrious and the honest ever found in him a kind adviser and beneficent assistant. Long will he be remembered as a pure man, a faithful friend, and an upright citizen, conscientious in the discharge of all his obligations and in the performance of all his duties. He was, for many years, a worthy elder in the Presbyterian Church, and died, as he had lived, a true christian, and with humble resignation, on the 1st of November, 1829, in the seventy-fifth year of his age. His mortal remains repose in a private cemetery, selected by General Graham and himself as a family burying ground, and near which has lately been built the church of Macpelah. He left seven children—Ephraim, Franklin, Harriet, Robert, Joseph, Theodore and Mary. Franklin and Joseph represented, at different times, the county of Lincoln in the State Legislature.

Joseph Brevard, the youngest son of John Brevard,

Sen., at the youthful age of seventeen, held the commission of Lieutenant in the Continental army. His brother Alexander said he was at that time quite small and delicate, and that he always pitied him when it was his turn to mount guard. General ———, who was in command at Philadelphia, discovering that he wrote a pretty hand, appointed him his private secretary. In this position he remained until he received the commission of Lieutenant in the Southern army, which he held until the close of the war. After the war he studied law, and settled in Camden, S. C., where he took a high stand both as a lawyer and a citizen. After filling several offices of public trust, he was elected one of the Judges, which position he occupied with distingaished honor.

After a few years he resigned his Judgship, and was twice elected to Congress from his district. He made a Digest of the Statute Laws of South Carolina, and also left one or two volumes of cases reported by himself. These books, particularly the latter, are still referred to as good legal authority. He died in Camden, and has left a name cherished and honored by all those who remember his numerous virtues.

Such is a brief and imperfect sketch of that family whose name is prefixed. Many events, of thrilling interest, connected with their revolutionary services, have, no doubt, sunk into oblivion; but enough has been presented to stimulate the rising generation to imitate their heroic example and admire their unfaltering devotion to the cause of American freedom.

COLONEL JAMES JOHNSTON.

Col. James Johnston, one of the earliest patriots of "Tryon," afterward Lincoln county, was born about the year 1742. His father, Henry Johnston, was of Scottish descent. During the many civil and ecclesiastical troubles which greatly agitated England preceding the ascent of William, Prince of Orange, to the throne in 1688, and the ruinous consequences of the defeat of Charles Edward, the "Pretender," at the battle of Culloden, in April, 1746, a constant tide of emigration was flowing from Scotland to the northern part of Ireland, or directly to the shores of the New World, then holding forth to the disturbed population of Europe peculiar features of attractiveness, accompanied with the most alluring prospects of future aggrandizement and wealth. Among the families who passed over during this period were some of the extensive clan of Johnstons (frequently spelled *Johnstone*); also, the Alexanders, Ewarts, Bells, Knoxes, Barnetts, Pattons, Wilsons, Spratts, Martins, with a strong sprinkling of the Davidsons, Caldwells, Grahams, Hunters, Polks, and many others whose descendants performed a magnanimous part in achieving our independence, and stand high on the "roll of fame" and exalted worth.

The name Johnston in Scotland embraces many distinguished personages in every department of literature. From one of the families who came directly to America in 1722 ("Lord William Johnston") have descended in different branches, the late General Albert Sidney Johnston and General Joseph E. Johnston—illustrious, patriotic names the Southern people and a disinterested posterity will ever delight to honor.

The Johnstons in their native "land o'cakes and brither Scots," had the reputation of being "heady," strong-minded, proud of their ancestral descent, and were regarded, at times, as being rather "rebellious"—a trait of character which, in this last respect, some of their descendants strongly manifested in the late Confederate struggle, but in accordance with the most honorable and patriotic motives.

When Henry Johnston and his youthful wife settled on the western banks of the Catawba river, the country was then covered with its native forests, and over its wide expause of territory, as yet but little disturbed by the implements of husbandry, the Indians and wild beasts held almost undisputed sway. The uplands were clothed with wild "pea vines," and other luxuriant herbage, and cattle literally roamed over and fed upon a "thousand hills." Every water course, too, bristled with cane-brakes, indicating the great fertility of the soil, and the sure road, under proper industrial efforts, to agricultural prosperity.

In the absence of family records we are left to infer Col. Johnston grew up to manhood, receiving as good an education as his own limited means and the opportunities of societies then afforded. It was then a gloomy period in our history. In 1765 the Stamp Act had been passed, which agitated the American Colonies from one extremity to the other. The dark cloud of discontent hung heavily over our people, too truly foreboding the storm of open rupture, and approaching revolution. During this exciting period he imbibed those patriotic principles, which, in subsequent years, governed his actions, and prepared him to cast in his lot, and heartly unite with those who pledged "their lives, their fortunes, and their sacred honor" in the cause of American freedom. He emphatically belonged to that class of ardent young men of the Revolutionary period

"Whose deeds were cast in manly mold,
For hardy sports or contest bol'd."

Tradition speaks of the wife of Henry Johnston as dying comparatively young, leaving two children—James, the immediate subject of this sketch, and Mary—who married Moses Scott, settled near Goshen Church, in the present county of Gaston, and there ended her days. Moses Scott had three children—James J., William and Abram Scott. Of these sons, James Johnston Scott married in 1803, Mary, a daughter of Captain Robert Alexander, a soldier of the Revolution, and of extensive usefulness. He (James) died in 1809, in the twenty-seventh year of his age, leaving two children—Abram and Mary Scott, the former of whom in this Centennial year (1876) still survives, having nearly completed his "three-score years and ten."

Col. Johnston first entered the service as Captain of a company, in the winter of 1776, Col. William Graham commanding, against a large body of Tories in the northwestern section of South Carolina. This expedition is known in history as the "Snow Campaign," from the unusually heavy snow, of that winter, and, in conjunction with the troops of that State, drove the Tory commanders, Cunningham and Fletcher, from the siege of the post of Ninety Six. On the retreat of these Tory leaders they surprised and defeated them with a loss of four hundred of their followers. The reader may be curious to know the origin of the name "Ninety Six" applied to this post, now constituting the village of Cambridge, in Abbeville county. It was so called because it was ninety-six miles from the frontier fort, Prince George, on Keowee river, in the present county of Pickens. No portion of South Carolina suffered more during the Revolution than the district around Ninety-Six. The Tories were numerous, bold and vindictive, and for that reason the gallant Whigs of that region frequently called upon their compatriots-in-arms in North Carolina, more particularly in Mecklenburg, Lincoln and Burke counties, for assistance in defending their homes and their property.

In this same year (1776) Gen. Rutherford called out a strong force of infantry and cavalry from Mecklenburg, Rowan, Tryon, (afterwards Lincoln), and other western counties to subdue the "Over-hill" Cherokee Indians, who were committing numerous depredations, and occasionally murdering the inhabitants on the frontier settlements. At that time the "Blue Ridge" constituted the bounds of organized civilization. The expedition, commanded by Gen. Rutherford, was completely successful, the Indians were routed, their towns destroyed, and a considerable number killed and made prisoners. Nothing short of this severe chastisement of the Indians for their depredations and murders would serve to teach them of the supremacy of the white man, and cause them to sue for peace. On this occasion many of the western patriots experienced their first essay in arms, and learned something of the toils and dangers of the soldier's life.

During the war several expeditions were sent from the border counties of North Carolina to assist in pulling down the Tory ascendancy of the disaffected portion of upper South Carolina. In one of these expeditions Col. Johnston experienced an adventure—a passage at arms, which, as an incident of the war and characteristic of his bravery, is here worthy of narration. On Pacolet river, near the place where the late Dr. Bivings erected a factory, Col. Johnston, in a skirmish, had a personal rencontre with Patrick Moore, a Tory officer, whom he finally overpowered and captured. In the contest he received several sword cuts on his head, and on the thumb of the right hand. As he was bearing his prisoner to the Whig lines, a short distance off, he was rapidly approached by several British troopers. He then immediately attempted to discharge his loaded musket against his assailants, but unfortunately it *missed fire*, in consequence of blood flowing from his wounded thumb and wetting the *priming*. This misfortune on his part enabled his prisoner to escape; and, perceiving his own dangerous and armless position, he promptly availed himself of a friendly thicket at his side, eluded his pursuers and soon afterwards joined his command.

On the 14th of June, 1780, Gen. Rutherford, whilst encamped near Charlotte, received intelligence that the Tories under Col. John Moore had assembled in strong force at Ramsour's Mill, near the present town of Lincolnton. He immediately issued orders to Col. Francis Locke, of Rowan; to Major David Wilson, of Mecklenburg, and other officers, to use every exertion to raise a sufficient number of men to attack the Tories at that place. On the 17th of June Gen. Rutherford marched from his encampment, two miles south of Charlotte, to the Tuckaseegee Ford, on the Catawba. He had previously dispatched an express to Col. Locke, advising him of his movement, and ordered him to join his army on the 19th or morning of the 20th of June, a few miles beyond that ford. The express, in some unaccountable way, miscarried. The morning of the 19th being wet, Gen. Rutherford did not cross the river until evening and encamped three miles beyond on Col. Dickson's plantation. Whilst there, waiting for Col. Locke's arrival, in obedience to the express, he received a notice from that officer, then encamped at Mountain Creek, informing him of his intention of attacking the Tories on the next morning at sunrise, and requested his co-operation. This notice was delivered to Gen. Rutherford by Col. Johnston at 11 o'clock of the night of the 19th of June, being selected for that duty by Col. Locke on account of his personal knowledge of the intervening country and undaunted courage. Col. Locke's encampment was then sixteen miles from Ramsour's Mill. Late in the evening of the same day, and soon after the departure of Col. Johnston to Gen. Rutherford's camp, Col. Locke marched with his forces, less than four hundred in number, stopped a short time in the night for rest and consultation, and arrived within a mile of Ramsour's at daylight without being observed by the Tories. The battle soon commenced by the mounted companies of Captains Falls, McDowell and Brandon. The Tories at first fought with considerable bravery, driving back the Whig cavalry. These, however, soon rallied, and, being supported by the advancing infantry, pressed forward under their gallant leaders with a courage which knew no faltering and completely routed the Tories, driving them, after an hour's contest, from their strong position, and capturing about fifty of their number. This victory, occurring soon after the surrender of Charleston, when the Tories had become bold and menacing in their conduct, greatly cheered the Whigs throughout the entire South, animated them with fresh hopes, and nerved them on to future deeds of "noble daring."

Gen. Rutherford, not leaving his encampment at Col. Dickson's before daylight of the morning of the 20th of June, failed to reach Ramsour's Mill until two hours after the battle. Col. Johnston there joined his command, and participated in the closing duties of this victorious engagement in the cause of American freedom.

At the battle of King's Mountain Col. Johnston commanded the reserves, about ninety in number, which were soon called into service after the battle commenced. The decisive and brilliant victory of that memorable day has been so frequently adverted to in history that it is deemed here unnecessary to enter into particulars. Suffice it to say, it completely broke down the Tory influence in Western North Carolina, and its more rampant manifestations in upper South Carolina. It is known that Cornwallis, then in Charlotte, in a few days after hearing of the defeat and death of Ferguson, one of his bravest officers, marched from that rebellious town in the night and hastily retreated to safer quarters in Winnsboro, S. C.

During the progress of the war Col. Johnston was frequently engaged in other minor expeditions, requiring promptitude of action and unflinching bravery, in assisting to disperse bodies of Tories wherever they might assemble, and arrest obnoxious individuals when the peace and welfare of society demanded such service.

At the Provincial Congress which met at Halifax on

the 4th of April, 1776, Colonel James Johnston and Colonel Charles McLean were the delegates from Tryon county. Colonel McLean was an early and devoted friend of liberty. He resided on the headwaters of Crowder's creek, in the present county of Gaston, and commanded the first regiment which marched from Lincoln county against the Tories of upper South Carolina. This Provincial Congress was one of the most important ever held in the State. The spirit of liberty was then in the ascendant, animating every patriotic bosom from the sea coast to the mountains. At this assembly the military organization of the State was completed, and the following patriotic resolution unanimously adopted:

"*Resolved*, That the Delegates from this Colony in the Continental Congress be empowered to concur with the Delegates from the other colonies in declaring independence and forming foreign alliances, reserving to this colony the sole and exclusive right of forming a constitution and laws for this colony."

This early action of the Provincial Congress of North Carolina is the first public declaration, by proper legislative State authority, on record, preceding the Virginia resolutions of the same character by more than a month, and of those of the National Congress at Philadelphia by nearly three months, now exulting in its *centennial celebration*. Near the close of the Revolution Col. Johnston acted for a considerable length of time as disbursing agent for the Western Division of the army. After the division of Tryon county in 1779 into Lincoln and Rutherford counties, he was elected to the Senate from the former county in 1780, '81 and '82. He also acted, for many years, as one of the magistrates of the county, and, by virtue of his office, was frequently called upon "*to make of twain one flesh*" in the holy bonds of matrimony."

Major John Davidson, who knew Col. Johnston long

and well, always summed up his estimate of his character by saying, "he was a most excellent man, and never shrunk from the performance of any duty when the welfare of his country demanded such service."

Several years previous to the Revolution Colonel Johnston married Jane Ewart, eldest daughter of Robert Ewart, a most worthy lady of Scotch-Irish descent. In 1775 Robert Ewart was appointed with Griffith Rutherford, John Brevard, Hezekiah Alexander, Benjamin Patton, and others, one of the Committee of Safety for the "Salisbury District," which included Rowan, Mecklenburg and other western counties. The marriage connections of other members of the Ewart family were as follows: Margaret married Joseph Jack; Mary married Robert Knox; Rachel married Thomas Bell; Betsy married Jonathan Price; Sallie married Thomas Hill; Robert married Margaret Adams At the battle of King's Mountain Robert Ewart, James Ewart, Robert Knox, Joseph Jack, Thomas Bell, Jonathan Price, Abram Forney, Peter Forney, and other brave spirits, were in the company commanded by Colonel James Johnston, and performed a conspicuous part in achieving the glorious victory on that occasion.

Previous to the war Colonel Johnston purchased valuable land on the Catawba river, one mile southwest of Toole's Ford, which became known in subsequent years as "Oak Grove" farm, deriving this name from several native denizens of the forest which stood near the family mansion and cast around their beneficent shade. Here he was blest with a numerous offspring, and permitted to enjoy much of that dignified ease and pleasures of a quiet home-life which his patriotic services had assisted to procure. For many years preceding his death he was a consistent member and Ruling Elder of the Presbyterian church at Unity, in Lincoln county. His large experience, general intelligence, disinterested benevolence, unsullied integrity and great decision of character, all combined to make him eminently useful in the different relations of society and secure for him the high regard and esteem of all who knew him.

Colonel Johnston died with calm resignation on the 23rd of July, 1805, aged about sixty-three years. His wife died on the 17th of August, 1795; and both, with other members of the family, are buried in a private cemetery on the "Oak Grove" farm.

GENEALOGY OF COL. JAMES JOHNSTON.

Col. James Johnston (sketch of his life and services previously given) married Jane Ewart, an estimable lady, daughter of Robert Ewart, of Scotch-Irish descent, and one of the early patriots of Mecklenburg county. Their descendants were, first generation:

1. Robert Johnston, who married Mary M., daughter of Capt. John Reid, a soldier of the Revolution, a Senator from Lincoln county in 1810 and 1811, and again in 1817 and 1818, and former proprietor of the Catawba Springs. He raised a family of twelve children, all of whom attained the age of maturity and survived their parents. The first death in the family was that of the late Rufus M. Johnston, of Charlotte. He was an industrious farmer, and upright member of society; for many years an elder of the Presbyterian church at Unity, and died with peaceful resignation on the 23d of May, 1854, in the seventy-seventh year of his age. His wife, Mary, died on the 30th of July, 1857, and both are buried in a private cemetery on the old homestead property, now owned by their grandson, John R. Johnston, Esq. His descendants were, 2d generation:

1. Sarah Johnston married Dr. Benjamin Johnson, of Virginia.

2. James A. Johnston married Jane Byers, of Iredell county.

3. Dr. Sidney X. Johnston married Harriet K. Connor, of Lincoln county.

4. Jane Johnston married first, John D. Graham, second, Dr. William B. McLean, of Lincoln county.

5. John R. Johnston married first, Delia Torrence, second, Laura E. Happoldt, of Burke county.

6. Robert Johnston married Caroline Shuford, of Lincoln county.

7. Dr. Thos. Johnston married Dorcas Luckey, of Mecklenburg county.

8. Harriet Johnston married William T. Shipp, of Gaston county.

9. Mary Johnston married Dr. William Davidson, of Mecklenburg county.

10. Martha Johnston married Col. J. B. Rankin, of McDowell county.

11. Col. William Johnston, present Mayor (1876) of Charlotte, married Ann Graham, of Mecklenburg county.

12. Rufus M. Johnston married Cecilia Latta, of York county, S. C.

2d. Margaret Ewart Johnston married Logan Henderson, Esq., youngest son of James Henderson, who moved from Pennsylvania to North Carolina at the first settlement of the country. He was the brother of Major Lawson Henderson, long and well known as one of the worthy citizens of Lincoln county, and of Col. James Henderson, a brave officer killed at the battle of New Orleans. The patriarchal ancestor, James Henderson, became the owner of a large body of land on the south fork of the Catawba river, in the present county of Gaston, embracing a valuable water-power, at which he erected a grist mill, then a new and useful institution. He lived to an extreme old age, and is buried on a high eminence near the eastern bank of the river, where a substantial stone wall surrounds the graves of himself, Adam Springs, the next owner of the property, and a few others.

In 1818, Logan Henderson joined the tide of emigration to Tennessee, and purchased much valuable land near Murfreesboro, in Rutherford county. In and near his last place of settlement, the most of his worthy descendants still reside. He died, after a brief illness, with calm composure, on the 8th of December, 1846, in the sixty-second year of his age. His wife survived him many years, and died with peaceful resignation on the 13th of August, 1863, in the seventy-fifth year of her age.

Their descendants were, second generation:

1. James F. Henderson married Amanda M. Vorhees, of Tennessee.
2. Violet C. Henderson married William F. Lytle, of Tennessee.
3. Jane E. Henderson married William S. Moore, of Tennessee.

The remaining children of Col. James Johnston were:

3. James Johnston, Jr., a promising young man, died near the age of maturity, in 1816, without issue.
4. Henry Johnston died in 1818 without issue.
5 Martha Johnston married Dr. James M. Burton. Soon after marriage they moved to Georgia, where they both died without issue.
6. Jane Johnston married Rev. John Williamson, pastor of Hopewell church, in Mecklenburg county, and died in 1817 without issue.
7. Catharine Johnston married John Hayes, Esq., who settled near Toole's Ford, on the Catawba river, about one mile from the old homestead of Col. James Johnston. He was a worthy christian citizen, long a subject of patient suffering from disease, for many years an elder of the Presbyterian church, and died peacefully on the

13th of April, 1846, aged seventy-two years. His wife, Catharine, a lady of great amiability and worth, died on the 17th of December, 1858, aged seventy-four years.

Their descendants were, second generation:

1. Jane C. Hayes married Dr. Sidney J. Harris, of Cabarrus county.

2. Martha E. Hayes married William Fulenwider, of Lincoln county.

3. Margaret J. Hayes married Dr. William Adams, of York county, S. C.

4. Minerva W. Hayes married Col. William Grier, of Mecklenburg county.

5. Elizabeth L. Hayes married Charles L. Torrence, of Rowan county.

6. John L. Hayes married Matilda Hutchinson, of Mecklenburg county.

7. Dr. William J. Hayes married Isabella Alexander, great-grand daughter of John McKnitt Alexander, a Signer and one of the Secretaries of the Mecklenburg Convention of the 20th of May, 1775.

8. Dr. William Johnston, youngest son of Col. James Johnston, married Nancy, daughter of Gen. Peter Forney, of Lincoln county.

Their descendants were, second generation:

1. Annie C. Johnston married Dr. Joseph W. Calloway, of Rutherford county.

2. Jane C. Johnston died at school in Greensboro, Guilford county.

3. Martha S. Johnston married Richard R. Hunley, Esq., of Alabama.

4. Capt. James F. Johnston, citizen of Charlotte.

5. Susan L. Johnston, citizen of Charlotte.

6. William P. Johnston, (died young).

7. Margaret Johnston married Col. Peter F. Hunley, of Alabama.

8. Gen. Robert D. Johnson married Johncie Evans, of Greensboro, N. C.

9. Dr. William H. Johnston married Cathleen Gage, of Chester county, S. C.

10. Capt. Joseph F. Johnston married Theresa Hooper, of Alabama.

11. Catharine Johnson died comparatively young.

12. Bartlett S. Johnston, now (1876) a merchant of New York city.

Most of the descendants of Colonel James Johnston performed a soldier's duty, and won military distinction in the late war between the States, but our prescribed limits forbid a more extended notice of their Confederate services. This will be the noble task of some future historian, illustrating, as it would, much heroic bravery, chivalric daring, and perseverance under difficulties seldom surpassed in the annals of any people. The preceding sketch and genealogy will serve to perpetuate the name and indicate the relationship of different branches of the family. It should awaken in every descendant emotions of veneration for the memory of a common patriarchal ancestor, who was one of the earliest and most unwavering patriots of the Revolutionary struggle for independence; contributed largely in council and in the field to its success, and whose mortal remains, with others of the family, now repose in the private cemetery of the "Oak Grove" farm, in Gaston county, N. C.

JACOB FORNEY, SR.

(Condensed from Wheeler's "Historical Sketches.")

Among the early settlers of Lincoln county (formerly Tryon) was Jacob Forney, Sr. He was the son of a Huguenot, and born about the year 1721. His life was checkered with a vicissitude of fortunes bordering on romance. At the revocation of the edict of Nantes, in 1685,.

his father fled from France, preferring self-expatriation to the renunciation of his religious belief, and settled in Alsace, on the Rhine where, under the enlightening influences of the reformation, freedom of opinion in matters of conscience was tolerated. The family name was originally spelt *Farney*, but afterwards, in Alsace, where the German language is generally spoken, was changed to *Forney*. Here his father died, leaving him an orphan when four years old. At the age of fourteen he left Alsace and went to Amsterdam in Holland. Becoming delighted whilst there with the glowing accounts which crossed the Atlantic respecting the New World, and allured with the prospect of improving his condition and enjoying still greater political and religious prvileges, he came to America by the first vessel having that destination, and settled in Pennsylvania. Here he remained industriously employed until until his maturity, when he returned to Germany to procure a small legacy. Having adjusted his affairs there he again embarked for America on board of a vessel bringing over many emigrants from the Canton of Berne in Switzerland. Among the number was a blithesome, rosy-cheeked damsel, buoyant with the chains of youth, who particularly attracted young Forney's attention. His acquaintance was soon made, and, as might be expected, a mutual attachment was silently but surely formed between two youthful hearts so congenial in feeling, and similarly filled with the spirit of adventure. Prosperous gales quickly wafted the vessel in safety to the shores of America, and soon after their arrival in Pennsylvania Jacob Forney and Mariah Bergner (for that was the fair one's name) were united in marriage. At this time the fertile lands and healthful climate of the South were attracting a numerous emigration from the middle colonies. Influenced by such inviting considerations, Forney joined the great tide of emigration a few years after his marriage, and settled in Lincoln county (formerly Tryon) about the year 1754.

The first settlers of Lincoln county suffered greatly by the depredations and occasional murders by the Cherokee Indians. On several occasions many of the inhabitants temporarily abandoned their homes, and removed to the more populous settlements east of the Catawba river Others, finding it inconvenient to remove, constructed rude forts for their mutual defence. A repetition of these incursions having occurred a few years after Forney's arrival, he removed his family to a place of safety east of the river until the Indians could be severely chastised by military force. On the next day he returned to his former residence, accompanied by two of his neighbors, to search for his cattle. After proceeding about a mile from home they spied a small Indian just ahead of them running rapidly, and not far from the spot now well known as the "Rocky Spring Camp Ground." Forney truly suspected more Indians were in the immediate vicinity. After progressing but a short distance, he and his party discovered, in an open space beyond them, ten or twelve Indians, a part of whom, at least, were armed with guns, apparently waiting their approach. Forney being a good marksman, and having a courage equal to any emergency, was in favor of giving them battle immediately, but his two companions overruled him, contending it would be impossible to disperse such a large number. It was therefore deemed advisable to retreat, and make their way to the fort, about two miles in their rear, where several families had assembled. After proceeding a short distance the Indians approached somewhat nearer and fired upon the party but without effect. Forney directed his companies to reserve their fire until the Indians approached sufficiently near to take a sure and deadly aim, and maintain an orderly retreat in the direction of the fort. Soon after they commenced retreating the Indians again fired upon them and unfortunately one of the party, Richards, was dangerously wounded. At this critical moment, when one or two well directed fires might have repulsed their enemy, the courge of F——, the other companion, failed him, and he made his *rapid departure*. Forney, however, continued his retreat, assisting his wounded companion as much as he could, and, although fired upon several times, managed to keep the Indians at some distance off by presenting, his unerring rifle when their timidity was manifested by falling down in the grass, or taking shelter behind the trees, each one, no doubt, supposing the well-aimed shot might fell him to the earth. At length poor Richards, becoming faint from loss of blood, and seeing the imminent danger of his friend's life, directed Forney to leave him, and, if possible, save himself. This advice he reluctantly complied with and pursued his course to the fort. But the Indians did not pursue him much farther, being probably satified with the murder of the wounded Richards.

In this unequal contest Forney only received a small wound on the back of his left hand, but, on examination, discovered that several bullets had pierced his clothes. This adventure shows what cool, determined bravery may effect under the most discouraging circumstances, and that an individual may sometimes providentially escape although made the object of a score of bullets or other missiles of destruction. When he reached the fort he found the occupants greatly frightened, having heard the repeated firing. After this adventure and narrow escape became generally known, a belief was widely entertained by the surrounding community that Forney was *bullet-proof*. It was even affirmed, and received *additions by repeating*, that after he reached the fort and unbuttoned his vest, a *handful of bullets dropped out*. In subsequent years Forney was accustomed to smile at this innocent credulity of his neighbors but frequently remarked that the impression of his being *bullet-proof* was of great service to him on more than one occasion preceding and during the Revolutionary war.

Few persons during the war suffered heavier losses than Jacob Forney. By persevering industry and strict economy he had surrounded himself and family with all the comforts, and, to some extent, luxuries of the substantial farmer. When Cornwallis marched through Lincoln county in the winter of 1781, endeavoring to overtake Morgan with his large number of prisoners captured at the Cowpens, he was arrested in his progress by the swollen waters of the Catawba river. Being thus foiled in his expectations, supposing he had Morgan *almost in his grasp*, Cornwallis fell back about five miles from the river to Forney's plantation, having been conducted there by a Tory well acquainted with the neighborhood. Here Cornwallis remained encamped for three days, consuming, in the meantime Forney's entire stock of cattle, hogs, sheep, geese, chickens, a large amount of forage, forty gallons of brandy, &c. His three horses were carried off, and many thousands of rails and other property destroyed. But the extent of his losses did not end here. Cornwallis had been informed that Forney had a large amount of money concealed somewhere in his premises, and that if diligent search were made it might be readily found. This information set the British soldiers to work, and, aided by the Tory conductor's suggestions, they finally succeeded in finding his gold, silver and jewelry buried in his distillery, the greater portion of which he had brought with him from Germany. Whilst this work of search was going on without, his Lordship was quietly occupying the upper story of the family mansion, making it his headquarters. Forney and his wife being old, were *graciously* allowed the privilege of living in the basement. As soon as he was informed his gold, silver and jewelry were found, amounting to one hundred and seventy pounds sterling, he was so exasperated for the moment that he seized his gun and rushed to the stair steps with the determination to kill Cornwallis, but his wife quickly followed and intercepted him, thus preventing the most deplorable consequences—the loss of his own life, and perhaps that of his family. But the prudent advice of his wife, "Heaven's last, best gift to man," had its proper, soothing effect, and caused him to desist from his impetuous purpose. It is hardly necessary to inform the reader he was punished in this severe manner because he was a zealous supporter of the cause of freedom, and his three sons were then in the "rebel army."

The log house in which his lordship made his headquarters for *three days* and *four nights* is still in existence, though removed, many years since, from its original site to a more level location in the immediate vicinity. In this humble building he, no doubt, cogitated upon the speedy subjugation of the "rebels," and that subsequent glorification which awaits the successful hero. Little did Cornwallis then allow himself to think that he and his whole army, in less than nine months from that time, would have to surrender to the "rebel army," under Washington, as prisoners of war!

It is said Cornwallis, after finishing his morning repast upon the savory beef and fowls of the old patriot's property, would come down from his headquarters, up stairs, and pass along his lines of soldiers, extending for more than a mile in a northwest direction, and reaching to the adjoining plantation of his son Peter, who kept "bachelor's hall," but was then absent, with his brother Abram, battling for their country's freedom. About midway of the extended lines, and only a few steps from the road on which the British army was encamped, several granite rocks protrude from the ground. One is about four feet high, with a rounded, weather-worn top—a convenient place to receive his lordship's cloak. Another rock, nearly adjoining, is about two feet and a half high, with a flat surface gently descending, and five feet across. At this spot Cornwallis was accustomed to dine daily with some of his officers upon the rich variety of food seized during his stay, and washing it all down, as might be aptly inferred, with a portion of the forty gallons of captured brandy previously mentioned. This smooth-faced rock, on which his lordship and officers feasted for three days, is known in the neighborhood to this day as "Cornwallis' Table." On visiting this durable remembrancer of the past quite recently, the writer looked around for a piece of some broken plate or other vessel, but sought in vain. The only mementoes of this natural table he could bear away were a few chips from its outer edge, without seriously mutilating its weather-beaten surface, now handsomely overspread with *moss* and *lichen*. Where once the tramp and bustle of a large army resounded, all is now quiet and silent around, save the singing of birds and gentle murmers of the passing breeze in the surrounding forest.

After Cornwallis left, Forney ascertained that the Tory informer was one of his near neighbors with whom he had always lived on terms of friendship. Considering the heavy losses he had sustained attributable to his agency, he could not overlook the enormity of the offence, and accordingly sent a message to the Tory that he must leave the neighborhood, if not, he would shoot him at *first sight.* The Tory eluded him for several days by lying out, well knowing that the stern message he had received *meant action.* At length Forney, still keeping up his search, came upon him unawares and *fast asleep.* He was immediately aroused from his slumbers, when beholding his perilous situation, he commenced pleading most earnestly for his life, and promised to leave the neighborhood. Forney could not resist such touching appeals to his mercy, and kindly let him off. In a few days afterward the Tory, true to his promise, left the neighborhood and never returned.

Jacob Forney, Sr., died in 1806, aged eighty-five. In his offspring flowed the blood of the Huguenot and the Swiss—people illustrating in their history all that is grand in heroic suffering and chivalric daring. His wife survived him several years; both were consistent and worthy members of the Lutheran Church, and are buried in the "old Dutch Meeting House" graveyard, about three miles from the family homestead, and near Macpelah Church.

GEN. PETER FORNEY.

Gen. Peter Forney, second son of Jacob Forney, Sr., was born in Tyron county (now Lincoln) in April, 1756. His father was the son of a French Huguenot, and his mother Swiss. His origin is thus traced to a noble class of people whose heroic bravery, unparalleled suffering and ardent piety are closely connected in all lands where their lots have been cast with the promotion of civil and religious liberty.

Gen. Forney was one of the earliest and most unwavering Whigs of the revolutionary struggle. He first entered the service about the first of June, 1876, in Capt. James Johnston's company and Col. William Graham's regiment. The command marched to Fort McFadden, near the present town of Rutherfordton, and found that the greater portion of the inhabitants had fled for protection against the Cherokee Indians. After remaining a short time at the fort, he joined a detachment of about one hundred men in pursuit of the Indians, under Captains Johnston, Cook and Hardin. They marched about one hundred miles, and not being able to overtake them, the detachment returned to the fort. In 1777, Gen. Forney voluntered as a Lieut. in Capt. James Reid's company, for the purpose of quelling a considerable body of Tories assemble not far from the South Carolina line. The detachment was commanded by Col. Charles M'Lean, who marched into South Carolina and pursued after the Tories until it was ascertained Gen. Pickens, considerably in advance with his forces, had commenced the pursuit of the same, and was too far ahead to be overtaken. The detachment then returned to North Carolina, and, having taken several prisioners on the way, suspected of being inimical to the American cause, Capt. Reid was ordered to convey them to Salisbury. Gen. Forney still remained in service, and attached himself to Capt. Kuykendal's company until some time in June. After this time he was frequently out in short expeditions for the purpose of intimidating and keeping down the rising spirit of the Tories, and arresting them, whenever the good of the country seemed to require it. In the fall of 1779 Gen. Forney voluntered with a party to go to Kentucky (Harrod Station) and after staying there a short time returned home. At this time, there being a call made upon the militia to march to the relief of Charleston, he voluntered as a Lieut. in Capt. Neals' company, which was ordered to rendezvous at Charlotte, whilst there, waiting for the assemblage of more troops, he was appointed Captain by Col. Hampton and Lieut. Col. Hambright, Capt. Neal being superseded in his command on account of intemperance. From Charlotte the assembled forces march by way of Camden to Charleston, under the command of Cols. Hall, Dickson and Major John Nelson, continental officers. The militia of North Carolina, at the time, was commanded by Gen. Lillington. The term of service of Gen Forney's company having expired shortly after his arrival at Charleston, and the British being in considerable force off that city, he induced the greater portion of his company to again volunteer for about six weeks longer, until fresh troops, then expected, would come to their relief. In the spring of 1780 Gen. Forney, immediately after his return from Charleston, volunteered under Lieut. Col. Hambright, and went in pursuit of Col. Floyd, a Tory leader on Fishing Creek, S. C. Hearing of their approach Floyd hastily fled to Rocky Mount, and the expedition, not being able to accomplish anything more at that time, returned to North Carolina On the night of his arrival at home Gen. Forney was informed that the Tories, under Col. John Moore, were embodied in strong force at Ramsour's Mill near the present town of Lincolnton. On the next day he left home and went up the Catawba river, when, encountering a considerable body of Tories near Mountain Creek, he returned and immediately hastened to inform Gen. Rutherford. He found him encamped at Col. Dickson's, three miles northwest of Tuckaseege Ford, with a strong force. He then attached himself to his army, and marched early next morning to Ramsour's, but did not reach there until two hours after the battle, the Tories having been completely defeated by Col. Locke and his brave associates. The dead and wounded were still lying where they had fallen, and Gen. Rutherford's forces assisted in the closing duties of that brilliant victory. Never afterwards in that county did Tory-loyalism present a formidable opposition to the final success of the American arms. Of the Whig officers the brave Captains Falls, Dobson, Smith, Knox, Bowman, Sloan and Armstrong were killed, and Captains Houston and McKissick wounded. Of the Tories, Captains Murray, Cumberland and Warlick were killed, and Capt. Carpenter wounded.

During the latter part of the year 1780 Gen. Forney was almost constantly in service in different portions of county. When Cornwallis entered the county in the last week of January, 1781, endeavoring to overtake Gen. Morgan with his prisoners captured at the Cowpens, he was providentially arrested in his march by the swollen waters of the Catawba river. He then fell back and encamped three days on the plantation of Jacob Forney, Sr., a well to-do farmer and *noted Whig*, consuming in the meantime, destroying or carrying off, every thing of value belonging to father or son, (Gen. Forney,) consisting of three horses, a large stock of cattle, hogs, sheep, fowls, forage, &c.

After the British army moved from this encampment, Gen. Forney commanded a company and placed themselves on the eastern bank of the river, endeavoring to oppose their crossing, and remained there until the light troops, under Col. Hall, effected a passage at Cowan's Ford. The militia being repulsed, and Gen. Davidson killed, he fled to Adam Torrence's, hotly pursued by Tarleton's troop of cavalry. At this place he found a considerable body of militia, but in great confusion in consequence of the death of Gen. Davidson, and greatly disheartened. After giving the British one discharge of their arms, and killing several, the militia were repulsed, with small loss, and fled in all directions. Gen. Forney then retreated across the Yadkin, and remained on Abbot's creek about six weeks, during which time he had no regular command, and co-operated with other soldiers, whenever it appeared any advantage could be rendered to the American cause.

In the spring of 1871, Gen. Forney commenced repairing his plantation which the British had entirely destroyed, together with that of his father's in the immediate vicinity, whilst encamped there. He remained at home until a call was made upon the militia to march to the relief of Wilmington, when he again volunteered and commanded a company of dragoons, associated with Captains White and Lemmonds. In this expedition Charles Polk was appointed Major of dragoons, Gen. Rutherford in chief command, and marched through the disaffected country around Cross creek, (now Fayetteville,) and on to the immediate vicinity of Wilmington. Here Gen Rutherford created a belief before his arrival that his forces were much larger than they really were. In consequence of this belief Major Craig, in command of the post, deeming his situation then insecure, immediately evacuated Wilmington and fled to Charleston. This was the only post in North Carolina held by the British, and with the flight of Craig all military operations ceased within her borders· This campaign closed the Revolutionary services of a gallant soldier and faithful patriot in the cause of American freedom.

In 1783 Gen. Forney married Nancy, daughter of David Abernathy, a lady of great moral worth and christian benevolence. The natural goodness of her heart made her the "cheerful giver." Her numerous acts of charity were free of all ostentation, and flowed silently forth like gentle streams from a pure fountain, imparting new vigor and refreshing everything in their course. After the close of the war, full of youthful enterprise, and anxious to engage in some useful business, he fortunately became the owner of the "Big Iron Ore Bank," seven miles east of Lincolnton. This is one of the best and most extensive deposits of iron ore, of the variety known as "magnetic," in the State. Aware of the inexhaustible supply of ore, Gen. Forney disposed of interests to other parties (Brevard and Graham) and they immediately proceeded to erect a furnace (called Vesuvius) on Anderson's creek, now owned by the heirs of the late J. M. Smith, Esq. After a few years the copartnership was dissolved, separate sites were purchased by Forney and Brevard, on Leeper's creek, additional furnaces were erected and thus the manufacture of cast metal, under its various forms, was vigorously and successfully carried into operation. Gen. Forney commenced building his ironworks in 1787, associated for several years with his brother Abram, laid in a supply of the necessary stock, (ore and coal,) as recorded in a small account book, produced hammered iron in his forge on the 26th of August, 1788. This is believed to be the *first* manufacture of iron in the western part of the State. Here Gen. Forney permanently settled for life, and prospered in his useful calling. His residence received the name of "Mount Welcome," an appellation appropriately bestowed, as his future history manifestly proved. The poor and needy of his own neighborhood were frequently the beneficiaries of his bounty; and the weary traveler was at all times made "welcome," and entertained beneath his hospitable roof "without money, and without price."

Gen. Forney was elected as a member to the House of Commons from 1794 to 1796 inclusively, and to the State Senate in 1801 and 1802. He was again called out from the shades of private life and elected as a Representative to Congress from 1813 to 1815. He also served as Elector in the Presidential campaigns of Jefferson, Madison, Monroe and Jackson. With these repeated evidences of popular favor his public services ended. Frequent solicitations were tendered to him afterwards, all of which he declined. The infirmities of old age were now rapidly stealing upon him, and rendering him unfit for the proper discharge of public duties. For several years previous to his decease his mental vigor and corporeal strength greatly failed. After a short illness, without visible pain or suffering, he quietly breathed his last on February 1st, 1834, in the seventy-eighth year of his age. Generosity, candor, integrity and freedom from pride or vain show were prominent traits in his character. Let his name and his deeds and his sterling virtues be duly appreciated and faithfully imitated by the rising generation.

MAJOR ABRAM FORNEY.

Major Abram Forney, youngest son of Jacob Forney, Sr., was born in Tryon county, (now Lincoln) in October, 1758. His father was a Huguenot, and his mother Swiss. His origin is thus connected with a noble race of people who were driven into exile rather than renounce their religious belief under the persecutions which disgraced the reign of Louis XIV, of France. Major Forney first entered the service about the 25th of June, 1776, as one of the drafted militia in Capt. James Johnston's company, and Col. William Graham's regiment. His company was then ordered to reinforce the troops at Fort McFadden, near the present town of Rutherfordton, and remained there until about the 1st of August, when he returned home to prepare for the expedition against the Cherokee Indians. The militia of Mecklenburg, Rowan Lincoln and other counties were called out by orders from Gen. Rutherford, who marched to Pleasant Gardens, where he was joined by other forces. From that place Major Forney marched into the Nation with a detachment under Col. William Sharpe as far as the Hiwassee river, where they met with a portion of Gen. Williamson's army from South Carolina. The expedition was completely successful; the Indians were routed, their towns destroyed, a few prisoners taken, and they were compelled to sue for peace. The prisoners and property taken by Gen. Rutherford's forces were turned over to Gen. Williamson, as falling within his military jurisdiction. The expedition then left the Nation, and he reached home on the 13th of October, 1776.

In February, 1777, Major Forney again volunteered as a private in Capt. James Reid's company for the purpose of quelling some Tories who had, or were about to embody themselves near the South Carolina line. The detachment was commanded by Col. Charles McLean. The

Tories were commanded by a certain John Moore, whom Col. McLean pursued into South Carolina until he ascertained Gen. Pickens was engaged in the same pursuit, and too far ahead to be overtaken. The detachment then returned to North Carolina, and having taken several prisoners on the way, suspected of being inimical to the American cause, Major Forney was ordered to take them to Salisbury. After this service he was dismissed and returned home in April, 1777.

At different times subsequently Major Forney volunteered in several short expeditions as far as the South Carolina line, for the purpose of intimidating and keeping down the rising spirit of the Tories, who were numerous in this section of country, and required a strict vigilance to hold them in a state of subjection. Early in June, 1780, when a call was made upon the militia, he volunteered in Capt. John Baldridge's company, marched to a temporary rendezvous at Ramsour's, and thence to Espey's, where they joined other troops under the command of Col. William Graham and Lieut. Col. Hambright. The united forces then proceeded to Lincoln "old Court House," near Moses Moore's, the father of Col. John Moore, the Tory leader, and marched and countermarched through that section of country. At this time, hearing that Ferguson was coming on with a strong force, it was deemed advisable to retreat and cross the Catawba at Tuckaseege Ford. Col. Graham then marched with his forces to that place, and there met some other troops from South Carolina, under Col. Williams, retreating before Cornwallis, whose army had just reached Charlotte. The two forces then united under Col. Williams and marched up the west side of the Catawba river, and thence across the country in a circuitous direction towards South Carolina in the rear of Ferguson, and thus were enabled to fall in with the "over mountain" troops under Campbell, Shelby, Cleaveland, Sevier, and others, at the Cowpens, afterwards rendered famous by the battle fought there. The officers having agreed upon the plan of operations, a select portion of the combined forces marched rapidly in pursuit of Ferguson, and found him encamped on King's Mountain on the 7th of October, 1780. The action immediately commenced, and resulted in one of the most decisive victories gained during the Revolutionary struggle, and constitutes the *turning point* of final triumph in the cause of American freedom. Soon after the battle, Major Forney and Capt. James Johnston were appointed to number the dead on the British side. They soon found Ferguson at the foot of the hill, dead, and covered with blood. His horse having been shot from under him, he continued to advance, sword in hand, cheering on his men by word and example, until five or six balls pierced his body and sealed his fate. Major Forney often stated he picked up Ferguson's sword, intending to keep it as a trophy, but some subordinate officer getting hold of it, made off with it, and thus deprived him of his prize. An incident connected with the closing scenes of this memorable battle is here worthy of being recorded:

As Major Forney was surveying the prisoners, through the guard surrounding them, he spied one of his neighbors, who only a short time before the battle had been acting with the Whigs, but had been persuaded by some of his Tory acquaintances to join the king's troops. Upon seeing him Major Forney exclaimed, "is that you, Simon?" The reply quickly came back, "Yes, it is, Abram, and I beg you to get me out of this *bull pen;* if you do, I will promise never to be caught in such a scrape again." Accordingly, when it was made to appear on the day of trial that he had been unfortunately wrought upon by some Tory neighbors, such a mitigation of his disloyalty was presented as to induce the officers holding the court-martial to overlook his offence and set him at liberty. Soon afterward, true to his promise, he joined his former

Whig comrades, marched to the battle of Guilford and made a good soldier to the end of the war.

Near the close of the year 1780, hearing that Col. Morgan was preparing to go upon an expedition into South Carolina, Major Forney attached himself to the command of Capt. James Little, with the intention of joining his forces, but did not come up with them until after the battle of the Cowpens. He then returned home, and remained there until the 27th of January, 1781, when all the Whigs in his section of the country had to fly before Cornwallis in pursuit of Morgan with his large number of prisoners on their way to Virginia. Major Forney then crossed the Catawba, and joined a detachment of troops on its eastern bank under Capt. Henderson, placed as a guard by Gen. Davidson at Cowan's Ford, where it was expected the British might attempt to cross. Having stood guard for some time at this point, and being relieved, he went a short distance to a house to procure refreshments of which he was much in need, and was not present when the guard was repulsed, and Gen. Davidson killed. He then fled with the other troops to Adam Torrence's, about ten miles distant, where a considerable body of militia had assembled, but were greatly disheartened on account of the death of Gen. Davidson. The day was damp and unfavorable to the use of firearms. The militia, without much order, fired once at the British, killing seven, and then dispersed in all directions. He then retreated until he reached Gen. Greene's army, in Guilford county. From this place he was advised to return home, and in doing so was furnished with a ticket to procure provisions on the way.

On the 25th of March, 1781, the militia being again called out, Major Forney attached himself to the command of Capt. Samuel Espey, acting as a Sergeant. The company then joined a detachment of militia under Gen. Thomas Polk, marched into South Carolina, and came up with Gen. Greene's army at Rugeley's Mill. The army was then placed under the command of Col. Dudley, and remained under him until Gen. Greene commenced his march to the post of Ninety Six. At this time, Capt. Espey being compelled to leave the service in consequence of a wound received at the battle of King's Mountain, went home with a part of his company, and then Major Forney joined the command of Capt. Jack, still acting as Sergeant. Soon afterward the expedition returned to Charlotte, when he was dismissed by Capt. Jack, about the 1st of July, 1781.

In a short time afterward, Major Forney attached himself to the company of Capt. John Weir, under orders to proceed to Wilmington. His company crossed the Catawba at Tuckaseege Ford on the 1st day of November, 1781, and encamped three or four miles beyond the river on the road leading to Charlotte. On the next day the company marched through Charlotte and encamped at Col. Alexander's, who had been ordered to take command of the detachment. Whilst there intelligence was received of the return of Gen Rutherford's forces. Major Forney was then sent to that officer for orders; receiving these, the company recrossed the Catawba. Capt. Loftin then took command in place of Capt. Weir, who had resigned and returned home. The company proceeded to form several stations in the county, and arrested some *suspected* persons. Capt. Thomas McGee having assumed command in place of Loftin, resigning, marched with the prisoners to Salisbury, and delivered them up to the proper authorities on the 31st of December, 1781.

Again, when a call was made upon the militia in 1782, to march against the Cherokee Indians, Major Forney was placed in command of a company, and ordered to rendezvous at Ramsour's Mill. He remained there from about the 1st of June until the 1st of August, when he marched to the head of the Catawba and joined the troops of

Burke and Wilkes. He then attached his company to Col. Joseph McDowell's regiment, marched across the Blue Ridge and met with the Rutherford troops on the Swannanoa river, under the command of Col. Miller. After the junction of the Rutherford troops, the expedition, under Gen. Charles McDowell, marched into the Nation, nearly on the trail of Gen. Rutherford in 1776, but proceeded some farther than where his army halted. The expedition was entirely successful; took a few prisoners, returned home and were dismissed in October, 1782.

This was the last service of a brave soldier, who fought long, and fought well, for the freedom of his country. Major Abram Forney died on the 22nd day of July, 1849, in the ninety-first year of his age.

His only surviving son, Capt. Abram Earhardt Forney, at the present time, (1876,) is still living at the old homestead, has already passed his "three score years and ten;" is an industrious farmer, and worthy citizen of Lincoln county.

REMARKS.

Among the curious revolutionary mementoes that Capt. A. E. Forney, son of Major Abram Forney, has in his possession is a small *leather memorandum pocket-book*, filled originally with twenty-four blank leaves; also a *powder horn*, made by his father preparatory to an expedition to the mountains. The front, or opening sides, is handsomely ornamented with numerous small stars, arranged diagonally across the surface and around the borders. The back side has the patriot's initials, A. F. distinctly impressed, and immediately beneath, the year 1775, the whole displaying considerable artistic skill; numerous entries appear on its pages, made at different times, and without reference to strict chronological order; brief notices of military and agricultural matters and occassionally a birth, death or marriage are harmoniously blended. On page 5 is this entry: "The first snow in the year 1775, was on December the 23rd day, and it was very deep."

On the same page it is recorded: "April the 28th day, Old John Seagle departed this world, 1780." On page 11 this entry appears: "May the 3rd day I sowed flax seed in the year 1779, and other entries relating to the same agricultural avocation are interspersed through the little book. The culture of flax was then an indispensible employment. Our soldiers then wore *hunting shirts*, made of flax, to the battle fields. Cotton was not generally cultivated until twenty years later. On page 24 it is recorded: "May the 1st day there was a frost in the year 1779." On page 22 is this entry: "Be it remembered the battle between the Whigs and Tories (at Ramsour's) was fought on the 20th day of June 1780." (Signed) Abram Forney. Had any doubt arisen as to the precise date of this important battle it could have been ascertained from this memorandum pocket-book of this distinguished patriotic soldier. On page 13 is an entry which, on its realization, sent a thrill of joy throughout the land: "April the 17th day, great talk of peace in the year 1783." The definite treaty was not signed until the 30th of September following, and a new Republic sprung into existence.

GENEALOGY OF THE FORNEY FAMILY.

Jacob Forney, Sr., (sketch of his life previously given) married Mariah Bergner, a native of Switzerland. Their descendants were three sons, Jacob, Peter and Abram, and four daughters. Catherine married Abram Earhardt, Elizabeth married John Young, Christina married David Abernathy and Susan married John D. Abernathy. Of the descendants of the daughters, who left the State soon after marriage, little is known.

Jacob Forney, the eldest son, married Mary Corpening, of Burke county, N. C. Soon after the Revolutionary war he purchased a valuable track of land on Upper creek, five miles northwest of Morganton, on which he settled and raised a large family. He lived a long, quiet and useful life. His tombstone, in a private cemetery on the old homestead property, bears this inscription: "Sacred to the memory of Jacob Forney, born Nov. 6th, 1754, died Nov. 7th, 1840, aged eighty-six years and one day." He had eleven children:

1. Elizabeth E. Forney, (died young.)
2. Thomas J. Forney married S. C. Harris, of Montgomery county.
3. Isaac Newton Forney, married M. L. Corpening, of Burke county.
4. Marcus L. Forney married S. Connelly, of Burke county.
5. Albert G. Forney married Eglantine Logan, of Rutherford county.
6. Fatima E. Forney married H. Alexander Tate, of Burke county.
7. Peter Bergner Forney married M. S. Connelly, of Caldwell county.
8. James Harvey Forney married Emily Logan, of Rutherford county.
9. Daniel J. Forney married S. C. Ramsour, of Lincoln county.
10. Mary L. Forney married W. P. Reinhardt, of Catawba county.
11. Catharine S. Forney married A. T. Bost, of Catawba county.

2. *General Peter Forney*, (sketch of his life previously given) married Nancy, daughter of David Abernathy, of Lincoln county. He had twelve children:

1. Daniel M. Forney married Harriet Brevard, of Lincoln county.
2. Mary Forney married Christian Reinhardt, of Lincoln county.
3. Moses Forney, (died in Alabama unmarried.)

4. Jacob Forney married Sarah Hoke, of Lincoln county.

5. Joseph Forney (died comparatively young.)

6. Eliza Forney married 1st, Henry T. Webb, Esq., of North Carolina, and 2nd, Dr. John Meek, of Alabama.

7. Susan Forney married Bartlett Shipp, Esq., of Lincoln county.

8. Lavinia Forney married John Fulenwider, of Lincoln county.

9. Nancy Forney married Dr. Willian Johnston, of Lincoln county.

10. Caroline Forney married Ransom G. Hunley, of South Carolina.

11. Sophia G. Forney married Dr. C. L. Hunter, of Lincoln county.

12. J. Monroe Forney married Sarah Fulenwider, of Cleaveland county.

3. *Major Abram Forney*, (sketch of his life previously given,) married Rachel Gabriel, of Lincoln county. He only had two children: 1. Abram Earhardt Forney, a worthy citizen of the same county, and now (1876) considerably past his "three score years and ten," and 2., John W. Forney, who died comparatively young.

Daniel M. Forney, eldest son of Gen. Peter Forney, received the appointment of Major in the war of 1812, and proceeded to the scene of conflict in Canada. He served as a Representative to Congress from 1815 to 1818, and as a Senator from Lincoln county to the State Legislature from 1823 to 1826. In 1834, he moved to Lowndes county, Ala., where he died in October, 1847, in the sixty-fourth year of his age. He had seven children:

1. Eloise Forney married Gen. Jones Withers, of Mobile, Ala.

2. Mariah Forney married Judge Moore, of Alabama.

3. Alexander B. Forney, (died comparatively young.)

4. Harriet Forney, (died young.)

5. Macon Forney, (died young.)
6. Susan Forney, married Dr. B. C. Jones, of Alabama.
7. Emma Forney married Col. M. Smith, of Alabama.

2. *Mary Forney*, who married Christian Reinhardt, had five sons and four daughters. One of the sons, Franklin M. Reinhardt, who remained in the State, was a worthy member of society, highly esteemed by all who knew him, and remarkable for his benevolent disposition and liberality to the poor. He married Sarah, daughter of the late David Smith, of Lincoln county. He died on the 12th of June, 1869, in the sixty-second year of his age.

3. *Jacob Forney*, who married Sarah Hoke, daughter of the late Daniel Hoke, formerly of Lincoln county, N. C., was an enterprising, useful and highly respected member of society, possessed many noble traits of character, and raised a large and interesting family. He moved in 1835, from Lincoln county to Alabama, and settled in Jacksonville, where he died on the 24th of April, 1856, in the sixty-ninth, year of his age. He had nine children:

1. Daniel P. Forney, of Jacksonville, Alabama.
2. Joseph B. Forney married Mary Whitaker, of Alabama.
3. William H. Forney married Eliza Woodward, of Alabama.
4. Barbara Ann Forney married P. Rowan, Esq., of Alabama.
5. Gen. John H. Forney married Septima Rutledge, grand-daughter of Edward Rutledge, one of the signers of the Declaration of Independence.
6. Emma E. Forney married 1st, Col. Rice, 2nd, Rev. Thomas A. Morris.
7. Col. George H. Forney, (killed at Spotsylvania Court House, Va.)
8. Catharine Amelia Forney, married J. M. Wylie, Esq., of Alabama.

9. Mariah Louisa Forney, ("Ida") married R. D. Williams, Esq., of Alabama.

The sons of Jacob Forney won military distinction and renown in the late Confederate war. Our prescribed limits forbid a more extended notice of their gallant services. Their chivalric courage and "deeds of noble daring" will justly claim the careful study of some future historian.

4. *Eliza Forney* married 1st, Henry Y. Webb, Esq., of Granville county, N. C. He was educated at the University of North Carolina, was a member of the Legislature in 1817; appointed by President Monroe, Territorial Judge of Alabama; elected to the same position by the State Convention of 1819, and died in September, 1823.

Eliza Forney, by first marrage with Henry Y. Webb, Esq., had five children.

1. Frances Ann Webb married Col. John R. Hampton, formerly of Charlotte, N. C., now a worthy and highly respected citizen of Bradley county, Ark. His wife Frances, died in 1842, leaving three children, of whom only one, (Susan) widow of Dr. Greene Newton, at present survives.

2. William P. Webb, Esq., married Martha Bell, of Alabama. His children are:

1. James E. Webb, of Hale county, Alabama, married Zemma Creswell.

2. Frances E. Webb married Robert Crawford, of St. Louis, Mo.

3. Judge William H. Webb married "Donna Louise Abrigo," of Monterey, Mexico.

4. Rev. Frank Bell Webb, pastor of the Presbyterian church, at Union Springs, Ala.

5. Wert Webb, commission merchant of St. Louis, Mo., and two daughters, now in their minority.

3. Col. James D. Webb, of the 51st Alabama Regiment, married Jessie Walton. He was frequently a member of the Legislature of Alabama, and was highly esteemed for his purity of character. He died of wounds

received in battle, July 3rd, 1863, near Winchester, Tenn., where he is buried. He left a widow and six children.

4. Susan E. Webb died in 1832, at the age of twelve years.

5. Dr. Henry Y. Webb, married Elizabeth S. Alexander, a great-grand draughter of Abraham Alexander, Chairman of the Mecklenburg Convention of the 20th of May, 1775. Most of the Alexanders in the United States have descended from seven brothers who fled from Scotland to the North of Ireland on account of civil and religious persecutions. From 1725 to 1740, many of their descendants emigrated to America, one of whom was William Alexander, who inherited an estate and earldom in Scotland, and became Lord Stirling, a distinguished General in the Revolutionary war. After a short sojourn in Pennsylvania, many of the Alexander families and their descendants emigrated south, and formed numerous settlements in Mecklenburg and adjoining counties.

Descendants of Eliza Forney (2nd marriage) and Dr. John Meek were:

1. Samuel T. Meek, married Miss Cabeen, of South Carolina.

2. John A. Meek, of Franklin, Ky., married Miss Newton, of Arkansas.

3. Lavinia Meek married, 1st, Col. Harry Williams, of Louisiana and 2nd, E. B. Cryer, of Trenton, Louisiana.

4. Nancy, and 5, Sarah Meek.

Bartlett Shipp, who married Susan Forney, served in the State Legislature from 1824 to 1830, and was one of the delegates from Lincoln county in 1835, to amend the constitution. He was an able lawyer, had a large practice for many years, and died in Lincolnton, on the 26th of May, 1869, in the eighty fourth year of his age. His descendants were:

1. Eliza Shipp married William Preston Bynum, Esq., at present one of the Judges of the Supreme Court of North Carolina.

2. William M. Shipp, Esq., married 1st, Catharine Cameron, of Hillsboro, and 2d, Margaret Iredell, of Raleigh.

3. Susan Shipp married V. Q. Johnson, Esq., of Virginia.

Descendants of John Fulenwider and Lavinia Forney were:

1. John M. Fulenwider married Frances Hudson, of Alabama.

2. Eliza Fulenwider married L. M. Rudisill, Esq., of Catawba county, N. C.

3. Robert Fulenwider married Mary Sellers of Alabama.

4. Daniel Fulenwider married Mary Ann Leslie of Alabama.

5. Jane Fulhnwider married Joshua Kirby, of Alabama.

6. Fannie Fulenwider, married James Gore, of Alabama.

7. Louisa Fulenwider married Robert Loyd, of Alabama.

8. Mary Fulenwider, (unmarried.)

For descendants of Dr. William Johnston and Nancy Forney see " Genealogy of Colonel James Johnston."

Descendants of Ransom G. Hunley and Carolina Forney, were:

1. Richard R. Hunley married Martha S. Johnston, of Lincoln county.

2. Col. Peter F. Hunley married Margaret Johnston, of Lincoln county.

3. Mary Hunley married Gen. E. W. Martin, of Alabama.

4. Annie Hunley married Alfred Agee, Esq., of Alabama.

5. Ransom Hunley, (died young.)

Descndants of Dr. C. L. Hunter and Sophia G. Forney, were:

1. Nancy Jane Hunter, (died young.)

2. Caroline Elmina Hunter, (died young.)

Henry Stanhope Hunter (severely wounded in the late war.)

4. Capt. George William Hunter, mortally wounded in the battle at Chancellorsville, Va.

5. Sophia F. Hunter married John H. Sharp, Esq., of Norfolk, Va.

CHAPTER VI.

GASTON COUNTY.

Gaston county was formed in 1846, from Lincoln county, and derives its name from William Gaston, one of the most distinguished men of North Carolina, and late one of the Judges of the Supreme Court. In the language of one who knew him well (the late Chief Justice Ruffin) "he was a great Judge, and a good man." Its capital, Dallas, is named in honor of the Hon. George M. Dallas, Vice-President of the United States in 1844.

The territory embraced in this county, contained many true and gallant Whigs during the Revolutionary war. Sketches of some of these will appear in the present chapter.

REV. HUMPHREY HUNTER.

[Condensed from Wheeler's "Historical Sketches."]

Rev. Humphrey Hunter was born in Ireland, near Londonderry, on the 14th of May, 1775. His paternal grandfather was from Glasgow, in Scotland. His maternal grandfather was from Brest, in France. His descent is thus traced to the Scotch-Irish, and Huguenots of France, forming a race of people who greatly contributed to the spread of civil and religious liberty wherever their lots were cast. In America, the asylum of the oppressed of all nations, many of their descendants occupy proud positions on the page of history, and acted a magnanimous part in the achievment of our independence.

At the early age of four years, Humphrey Hunter was

deprived by death of his father. In a short time afterward, his mother joined the great tide of emigration to the new world, and in May 1759, embarked on the ship Helena, bound for Charleston, S. C. After a long and boisterous voyage, the vessel at length reached its destination in safety. His mother then procured a cheap conveyance and proceeded to the eastern part of Mecklenburg county, (now in Cabarrus) where she purchased a small tract of land, and spent the remainder of her days.

In the manuscript journal of the Rev. Humphrey Hunter, we are furnished with some interesting facts respecting his life and services. He informs us he grew up in the neighborhood of Poplar Tent, inhaling the salubrious air of a free clime, and imbibing the principles of genuine liberty. At this stage of his early training, he pays a beautiful tribute to the patriotism of the mothers of the Revolution. He says: " Neither were our mother's silent at the commencement of the Revolution." "Go son, said his mother, and join yourself to the men of our country. We ventured our lives on the waves of the ocean in quest of the freedom promised us here. Go, and fight for it, and rather let me hear of your *death* than of your *cowardice.*"

In a short time afterward this patriotic advice of his mother was called into action. "Orders were presently issued," continues his journal, "by Colonel Thomas Polk to the several militia companies of the county for two men, selected from each *beat* or district to meet at the Court House in Charlotte, on the 19th day of May, 1775, in order to consult upon such measures as might be thought best to be pursued. Accordingly, on said day, a far greater number than two out of each company were present." Drawn by the great excitement of the occasion, surpassing that of any other preceding it, he attended the Convention on the appointed day. He was then a few days over twenty years of his age, and mingled with the

numerous crowd of interested spectators. He then had
the pleasure of listening to the reading of the *first Declaration of Independence* in the United States, and joined in the
shout of approval which burst forth from the assembled
multitude. In a short time after the Convention in
Charlotte, Col. Thomas Polk raised a regiment of infantry
and cavalry, and marched in the direction of Cross creek
(now Fayetteville) to disperse a body of Tories. In this
service, he joined a corps of cavalry under Captain Chas.
Polk. Soon after the return of this expedition, he commenced his classical studies at Clio Academy, in the western part of Rowan county, (now Iredell) under the instruction of the Rev. James Hall.

About this time the Cherokee Indians were committing numerous depredations and occasional murders near
the head sources of the Catawba river. Upon this information, Gen. Rutherford called out a brigade of militia from Guilford, Mecklenburg, Rowan, Lincoln and
other western counties, composed of infantry and three
corps of cavalry. In one of the companies commanded
by Captain, afterwards Col. Robert Mebane, he acted as
Lieutenant. Two skirmishes took place during this campaign, in which several Indians were killed and a considerable number made prisoners, among the latter, Hicks
and Scott, two white traders, who had married Indians
and espoused their cause. After his return from the
Cherokee expedition, he resumed his classical education
at Queen's Museum, in Charlotte, under the control of
Dr. Alexander McWhorter, an eminent Presbyterian
clergyman from New Jersey. In the summer of 1780,
this institution, having assumed in 1777, the more patriotic name of "Liberty Hall Academy," was broken up by
the approach of the British army under Lord Cornwallis.
The school, then in a flourishing state, was dismissed;
the young men were urged by Dr. McWhorter with
patriotic appeals, to take up arms in defence of their

country; and upon all he invoked the blessings of Heaven. At this time Gen. Gates was on his way to the Southern States. Under orders from Gen. Rutherford, a brigade was promptly raised to rendezvous at Salisbury. In this brigade Hunter acted for a short time as Commissary, and afterward as Lieutenant in the company of Capt. Givens. This force first marched from Salisbury down the northeast side of the Yadkin, scouring the Tory settlements of the Uwharrie and Deep rivers, previous to its junction with Gen. Gates at Cheraw. From this place Gen. Gates moved forward to Clermont, where he arrived on the 12th of August. On the 15th he marched towards Camden, progressing as far as the Gum Swamp, where sharp skirmishing took place in the night between advanced parties of the Americans and the British. On the 16th of August, 1780, the unfortunate battle of Camden was fought. A contagious panic seized most of the militia early in the action, and a precipitate retreat was the natural consequence. The regulars of Maryland and Delaware, with a small portion of the North Carolina militia, firmly stood their ground until surrounded with overwhelming numbers. The subject of this sketch was there made a prisoner and stripped of most of his clothes. Soon after his surrender he witnessed the painful incidents of battle, resulting in the death of Baron DeKalb. He informs us he saw the Baron without suite or aid, and without manifesting the designs of his movements, galloping down the line. He was soon descried by the enemy, who, clapping their hands on their shoulders in reference to his epaulettes, exclaimed "a General, a rebel General." Immediately a man on horseback (not Tarleton) met him and demanded his sword. The Baron reluctantly presented the handle towards him, inquiring in French, " Are you an officer, sir." His antagonist not understanding the language, with an oath, more sternly demanded his sword. The Baron then rode on with all possible speed, disdaining to surrender to any one but an officer. Soon the cry, "a rebel General," sounded along the line. The musketeers immediately, by platoons, fired upon him. He proceeded about twenty-five rods, when he fell from his horse, mortally wounded. Presently he was raised to his feet, stripped of his hat, coat and neckcloth, and placed with his hands resting on a wagon. His body was found, upon examination, to have been pierced by seven musket balls. Whilst standing in this position, and the blood streaming through his shirt, Cornwallis, with his suite, rode up. Being informed that the wounded man was Baron De Kalb, he addressed him by saying: "I am sorry, sir, to see you; not sorry that you are vanquished, but sorry to see you so badly wounded." Having given orders to an officer to administer to the wants of the Baron, Cornwallis rode on to secure the fruits of his victory. In a short time the brave and generous De Kalb, who had served in the armies of France and embarked in the American cause, breathed his last. He is buried in Camden, where a neat monument has been erected to his memory.

After being confined seven days in a prison-yard in Camden, Hunter was taken, with many other prisoners, including about fifty officers, to Orangeburg, where he remained until the 13th of November following, *without hat or coat*. On that day, without any intention of transgressing, he set out to visit a friendly lady in the suburbs who had promised to give him a homespun coat. Before he reached her residence, he was stopped by a horseman, armed with sword and pistols, who styled himself a Lieutenant of the station at the Court House, under Col. Fisher. The horseman blustered and threatened, and sternly commanded him to march before him to the station to be tried for having broken his parole. No excuse, apology or confession would be received in extenuation of his transgression. "To the station," said the horseman, "you shall go—take the road." The Tory loyalist was evidently exercising his brief authority over a real Whig. Up the road his prisoner had to go, sour and sulky, with much reluctance, being hurried in his march by the point of the Tory's sword. Hunter pursued his course, but constantly on the look-out for some means of self-defence. Fortunately, after they progressed a short distance, they approached a large fallen pine tree, around which lay a quantity of pine-knots, hardened and blackened by the recent action of fire. Hunter, in an instant, saw "his opportunity," immediately jumped to the further side of said tree, and, armed with a good pine-knot, prepared for combat. The Tory instantly fired one of his pistols at him, but without effect. He then leaped his horse over the tree. Hunter, with equal promptness, exchanged sides, being fired at a second time by his would-be conqueror, but again without effect. Much skilful manœuvoring took place, whilst the Tory was thus kept at bay. Hunter then commenced a vigorous warfare with the pine-knots so opportunely placed at his command, and dealt them out with profuse liberality. The accurate aim of two or three pine-knots against the horseman's head soon disabled him and brought him to the ground. He was then disarmed of his sword, and capitulated on the following terms: That Hunter should never make known the conquest he had gained over him, and give back the captured sword; and that he, (the Tory loyalist) would never report to headquarters that any of the prisoners had ever crossed the boundary line, or offended in any other manner. But secrecy could not be preserved, for during the combat the horse, without his rider, galloped off to the station and created considerable anxiety respecting the horseman's fate. All serious apprehensions, however, were soon removed as the dismounted horseman presently made his appearance, with several visible bruises on his head, bearing striking proof of the effective precision of the pine-knots. A close examination was soon instituted at the station, and numerous searching questions propounded to the wounded horseman, when the history of the contest had to be given, and all concealment no longer attempted. The rencounter took place on a Friday evening. On the Sabbath following, orders were issued by Col. Fisher to all the prisoners to appear at the Court House on Monday by twelve o'clock. On the evening of that Sabbath, Hunter, expecting close confinement, or, perhaps, the loss of his life, made his escape with five or six others from Mecklenburg, and commenced their way to North Carolina. They concealed themselves by day to avoid the British scouts sent in pursuit, and traveled during the night, supporting themselves principally on the *raw corn* found by the way-side. On the ninth night after they set out from Orangeburg, they crossed the Catawba and arrived safely in Mecklenburg county.

After remaining a few days at his mother's residence, he again entered the service, and joined a cavalry company, acting as lieutenat under Colonel Henry Lee. In a short time, the battle of the Eutaw Springs, the last important one in the extreme South, took place. In this engagement, where so much personal bravery was displayed, he performed a gallant part, and was slightly wounded. With this campaign, his military services ended. Among the variety of incidents which occurred during this year he was gratified in revisiting his old prison-bounds, and in witnessing the reduction of the station at Orangeburg. But greater still was the gratification he experienced in again beholding the identical sword he had taken from his Tory antagonist, as previously stated.

Soon after the close of the war he resumed his classical studies under the instruction of the Rev. Robert Archibald, near Poplar Tent Church. During the summer of

1785, he entered the Junior Class at Mount Zion College, in Winnsboro, S. C., and graduated in July, 1787. In a short time afterward he commenced the study of Thelogy under the care of the Presbytery of South Carolina, and was licensed to preach in October, 1789. In 1796 he removed from South Carolina to the south-eastern part of Lincoln county (now Gaston) where he purchased a home for his rising family. His ministeral labors extended through a period of nearly thirty-eight years, principally at Goshen and Unity churches in Lincoln county (under its old boundaries) and Steele Creek church, in Mecklenburg county. In 1789 he married Jane, daughter of Dr. George Ross, of Laurens District, S. C.—an estimable lady, noted for her amiable disposition, numerous acts of charity, and fervent piety.

In his preaching Mr. Hunter was earnest, persuasive and often eloquent. He possessed, in a remarkable degree, a talent for refined sarcasm, and knew how to use most effectively its piercing shafts against the idle objections, or disingenuous cavils of all triflers with the great truths of religion. In his advanced years the infirmities of old age greatly contracted the extent of his useful labors without impairing the vigor of his mental powers or the fervency and faithfulness of his preaching. He died, with christian resignation, on the 21st of August, 1827, in the 73rd year of his age. The Rev. Humphrey Hunter had ten chrilden, of whom, at the present time (1876) only one, the author and compiler of these sketches, survives.

DR. WILLIAM M'LEAN.

Dr. William McLean was born in Rowan county, N. C., on the 2nd day of April, 1757. His father, Alexander McLean, was a native of Ireland, who emigrated to America, landing at Philadelphia, between the years 1725

and 1730. Some time after his arrival in Pennsylvania
he married Elizabeth Ratchford, whose father emigrated
from England shortly after McLean left Ireland. Three
of his daughters, Jane, Margaret and Agnes, were born in
that State. He then joined the great tide of emigration
to the more enticing fields and genial climate of the
southern colonies, and settled in the Dobbin neighborhood,
eight miles from Salisbury, Rowan county, N. C.
Here he remained for a few years, during which time
his eldest son John, and William, the immediate subject
of this sketch, were born. He then moved to a tract of
land he purchased near the junction of the South
Fork with the main Catawba river, in Tryon, (now Gaston
county,) where three more sons were born, Alexander,
George and Thomas. This place he made his permanent
abode during the remainder of his life, surrounded with
the greater portion of his rising family. He attained a
good old age, his wife surviving him a few years; both
were consistent members of the Presbyterian church, and
are buried at the old " Smith graveyard," near the place
of his last settlement. Soon after the Revolutionary war,
Alexander McLean, Jr., moved to Missouri, and George
McLean to Tennessee Thomas McLean, the youngest
son, retained the old homestead, where, at an advanced
age, he ended his earthly existence. Although only
thirteen years old at the time of the battle of King's
Mountain, he could give a glowing account of the heroic
bravery which characterized that brilliant victory in
which many of his neighbors, under the brave Lieut.
Col. Hambright and Maj. Chronicle, actively participated.
John McLean, the eldest son, performed a soldier's duty
on several occasions during the war. Upon the call of
troops from North Carolina for the defence of Charleston,
he attached himself to Col. Graham's regiment, under
Gen. Rutherford, and was there captured. Immediately
after being exchanged, he returned to North Carolina

and joined the command of Capt. Adlai Osborne, and about three month's afterward was killed in a skirmish at Buford's Bridge, S. C.

After the removal of Alexander McLean to his final settlement on the south fork of the Catawba, as previously stated, William assisted him on the farm, and when a favorable opportunity offered, went to school in the neighborhood, acquiring as good an education as the facilities of the country then afforded. His instructor for the last three months in this early training was a Mr. Blythe, who, noticing his rapid advancement in learning, and capacity for more extended usefulness, advised him to go to Queen's Museum, in Charlotte. This institution was then in high repute under the able management of Dr. Alexander and Rev. Alexander McWhorter, a distinguished Presbyterian clergyman from New Jersey.

Dr. McLean complied with the advice of his instructor, and became a pupil of Queen's Museum. In this venerated institution, shedding abroad its enlightening influence on Western North Carolina, many of the leading patriots of the Revolution acquired their principal educational training. Its president, Dr. McWhorter, was not only an eminent preacher of the gospel, but was also an ardent patriot, and never failed, on suitable occasions, to discuss the politics of the day, and instil into the minds of his youthful pupils the essential principles of civil and religious liberty. His sentiments in this respect were so generally known, that it is said Cornwallis previous to his entrance into Charlotte in 1780, was extremely anxious to *enfold him in his embraces*. Dr. McLean remained in this institution of learning about two years and then returned home. Having made up his mind to become a physician during his collegiate course, he gathered all the medical books he could procure at that period, and diligently devoted his time to their study. In this stage of his early preparation for future usefulness,

Dr. Joseph Blythe, a distinguished surgeon in the Continental Army, wrote to him in terms of warmest friendship, and offered him the position of "surgeon's mate." This offer he accepted, repaired to Charlottte, and they both marched with the army to James Island, near Charleston. In this immediate vicinity at Stono (the narrow river or inlet, which separates John's Island from the main land) a severe but indecisive battle had been fought between a detachment of General Lincoln's army and the British, under General Prevost, in June, 1779. At the time of Dr. McLean's arrival at James Island, many soldiers were sick with the pestilental "camp fever" of that sultry climate, or were suffering from the wounds of battle at the army hospital. Some of these sufferers were from Lincoln and Mecklenburg counties, with whom he was personally acquainted. Under judicious medical treatment he was pleased to see most of them, in a short time, restored to health and ready for the future service of their country.

In the summer and fall of 1780 Dr. McLean was constantly with the Southern army watching the movements of Ferguson in the upper Tory settlements of South Carolina, previous to his defeat and death at King's Mountain. After that battle he went to Charlotte to wait on the sick and the wounded at that place.

In 1781 he was with General Greene's army, near Camden, and at other military encampments requiring his services. In all of these responsible positions he continued to faithfully discharge the duties of "Surgeon's Mate," or Assistant Surgeon, until the close of the Revolution.

Having completed his preparatory studies Dr. McLean went to the medical University of Pennsylvania at Philadelphia, and received from that venerable institution his diploma in 1787. In a short time after his arrival at home he purchased a farm in the "South Point" neighborhood, soon engaged in an extensive practice frequently charitable) and became eminent in his profession.

On the 19th of June, 1792, Dr. McLean married Mary, daughter of Major John Davidson, one of the signers of the Mecklenburg Declaration of Independence. In 1814 he was elected to the Senate from Lincoln county. In 1815 he delivered an address at King's Mountain, commemorative of the battle at that place, and caused to be erected, at his own expense, a plain headstone of dark slate rock, with appropriate inscriptions on both sides. The inscription on the east side reads thus: Sacred to the memory of Major William Chronicle, Capt, John Mattocks, William Robb and John Boyd, who were killed here on the 7th of October, 1780, fighting in defence of America." The inscription on the west side reads thus: "Colonel Ferguson, an officer belonging to his Brittanic Majesty, was here defeated and killed."

Dr. McLean, after a life of protracted usefulness, died with peaceful resignation on the 25th of October, 1828, in the seventy-second year of his age. His wife survived him many years, being nearly ninety-seven years old at the time of her death. They were both long, worthy and consistant members of the Presbyterian church, dignified their lives with their professions, and are buried in Bethel Graveyard, York county, S. C.

MAJOR WILLIAM CHRONICLE.

Major William Cronicle, the soldier and martyr to the cause of liberty at King's Mountain, was born in the south eastern part of Lincoln county (now Gaston) about 1755. His mother was first married to a Mr. McKee in Pennsylvania, who afterwards removed to North Carolina and settled in Mecklenburg county. By this marriage she had one son, James McKee, a soldier of the revolution, and ancestor of the several families of that name in the neighboehood of Armstrong's Ford, on the South Fork of the Catawba. After McKee's death, his widow married Mr. Chronicle, by whom she had an only son, William, who afterward performed a magnanimous part in defence of his country's rights. The site of the old family mansion is still pointed out by the oldest inhabitants with feelings of lingering veneration. "There," they will tell you, "is the spot where old Mr. Chronicle lived and his brave son, William, was brought up." The universal testimony of all who knew Major Chronicle represented him as the constant, never-tiring advocate of liberty, and as exerting a powerful influence in spreading the principles of freedom throughout the whole lower portion of old Lincoln county. His jovial turn of mind and winning manners, by gaining the good will of all, greatly assisted in making successful his appeals to their patriotism, and promoting the cause of liberty in which he had so zealously embarked.

Major Chronicle's first service was performed as Captain of a company at Purysburg in South Carolina. Early in the fall of 1780, a regiment was raised in Lincoln county, over which Col. William Graham was appointed Colonel; Frederick Hambrite, Lieut. Colonel, and William Chronicle, Major. It is well known that Col. Graham, on account of severe sickness in his family, was not present at the battle of King's Mountain. The immediate command of the regiment, assisted by Col. Dickson of the county, was then gallantly assumed by these officers, and nobly did they sustain themselves by word and example, in that ever-memorable conflict. Major Chronicle was brave, perhaps to a fault, energetic in his movements, self possessed in danger, and deeply imbued with the spirit of liberty. His last words of encouragement in leading a spirited charge against the enemy, were "Come on my boys, never let it be said a Fork boy run," alluding to South Fork, near which stream most of them resided.

This patriotic appeal was not given in vain. It nerved evey man for the contest. Onward his brave boys steadily moved forward, Major Chronicle in the advance, and approached within gun-shot of the British forces. Just at this time, a few sharp shooters of the enemy discharged their pieces, and retreated. The brave Chronicle fell mortally wounded, receiving a fatal ball in the breast. Almost at the same time, Capt. John Mattocks and Lieutenants William Rabb and John Boyd, also fell. Major Chronicle was only about twenty-five years old at the time of his death. The late Capt. Samuel Caldwell and his brother William, were both in this battle. William Caldwell brought home Major Chronicle's horse; his sword and spurs passed into the hands of his half brother, James McKee, and the venerated memorials are still in possession of one of his sons, who moved many years ago to Tennessee.

CAPTAIN SAMUEL MARTIN.

Captain Samuel Martin was a native of Ireland, and born in the year 1732. When a young man, he emigrated to America, and first settled in Pennsylvania. After remaining a short time in that State, he joined the great tide of emigration to the southern colonies. He first entered the service as a private in Captain Robert Alexander's company, in June 1776, Colonel Graham's Remiment, and marched to Fort McGaughey, in Rutherford county, and thence across the Blue Ridge Mountains against the Cherokee Indians, who were committing murders and depredations upon the frontier settlements. In January 1777, he attached himself to the command of Captain William Chronicle, and marched to the relief of the post of Ninety Six, in Abbeville county, S. C., and after this service he returned to North Carolina.

About the 1st of November, 1779, his company was

ordered to Charlotte, at that time a place of rendezvous of soldiers for the surrounding counties, and while there he received a special commission of captain, conferred on him by General Rutherford. With his special command he marched with other forces from Charlotte by way of Camden, to the relief of Charleston, and fell in with Col. Hampton, at the Governor's gate, near that city. Finding that place completely invested by the British army, he remained but a short time, and returned to North Carolina with Colonel Graham's regiment, about the 1st of June, 1780.

Being informed on the night of his arrival at home that the Tories were embodied in strong force at Ramsour's Mill, near the present town of Lincolnton, he immediately raised a small company and joined General Davidson's battalion, General Rutherford commanding, encamped at Colonel Dickson's plantation, three miles northwest of Tuckaseege ford. General Rutherford broke up his encampment at that place, early on the morning of the 20th of June, 1780, then sixteen miles from Ramsour's Mill, and marched with his forces, expecting to unite with Colonel Locke in making a joint attack upon the Tories, but failed to reach the scene of conflict until two hours after the battle. The Tories had been signally defeated and routed by Colonel Locke and his brave associates, and about fifty made prisoners, among the number a brother of Colonel Moore, the commander of the Tory forces.

Immediately after this battle he received orders from Colonels Johnston and Dickson to proceed with his company to Colonel Moore's residence, six or seven miles west of the present town of Lincolnton, and arrest that Tory leader, but he had fled with about thirty of his follower's to Camden, S. C., where Cornwall's was then encamped. Soon after this service Captain Martain was ordered to proceed with his company to Rugeley's Mill, in

Kershaw county, S. C. Here Colonel Rugeley, the Tory commander, had assembled a considerable force, and fortified his log barn and dwelling house. Colonel Washington, by order of General Morgan, had pursued him with his cavalry, but having no artillery, he resorted to an ingenious stratagem to capture the post without sacrificing his own men. Accordingly he mounted a *pine log*, fashioned as a cannon, elevated on its own limbs, and placed it in position to command the houses in which the Tories were lodged. Colonel Washington then made a formal demand for immediate surrender. Colonel Rugeley fearing the destructive consequences of the formidable cannon bearing upon his command in the log barn and dwelling house, after a stipulation as to terms, promptly surrendered his whole force, consisting of one hundred and twelve men, without a gun being fired on either side. It was upon the reception of the news of this surrender that Cornwallis wrote to Tarleton, "Rugeley will not be made a Brigadier."

After this successful stratagem, seldom equaled during the war, Captain Martin was ordered to march with his company in pursuit of Colonel Cunningham, (commonly called "bloody Bill Cunningham") a Tory leader, encamped on Fishing creek, but he fled so rapidly he could not overtake him. During the latter part of August and the whole of September, Captain Martin was rarely at home, and then not remaining for more than two days at a time. About the last week of September he marched with his company by a circuitous route, under Colonel Graham, to the Cowpens. There he united with Colonels Campbell, Shelby, Sevier, Cleaveland and other officers and marched with them to King's Mountain. In this battle Captain Martin acted a conspicuous part, was in the *thickest of the fight*, and lost six of his company. After this battle he continued in active scouting duties wherever his services were needed.

When Cornwallis marched through Lincoln county in pursuit of General Morgan, encumbered with upwards of five hundred prisoners, captured at the Cowpens, he was ordered to harass his advance as much as possible. A short time after Cornwallis crossed the Catawba at Cowan's Ford, he marched as far as Salisbury, when he was ordered by Colonel Dickson to convey some prisoners to Charlotte. Having performed this service, he proceeded to Guilford Court house, but did not reach that place until after the battle. He then returned home, and was soon after discharged.

In October 1833, Captain Martin, when *one hundred and one years* old, was granted a pension by the general government. He was a worthy and consistent member of the Associate Reformed Church, and died on the 26th of November, 1836, aged *one hundred and four years!* He married in Ireland, Margaret McCurdy, who also attained an extreme old age, and both are buried in Goshen grave yard, in Gaston county.

CAPTAIN SAMUEL CALDWELL.

Samuel Caldwell was born in Orange County, N. C., on the 10th of February, 1759, and moved to Tryon county, afterward Lincoln, in 1772. He first entered the service in Captain Gowen's company in 1776, and marched against the Cherokee Indians beyond the mountains. In 1779, he volunteered in Captain William Chronicle's company) in the "nine months service," and joined General Lincoln's army at Purysburg, S. C. In March, 1780, he joined Captain Isaac White's company, and marched to King's Mountain. In the battle which immediately followed, he and his brother, William actively participated. Shortly after this celebrated victory, he attached himself to Captain Montgomery's company and was in the battle of the Cowpens, fought on the 17th of January, 1781. Soon afterward he marched to Guilford, and was in the battle fought there on the 15th of March, 1781. In the following fall, he substituted for Clement Nance, in Captain Lemmonds cavalry company in the regiment commanded by Col. Robert Smith and Major Joseph Graham.

At the Raft Swamp, they attacked and signally defeated a large body of Tories; and in two days afterward defeated a band of Tories on Alfred Moore's plantation opposite Wilmington. On the next day, the same troops made a vigorous attack on the garrison, near the same place. After this service, he returned home and was frequently engaged in other minor but important military duties until the close of the war.

After the war, Captain Caldwell settled on a farm three miles southwest of Tuckaseege Ford where he raised a large family. He was a kind and obliging neighbor, attained a good old age, and is buried in the graveyard of Goshen church, Gaston county N. C.

CAPTAIN JOHN MATTOCKS.

Captain John Mattocks was one of the brave soldiers who fell at King's Mountain. He belonged to a family who resided a few miles below Armstrong's Ford, on the south fork of the Catawba river, at what is now known as the "Alison old place." There were three brothers and two sisters, Sallie and Barbara. The whole family, men and women, had the reputation of being "*uncommonly stout.*" John and Charles Mattocks were staunch Whigs, ever ready to engage in any enterprise in defence of the freedom of their country, but Edward Mattocks (commonly called Ned Mattocks) was a Tory. All of the brothers were at the battle of King's Mountain, in which Captain Charles Mattocks was killed early in the action when pressing forward with undaunted courage against the enemy. Among the severely wounded, was Ned Mattocks, the Tory brother. After the battle and signal victory, Charles Mattocks, fearing his brother might be hung with some others who suffered this penalty on the next day, kindly interceded in his behalf, took him home and nursed him carfully until he recovered of his wound. It is said, this *extraction of blood* so effectually performed by some one of the gallant Whigs on that occasion, completely *cured* Ned Mattocks of *Toryism* and caused him never afterward to unite with the enemies of his country.

The whole surviving family a few years after the war moved to Georgia, where they have descendants at the present time.

Major Chronicle, Captain Mattocks, William Rabb and John Boyd, all from the same South Fork neighborhood, are buried in a common grave at the foot of the mountain.

A plain head-stone of dark slate rock, commemorates the hallowed spot with the following inscription:

"Sacred to the memory of

MAJOR WILLIAM CHRONICLE,
CAPTAIN JOHN MATTOCKS,
WILLIAM RABB,
JOHN BOYD,

Who were killed here fighting in defence of America, On the 7th of October, 1780."

Many fragmentary but interesting incidents connected with the battle of King's Mountain have come down to our own time and unfortunately, many others have been buried in oblivion. The following incident was related to the author by a grandson of a brave soldier in that battle. Moses and James Henry both actively participated in that hotly contested engagement.

A few days after the battle, as James Henry was passing through the woods near the scene of conflict, he found a very fine horse, handsomely equipped with an elegant saddle, the reins of the bridle being broken. The horse and equipments were, as he supposed, the property of an officer. He took the horse home with him, considerably elated with his good luck; but his mother met him at the gate, and immediately inquired whose horse it was he had in charge, he replied, he supposed it belonged to some British officer. "James," said the mother, "turn it loose and drive it off from the place, for I will not have the hands of my household stained with British plunder."

The incident illustrates the noble Christian spirit which actuated our good mothers of the Revolutionary period.

The other brother, Moses Henry, evinced great bravery in the same engagement, and was mortally wounded. He was taken to the hospital in Charlotte, and was attentively waited upon by Dr. William McLean until he died. His widow, with several others under similar bereavement, was granted a liberal allowance by the county court of Lincoln. Moses Henry is the grandfather of Col. Moses Henry Hand, a worthy citizen of Gaston county, N. C.

WILLIAM RANKIN.

William Rankin was born in Pennsylvania, on the 10th of January, 1761, and at an early age joined the tide of emigration to the Southern States, and settled in "Tryon," afterward Lincoln county, N. C.

He first entered the service as a private in Captain Robert Alexander's company, Colonel William Graham's regiment, and marched to Montfort's Cove against the Cherokee Indians. In 1779 he volunteered under the same officer, and marched by way of Charlotte and Camden to the relief of Charleston, but finding the city completely invested by the British army, the regiment returned to North Carolina. In 1780, he again volunteered under Major Dickson, and marched against Col. Floyd, a Tory leader of upper South Carolina. After this service he returned home, and soon afterward marched under the same officer, General Rutherford commanding, to Ramsour's Mill, where a large body of Tories had assembled under Colonel John Moore. The forces under General Rutherford were encamped on Colonel Dickson's plantation, three miles north-west of Tuckaseege Ford, and about sixteen miles from Ramsour's. Early on the morning of the 20th of June, 1780, they broke up camp and moved forward, but did not reach the battle-field until two hours after the action had taken place, and the Tories defeated by Colonel Locke and his brave associates, with a force greatly inferior to that of the enemy. Immediately after this battle, he substituted for Henry E. Locke, in Captain William Armstrong's company, marched to Park's Mill, near Charlotte, and thence to General Rutherford's army, encamped at Phifer's plantation.

The Tories having assembled a considerable force at Coulson's Mill, General Davidson with a detachment of troops vigorously attacked them, in which skirmish he (Davidson) was severely wounded, detaining him from the service about two months. Soon afterward he marched with General Rutherford's command to Camden and participated in the unfortunate battle at that place on the 16th of August, 1780. While the British army were in Charlotte he served under Captain Forney and Major Dickson, watching the movements of the enemy. Shortly afterward he volunteered under Captain James Little, marched to Rocky Mount, and thence to the Eutaw Springs. In this battle, one of the most severely contested during the Revolution, his company was placed under the command of Colonel Malmedy, a Frenchman. Soon after his return home he was placed in charge of a considerable number of prisoners, and in obedience to orders, conveyed them to Salisbury. Here he remained until his time of service expired, and then received his discharge from Colonel Locke.

William Rankin attained the good old age of nearly ninety-three, and was at the time of his death the last surviving soldier of the Revolution in Gaston county. He married Mary Moore, a sister of General John Moore, also a soldier of the Revolution. His wife preceded him several years to the tomb.

His son, Colonel Richard Rankin, is now (1876) living at the old homestead, having passed "his three score years and ten." He served several times in the State Legislature, is an industrious farmer and worthy citizen of Gaston county.

GEN. JOHN MOORE.

General John Moore was born in Lincoln county, when a part of Anson, in 1759. His father, William Moore, of Scotch-Irish descent, was one of the first settlers of the county and a prominent member of society. He had four sons, James, William, John and Alexander, who, inheriting the liberty-loving principles of that period, were all true patriots in the Revolutionary war.

John Moore performed a soldier's duty on several occasions and was one of the guards stationed at Tuckaseege Ford, watching the movements of Lord Cornwallis after his entrance into Lincoln county. He also acted for a considerable length of time as Commissary to the army. General Moore married a sister of General John Adair, of Kentucky, by whom he had many children. Several years after her death, he married Mary Scott, widow of James Scott, and daughter of Captain Robert Alexander, by whom he had two children, Lee Alexander and Elizabeth Moore. He was a member of the House of Commons as early as 1788, and served for many years subsequently with great fidelity and to the general acceptance of his constituents.

To remove a false impression, sometimes entertained by

persons little conversant with our Revolutionary history, it should be here stated that General John Moore was in no way related to the *Colonel John Moore*, (son of Moses Moore), who lived about seven miles west of Lincolton, and commanded the Tory forces in the battle of Ramsour's Mill.

General Moore, after a life of protracted usefulness, died in 1836, with Christian resignation, aged about seventy-seven years, and lies buried near several of his kindred in Goshen graveyard, Gaston county, N. C.

ELISHA WITHERS.

Elisha Withers was born in Stafford county, Va., on the 10th of August, 1762. His first service in the Revolutionary war was in 1780, acting for twelve months as Commissary in furnishing provisions for the soldiers stationed at Captain Robert Alexander's, near the Tuckaseege Ford on the Catawba river, their place of rendezvous. After this service, he was drafted and served a tour of three months under Captain Thomas Loftin and Lieut. Robert Shannon, and marched from Lincoln county to Guilford Court-house under Colonels Locke and Hunt. His time having expired shortly before the battle, he returned home.

He again served another tour, commencing in August, 1781, as a substitute for James Withers, under Captain James Little, at the Eutaw Springs, where he was detailed with a few others, to guard the baggage wagons during the battle. He again volunteered under Captain Thomas Loftin and Lieut. Thomas McGee and was actively engaged in the "horse service," in several scouting expeditions until the close of the war.

After the war, he was for a long time known as "old Constable Withers," was highly respected, and died at a good old age.

CHAPTER VII.

CLEAVELAND COUNTY.

Cleaveland county was formed in 1841, from Lincoln and Rutherford counties and derives its name from Col. Benjamin Cleaveland, of Wilkes county, who, with a detachment of men from that county and Surry, under the commands of himself, and Major Joseph Winston, performed a magnanimous part in the battle of King's Mountain. Shelby, the capital of this county, derives its name from from Col. Isaac Shelby, a sketch of whose services with those of Colonels Campbell, Graham, Hambright and Williams will appear in the present chapter.

BATTLE OF KING'S MOUNTAIN.

> "O'er the proud heads of free men, our star banner waves ;
> Men firm as their mountains, and still as their graves,
> To-morrow shall pour out their life-blood like rain ;
> We come back in triumph, or come not again."

After the defeat of General Gates at Camden, on the 16th of August, 1780, and the surprise and defeat of Gen. Sumter, two days after at Fishing Creek, by Col. Tarleton, the South was almost entirely abandoned to the enemy. It was one of the darkest periods of our Revolutionary history. While Cornwallis remained at Camden, he was busily employed in sending off his prisoners to Charleston and Orangeburg ; in ascertaining the condition of his distant posts at ninety-six and Augusta, and in establishing civil government in South Carolina. Yet his success did not impair his vigilance in concerting measures for its continuance. West of the Catawba river, were bands of active Whigs, and parties of those who were defeated at Camden, were harrassing their enemies and defending on every available occasion, the suffering inhabitants of the upper country. Cornwallis, becoming apprised of this rebellious spirit of upper Carolina, detached Col. Patrick Ferguson, one of his most favorite officers, with one hundred and ten regulars and about the same number of Tories, under captain Depeyster, a loyalist, with an ample supply of arms and other military stores. He was ordered to embody the loyalists beyond the Catawba (or Wateree as the same river is called opposite Camden) and the Broad rivers; intercept the "mountain men", who were retreating from Camden, and also, the Americans under Col. Clarke, of Georgia, falling back from an unsuccessful attack upon Augusta. Ferguson's special orders were to crush the spirit of rebellion still too rife and menacing; and after scouring the upper part of South Carolina, toward the mountains of North Carolina, to join his Lordship at Charlotte. He at first made rapid marches to overtake the mountain men—the "Hornets," from the "Switzerland of America," and cut off Col. Clarke's forces. Failing in this, he afterward moved more slowly and frequently halted to collect all the Tories he could pursuade to join him. He crossed Broad river, ravaging the country through which he marched. About the last of September he encamped at Gilberttown, near the present town of Rutherfordton. In his march to this point, his force increased to upwards of one thousand men. All of his Tory recruits were furnished with arms, most of them with rifles, and a smaller portion with muskets, to the muzzles of which they fixed the large knives they usually carried with them to be used as bayonets, if occasion should require.

Although Ferguson failed to overtake the detachment of "mountain men," previously alluded to, he took two of them prisoners who had become separated from their command. These he paroled and sent off, enjoining them to tell the officers on the western waters that if they did not desist from their opposition to the British arms, and take protection under the royal standard, he would march his army over the mountains and lay waste their country with fire and sword. This was no idle threat, and its execution would have been attempted had not a brief stay in Gilberttown satisfied him from the reports of his spies that a storm of patriotic indignation was brewing among and beyond the mountains that was destined soon to descend in all its fury upon his own army. He knew that most of the inhabitants were of Scotch-Irish and Huguenot descent, mingled with many Germans, whose long residence in the wilds of America had greatly tended to increase their love of liberty.

As soon as General McDowell heard that Gates was defeated, he broke up his camp at Smith's Ford on Broad River, and passed beyond the mountains, accompanied by a few of his unyielding patriots. While there in consultation with Colonels Sevier and Shelby as to the best means for raising troops and repelling the invaders, the two paroled men arrived and delivered the message from Ferguson· It produced no terrific effects on the minds of these well-tried officers, but on the contrary tended to stimulate and quicken their patriotic exertions. It was soon decided that each one should use his best efforts to raise all the men that could be enlisted, and that these forces should assemble at the Sycamore Shoals of the Watauga river, on the 25th of September. The plans for raising a sufficient number of men to accomplish their purpose were speedily devised and carried into execution. To Col. Sevier was assigned the duty of communicating with Col. McDowell and other officers in voluntary exile beyond the mountains. To Col. Shelby was assigned a similar duty of writing to Col. Compbell of the adjoining county of Washington, in Virginia. Among the refugees beyond the mountains was Col. Clarke, of Georgia, with about one hundred of his overpowered but not subdued men. Their story of the sufferings endured by the Whig inhabitants of upper South Carolina and Georgia served to arouse and intensify the state of patriotic feeling among the hardy sons of Western North Carolina.

The enlisted troops assembled at the Sycamore Shoals, marched from that place on the 26th of September. They were all mounted, and unemcumbered with baggage expecting to support themselves partly by their trusty rifles from the game of the forest, as they progressed and partly by compelling the Tories to minister to their wants. The assembled forces placed under marching orders, were as follows : From Washington county, Va., under Col. William Campbell, four hundred men. From Sullivan county, N. C. (now in Tennessee) under Col. Isaac Shelby, two hundred and forty men. From Washington county, N. C. (now in Tennessee) under Col John Sevier, two hundred and forty men. From Burke and Rutherford counties, N. C., under Col. Charles McDowell, one hundred and sixty men. On the second day's march, two of their men deserted, and went ahead to the enemy. It is probable their report of the Whig strength accelerated Ferguson's retreating movements. On the 30th of September, they crossed the mountains and were joined at the head of the Catawba river by Col. Benjamin Cleaveland and Major Joseph Winston, with three hundred and fifty men from Wilkes and Surry counties. Upon the junction of these forces, the officers held a council and as they were all of equal grade, it was agreed that a messenger be dispatched immediately to head-quarters, supposed to be between Charlotte and Salisbury to get General Sumner or Gen. Davidson to assume the chief command. They were now in Col Charles McDowell's military district, and being the senior officer, the chief command properly devolved upon him, unless his right, for the present, should be waived, and by agreement, turned over to another. Col. Shelby proposed, mainly through courtesy, that Col. William Campbell, who had met them with the largest rigiment from a sister State, should assume the chief command until the arrival of some superior officer. This proposition was readily assented to, and Col. Charles McDowell volunteered his services to proceed to head-quarters, and requested his brother, Major Joseph Mc-Dowell, to take command of his regiment until his return.

On the 4th of October the riflemen—the "mountain boys,"—advanced to Gilberttown, unwilling that Ferguson should be at the trouble to "cross the mountains and hang their leaders," as boastfully promulgated only a few days before.

Ferguson's abrupt departure and retrograde movement from Gilberttown, like that of Cornwallis from Charlotte two weeks later, clearly betrayed his apprehensions of formidable opposition by the enraged "hornets" of the mountains. Pursuit was immediately determined upon, and the Whig forces reached the celebrated Cowpens on the 6th of October, where they were joined by Col. James D. Williams, of South Carolina, with nearly four hundred men, and about sixty men from Lincoln county, under Lieut. Colonel Hambright. (Col. William Graham, of the same regiment, on account of severe sickness in his family, was not in the battle fought on the next day.) It is also known a company was raised under Capt. Shannon, from the same county, but failed to reach the battle-ground in time for the engagement.

On the evening of the 6th of October the Colonels in council unanimously resolved that they would select all the men and horses fit for service, and immediately pursue Ferguson until they should overtake him, leaving the remaining troops to follow after them as fast as possible. Accordingly, nine hundred and ten men a mounted infantry, were selected, who set out about eight o'clock on the same evening and marched all night, taking Fergusons trail toward Deer's Ferry, on Broad river. Night coming on, and it being very dark, they got out of the right way, and for some time were lost, but before daylight they nearly reached the ferry. The officers thinking it probable that the enemy might be in possession of the eastern bank of the river, directed the pilot to lead them to the Cherokee ford, about one mile and a half below. It was on the morning of the 7th of October, before sunrise, when they crossed the river and marched about two miles to the place where Ferguson had encamped on the night of the 5th. There they halted a short time and took such breakfast as their wallets and saddlebags would afford. Every hour the trail of the enemy became more clearly visible, which served to quicken their movements and exhilarate their patriotic spirits. About the time they marched from the Cowpens they were informed a party of four or five hundred Tories were assembled at Major Gibbs, about four miles to the right; these they did not turn aside to attack. The riflemen from the mountains had turned out to *catch Ferguson.* This was their rallying cry from the day they left the Sycamore Shoals, on the Watauga, to the present opportune moment for accomplishing their patriotic purpose. For the last thirty six hours they had alighted from their horses but once at the Cowpens for one hour's rest and refreshment. As soon as their humble repast was finished on the morning of the 7th, at Ferguson's encampment, on the 5th just alluded to, the riflemen resumed their eager march. The day was showery, which compelled them to use their blankets and overcoats to prevent their arms from getting wet.

After marching about ten miles, the riflemen met a young man named John Fonderin, riding in great haste from Ferguson's camp, then scarcely three miles distant

Col. Hambright being acquainted with him and knowing that he had relatives in the enemy's camp, caused him to be arrested. Upon searching his person, he was found to have a fresh dispatch from Furguson to Cornwallis, then at Charlotte, in which he manifested great anxiety as to his situation and earnestly solicited aid. The contents of the dispatch was read to the privates, without stating Ferguson's superior strenght to discourage them. Col. Hambright then interrogated the young man as to Ferguson's uniform. He replied by saying, "Ferguson was the best uniformed man on the hill, but they would not see his uniform as he wore a checked shirt (duster) over it." Col. Hambright immediately called the attention of his men to this distinguishing feature of Furgusons dress. " *Well poys*, says he, in broken German, *when you see that man mit a pig shirt on over his clothes you may know who him is.*" Accordingly after the battle, his body was found among the dead, wearing the checked shirt, now crimsoned with blood and pierced with numerous balls. After a brief consultation of the chief officers upon horseback, the plan of attack was quickly arranged. Several persons present were well acquainted with the ground upon which the enemy was encamped. Orders were promptly given and as promptly obeyed. The Whig forces moved forward over King's Creek, and up a ravine, and between two rocky knobs, when soon the enemy's camp was seen about one hundred poles in front. Furguson, aware that he was hotly pursued by a band of patriots of determined bravery, had chosen this mountain elevation as one from which he boastingly proclaimed he could not be driven.

It was about 3 o'clock in the afternoon when the Whig forces reached the battle ground. The rain had ceased, the clouds had nearly passed away, the sun now shone brightly, and nature seemed to smile propitiously upon the sanguinary conflict soon to take place. On the march, the following disposition was made of the Whig forces.

The central column was commanded by Colonels Campbell and Shelby; the right, by Colonel Sevier and Major McDowell; and the left by Colonels Cleaveland and Williams. In this order the Whig forces advanced and came within a quarter of a mile of the enemy before they were discovered. Colonels Campbell's and Shelby's regiments commenced the attack, and kept up a galling fire on the enemy, while the right and left wings were advancing forward to surround them, which was done in about five minutes. The fire soon became general all around and maintained with the greatest bravery.

The engagement lasted a little over an hour, during which time, a heavy and incessant fire was kept up on both sides.

The Whigs, in some parts where the British regulars fought, were forced to give way two or three times for a short distance, before the bayonet charges of the enemy, but soon rallied and returned with additional arder and amination to the attack. The troops of the right having gained the summit of the mountain, compelled the enemy to give way and retreat along the top of the ridge, where Col. Cleaveland commanded and were soon stopped by his brave men. Some of the regiments suffered severely under the galling fire of the enemy, before they were in a proper position to engage in the action. The men led by Col. Shelby and Major McDowell were soon closely engaged and the contest throughout was very severe, and hotly contested. .

As Ferguson would advance towards Campbell, Sevier, Hambright and Winston, he was quickly pursued by Shelby, Cleaveland, McDowell and Williams. Thus Ferguson continued to struggle on, making charges with the bayonet and then retreating to make a vigorous attack at some other point; but, his men were rapidly falling before the fatal aim and persistent bravery of the Whigs.

Even after Ferguson was severely wounded and had three horses shot from under him, he continued to fight on, and animate his men by his example and unyielding courage—"extricate himself, he could not, and surrender, he would not," although requested to do so, near the close of the action by Captain De Peyster, his second in command. At length he received a fatal shot in the breast, which closed his earthly career forever.

Captain De Peyster then took command, and immediately ordered a white flag to be raised in token of surrender. The firing however did not entirely cease until Cols. Shelby and Sevier went inside the lines and ordered the men to desist. The Whigs were still greatly exasperated when they called to remembrance Tarleton's cruelty at Buford's defeat, where no quarter was given. The victory was complete, and reanimated the Whigs throughout the whole country. The Tory element of western Carolina, before strong and menacing, was broken up and greatly humbled, and Cornwallis himself when he received intelligence of the battle and its result, became so seriously alarmed at his perilous situation in a land of *assailing hornets*, that he suddenly decamped from Charlotte to safer quarters at Winnsboro, South Carolina.

According to the official statemant furnished to Gen Gates, encamped at Hillsboro, and signed by Colonels Campbell, Shelby and Cleaveland, the enemy sustained the following loss: "Of the regulars, one major, one captain, two Lieutenants and fifteen privates killed, thirty-five privates wounded and left on the ground not able to march; two captains, four lieutenats, three ensigns, one surgeon, five sergeants, three corporals, one drummer and fifty-nine privates taken prisoners.

Loss of the Tories, two colonels, three captains and

two hundred privates killed; one major, and one hundred and twenty-seven privates wounded and left on the ground not able to march; one colonel, twelve captains, eleven lieutenants, two ensigns, one quarter-master, one adjutant, two commissaries, eighteen sergeants and six hundred privates taken prisoners.

Total loss of the enemy eleven hundred and five men at King's Mountain."

The loss on the Whig side was, one colonel, one major, one captain, two lieutenants, four ensigns, and nineteen privates killed, one major, three captains, three lieutenants, and fifty-three privates wounded. Total Whig casualties, twenty-eight killed and sixty wounded. Of the latter, upwards of twenty died of their wounds, making the entire Whig loss about fifty men.

The victory of King's Mountain was the "turning point of the fortunes of America," and foreshadowed more clearly than ever before, *final success.*

As soon as the battle was over, a guard was placed around the prisoners and all remained on the mountain that night. On the next day, after the dead were buried and the wounded properly cared for, the cumbrous spoils of victory were drawn into a pile and burned. Colonels Campbell, Shelby and Cleaveland then repaired, with as little delay as possible, to the headquarters of General Gates, at Hillsboro, and made out to that officer on the 1st of November, an official statement of their brilliant victory. Col. Sevier, Major McDowell and other officers returned to the mountains and to their own neighborhoods, ready at all times, to obey any future calls of their country. The prisoners were turned over to the "mountain men" for safe keeping. Having no conveyances, they compelled the prisoners to carry the captured arms (about fifteen hundred in number) two guns each being assigned to most of the men. About sunset the Whigs who had fought the battle, being extremely hungry, had the pleasure of meeting the footmen, who had been left behind at Green river on their march to King's Mountain, pressing forward with a good supply of provisions.

Having appeased the cravings of hunger, they all marched to Bickerstaff's old field, in Rutherford county, where the principal officers held a court-martial over the "most audacious and murderous Tories." Thirty-two were condemned to be hung; after nine were thus disposed of, three at a time, the remainder, through mitigating circumstances and the entreaties of their Whig acquaintances, were respited. Several of the Tories, thus leniently dealt with, afterward joined the Whig ranks, and made good soldiers to the end of the war.

In 1815, through the instrumentality of Dr. William M'Lean, of Lincoln county, a head-stone of dark slate rock, was erected at King's Mountain, near the spot where Ferguson fell. It bears this incription: On the east: "Sacred to the memory of Maj. Wm. Chronicle, Capt. John Mattocks, William Robb and John Boyd, who were killed at this place on the 7th of October, 1780, fighting in defence of America."

On the west side:—"Col. Ferguson, an officer of his Brittanic Majesty, was defeated and killed at this place on the 7th of October, 1780."

Incidents:—Among the captured Tories were Captain W— G— and his lieutenant J— L—, both of whom were sentenced to be hung next morning at sunrise. They were first tied separately, with leather strings, and then closely together. During the night they managed to crawl to the waters edge, near their place of confinement, and wet their strings; this soon caused them to stretch so greatly as to enable the *leather-bound prisoners* to make their escape, and thereby deprive the "Mountain Boys" of having some contemplated fun. Like the Irishman's pig, in the morning "they came up *missing*."

As a foraging party of Tories, belonging to Ferguson's

army, was passing up King's Creek, they took old Arthur Patterson and his son Thomas prisoners; who, being recognized as noted Whigs, were carried to Ferguson's camp, threatened with hanging, and a guard placed over them. As the battle waxed warm and the issue of the contest seemed to be turning in favor of the American arms a call was made upon the guard to fall into line and assist their comrades in averting, if possible, their approaching defeat. During the commotion the old man Patterson moved gently to the back ground and thus made his escape. Thomas Patterson, not liking the *back movement*, watched his opportunity, *between fires* and change of the enimies position, dashed off boldly to the Whig lines, about one hundred yards distant, and reached them safely. He immediately called for a gun, which being furnished he fought bravely to the close of the engagement.

For several particulars connected with the battle of Kings Mountain, hitherto unknown, the author acknowledges his indebtedness to Abraham Hardin, Esq., a native of Lincoln County, N. C., and relative of Col. Hambright, now (1876) a worthy, intelligent, and christian citizen of York County, S. C., aged eighty-seven years.

COLONEL WILLIAM CAMPBELL.

Colonel William Campbell was a native of Augusta County, Va. He was of Scottish decent (his grandfather coming from Inverary) and possessed all the fire and sagacity of his ancestors. He assisted in raising the first regular troops in Virginia in 1775, and was honored with a Captain's commission. In 1776 he was made Lieutenant Colonel of the militia of Washington County, Va., and on the resignation of Evan Shelby, the father of Governor Shelby, he was promoted to the rank of Colonel, that rank he retained until after the battles of King's Mountain and Guilford Court-House, in both of which he distinguished himself, when he was promoted by the Virginia Legislature, for gallantry and general high merit, to the rank of Brigadier General in the Continental service. LaFayette, perceiving his fine military talents, gave him the command of a brigade of riflemen and light infantry, and he was ordered to join that officer below Richmond, who was covering Washington's approach to Yorktown in September 1781, previous to the surrender of Cornwallis at Yorktown on the 19th of October following.

Colonel Campbell, suffering from the severe wound received in the battle of Guilford, was taken ill and soon after died at La Fayette's head-quarters, about twenty-five miles above Williamsburg, in the thirty-sixth year of his age. His military career was short, but brilliant; and on all occasions, bravery, unsullied patriotism and manly rectitude of conduct marked his movements. La Fayette's general order, on the occasion of his decease is most highly complimentary to his efficient services and exalted worth. He is buried at Rocky Mills, in Hanover county, Va. About forty years afterward, his remains were removed to Washington county, to repose with those of his family.

Col. Campbell married a sister of Patrick Henry and left but one child, the mother of the late Hon. William C. Preston and Col. John S. Preston, both of Columbia, S. C. He was a man of high culture, a good classical scholar, but was chiefly given to the accurate sciences and *practically* to land surveying for himself and his kindred who were large land-holders in Virginia, east Tennessee and Kentucky. When under thirty years of age, he commanded a company in the Point Pleasant expedition on the Kenhawa river, in which occurred one of the most sanguinary battles in the history of Indian warfare and there acquired that early experience in arms which qualified him to perform a conspicuous part in the Revolutionary War

When the emergency arose for expelling the boasting Furguson from the soil of the Carolinas, Col. Sevier sought the assistance and co-operation of Col. Campbell, of Virginia, whose bravery and gallantry had become widely known. On the first application, Col. Campbell deemed it imprudent to withdraw his forces from their place of rendezvous, for fear of an attack from the neighboring Indians, but on a second urgent application, his assent yielded to the appeals of patriotism and he promptly marched with his regiment to co-operate with Colonels Sevier, Shelby and other officers to gain an undying fame, and glorious victory at King's Mountain.

The preceding statement of facts, corrects an error into which several historians have unintentionally fallen by confounding Lieut. Col. Campbell, a brave officer of a South Carolina regiment, who was mortally wounded at the battle of the Eutaw Springs, with Col. Wm. Campbell, of Virginia, one of the heroes of King's Mountain, who died a natural death in his native State a few weeks before the surrender of Cornwallis at Yorktown. The two officers were of no close family relationship, but resembled each other in unflinching bravery and genuine exhibitions of true patriotism.

COLONEL ISAAC SHELBY.

Col. Isaac Shelby was born in Maryland, near the North mountain, a few miles from Hagerstown, on the 11th of December, 1750. He was the son of General Evan Shelby, a native of Wales, who came to America when a mere youth. General Shelby was distinguished for his indomitable courage, iron constitution, and clear intellect. He served as a Captain of Rangers under Gen. Braddock, and acted bravely in the attack under General Forbes in

1758, in which he led the advance, and took from the French Fort Du Quesne. In 1772, he removed to the west and in 1774, commanded a company under Colonel Lewis and Governor Dunmore against the Indians, on the Scioto river. He was in the sanguinary battle of Kenhawa, October 10th 1774, when Colonels Lewis, Fleming and Field were killed and he was left the commanding officer.

In 1779, he led a strong force against the Chickamauga Indians, on the Tennessee river; and for his services and gallantry, was appointed a Brigadier General by the State of Virginia; the first officer ever vested with that grade on the western waters.

Thomas Shelby, a brother of Gen. Evan Shelby, joined the great tide of southern emigration and settled on Caldwell's Creek, in the eastern part of Mecklenburg county (now Cabarrus) about 1760. He died near the beginning of the Revolutionary war, leaving four sons, William, John, Evan and Thomas. One of these sons (Thomas) served as a private in Captain Charles Polk's company in the spring of 1776, in the Wilmington campaign.

Col. Isaac Shelby, the immediate subject of this sketch was born to the use of arms, blessed with a strong constitution and capable of enduring great exposure and fatigue. His whole educational training was such as fitted him for the stiring scenes in which he was destined by Providence to become so prominent an actor.

His first essay in arms was as a Lieutenant in a company commanded by his father, in the celebrated battle, previously mentioned, at the mouth of the Kenhawa, the most sanguinary conflict ever maintained against the northwestern Indians, the action lasting from sunrise to sunset, with varying success.

Night closed the conflict and under its cover, the celebrated chief *Cornstalk*, who commanded the Indians, abandoned the ground. In July, 1776, he was appointed Captain of a company of minute men by the Virgina committee of safety. In 1777, he was appointed by Governor Henry, a commissary of supplies for an extensive body of troops to guard the frontiers and one of the commissioners appointed to form a treaty with the Cherokees at the Long Island of the Holston river. In 1778, he was elected a member of the Virginia Legislature from Washington county, and was appointed by Thomas Jefferson, then Governor of that State, a Major in the escort of guards for the commissioners, engaged in running the line between Virginia and North Carolina. On the completion of that line, his residence was found to be in North Carolina, which circumstance induced Richard Caswell, then Governor of the State, to appoint him Colonel of the militia of Sullivan county. In the summer of 1780, he was engaged in Kentucky in surveying, locating and securing the lands which five years previously, he had marked out, and improved. It was at this time, that he heard of the surrender of Charleston. This disaster aroused his patriotic spirit, and caused him to return home, determined to enter the service of his bleeding country and never to leave it until her liberty and independence were secured. On his arrival at home, he found a requisition from General Charles McDowell to furnish all the aid in his power to check the enemy, who flushed with their late success in overrunning South Carolina and Georgia, had entered North Carolina with a similar object in view. He immediately sought enlistments from the militia of Sullivan county and in a few days crossed the mountains at the head of two hundred and forty riflemen.

He reported to Gen. McDowell near the Cherokee Ford, on Broad river, and was by that officer detached, with Colonels Sevier and Clarke, to surprise and take a fort held by Captain Patrick Moore, a noted Tory leader, on the Palcolet river. This service was promptly executed without losing any of his men. The fort was surrounded, and, after a short parley as to terms the enemy surrendered as prisoners of war.

Captain Moore, one British Major, ninety-three Tories and two hundred and fifty stands of arms and their amunition, greatly needed at that time, were the fruits of this victory.

It was at this period that Major Ferguson of the British army, in his progress to the mountains of North Carolina, made several attempts to surprise Col. Shelby, but in every instance, he was baffled through his vigilance and activity.

On the first of August, 1780, the advance of the British force came up and attacked Shelby at Cedar Springs. The situation had been chosen by Shelby and his martial, adventurous spirit did not avoid the issue of battle. A sharp and animated conflict ensued, which lasted half an hour, when the whole force of Ferguson advanced to the scene of action. Shelby deemed it prudent to retreat before superior numbers, carrying off as the fruits of his victory thus far obtained, fifty prisoners, including two British officers. The enemy made a rapid pursuit, but Shelby, availing himself of every advantageous ground, completely eluded their efforts to overtake him and soon afterward joined Gen. McDowell with only a loss of ten or twelve killed and wounded.

On the 19th of August, 1780, Colonels Shelby, Williams and Clarke, under orders from Gen. McDowell, again attacked, with seven hundred mounted men, a large body of Tories near Musgrove's Mill, on the south side of the Ennoree river. On the night of the 18th of August, these officers left Smith's Ford on Broad river, took a circuitous route through the woods to avoid Ferguson, whose whole force lay between, and at dawn of day, after riding about forty miles, attacked the patrol of the Tories, about half a mile from their camp. A brisk skirmish ensued, several were killed, and the patrol driven in. At this moment, a countryman living near informed Col. Shelby the enemy on the night before had been re-inforced by a body of six hundred regulars (the Queen's American regiment from New York) under Col. Innis. This was unexpected news. Fatigued as were their horses, retreat was impracticable; and to attack an enemy of such superior force, would have been an act of rashness and the certain defeat of his own little band of patriots.

Col. Shelby met the trying emergency with unflinching courage and great promptness of action. It was agreed that Colonel Williams should have the chief command. Accordingly, the whole Whig force, except Capt. Inman's command, was ordered to form a breastwork of old logs and brush, and make as brave a defence as circumstances permitted. Capt. Inman, with twenty-five men was directed to proceed to the ford of the river, fire across upon the enemy, and retreat when they appeared in strong force. This stratagem being the suggestion of the brave Capt. Inman, was successful. Col. Innis immediately crosssd the river to dislodge the "rebels." Capt. Inman and his little force instantly retreated, hotly pursued by Innis until within the area of the patriot ambuscade when a single shot by Col. Shelby gave the signal for attack. The Whig riflemen, with sure and steady aim, opened a destructive fire which was kept up for an hour, during which time Col. Innis was wounded; all the British officers except a subaltern were killed or wounded. The Tory Captain, Hawsey, and Major Fraser, of the British regulars, with sixty-three privates were killed, and one hundred and sixty made prisoners. The American loss was only four killed and nine wounded. In the pursuit Captain Inman was killed fighting hand to hand with the enemy. After this victory Col. Williams, with the prisoners, encamped at the Cedar Spring, in Spartanburg County and from thence proceeded to Charlotte, N. C. Colonels Williams and Clarke then returned to the western frontier and the prisoners under Maj. Hammond marched to Hillsboro.

Excited by this brilliant victory Col. Shelby prepared to attack the British force at Ninety-six, about thirty miles distant, when an express arrived from Gen. McDowell, with a letter from Governor Caswell, dated on the battle ground of Camden, informing him of Gates' defeat and advising him to get out of the way. This advice came in good time, for on the next day a strong detachment from Ferguson's army sallied forth to overtake the victors, but through the energy and activity of Col. Shelby the designs of the enemy were completely baffled·

The brilliancy of the affair shone more brightly by the dark gloom which now overspread the public mind in consequence of the defeat of Gen. Gates at Camden. This caused Gen. Mcdowell to disband for the present his little force and retire beyond the mountains. The whole country was now apparently subjugated, the hopes of the patriot were dimmed, and many took protection under the British standard. But the brave spirits of the west, as firm as their native mountains, were still undismayed ; and, if for a moment subdued, they were not conquered, and the fire of freedom glowed deeply in their patriotic bosoms.

At this gloomy period, Col. Shelby, in consultation with Col. Charles McDowell, proposed to Colonels Sevier and Campbell to raise a force as quickly as possible from their several counties, and attack the boasting Ferguson. A concert of action, and junction of their forces were promptly agreed upon, the battle of Kings Mountain followed soon thereafter, and the result is well known. It will be seen, the first movement for organizing forces and bringing to a speedy accomplishment this most decisive victory of the South originated in Western North Carolina.

Inspired by this victory, the forces of North Carolina assembled under General Davidson at New Providence, in Mecklenburg County, near the South Carolina line. Gen. Smallwood, with Morgan's light corps and the Maryland line advanced to the same point. Gen. Gates, with the remnant of his army, and General Stevens with levies from Virginia enabled General Greene, after he assumed the chief command in December, 1780, to hold Cornwallis in check and frustrate his design, at that time, of marching to Charlotte.

It was at the suggestion of Col Shelby that General Greene sent out the expedition which achieved the brilliant victory at the Cowpens. In 1781, Col. Shelby served under Gen. Marion, and with Col. Mayhem, was in the skirmish near Monk's Corner. On attacking this post it immediately surrendered with one hundred and fifty prisoners. Soon afterward he obtained leave of absence from Gen. Marion to attend the General Assembly of North Carolina, of which he was a member from Sullivan County.

In 1782 he was again a member, and was appointed a Commissioner to settle the preemption claims upon the Cumberland, and lay off the lands allotted to the officers and soldiers south of where Nashville now stands. He returned to Boonsboro on the April following where he married Susanna Hart, whose father was one of the partners of Judge Henderson. The liberties of his Country being nearly established he devoted himself to his farm on the first pre-emption and settlement granted in Kentucky. In May, 1792, he was elected the first Governor of the new State. In 1812, a stormy period in our history, he was again elected to the same position. When the war with Great Britain broke out his well known energy and Revolutionary fame induced the Legislature of Kentucky to solicit his services in the field. At the head of four thousand volunteers he marched to the shores of Lake Erie to assist Gen. Harrison in the celebrated battle of the Thames. For his bravery in this battle, Congress honored him with a gold medal. In 1817 President Monroe appointed him his Secretary of War, but on account of his advanced age he declined the honor. His last public act was that of holding a treaty with the Chickasaw Indians, in 1818, in which General Jackson was his colleague. In 1820 he was attacked with a paralytic affection but his mind still remained unimpaired. In July, 1826, he expired from a stroke of apoplexy, in the seventy-sixth year of his age, enjoying the love and respect of his country and consoled by the rich hopes of a joyful immortality. Worthily is his name preserved in North Carolina in a region that witnessed his exalted patriotism and valor.

COLONEL JAMES D. WILLIAMS.

Col. James D. Williams, a brave and meritorious officer, was mortally wounded at King's Mountain, near the close of the action. He died on the next morning, and is buried within two miles of the place where he so gallantly fell. Tradition says his first words, after reviving a little, were, "For God's sake, boys, don't give up the hill."

He was a native of Granville county, N. C. He moved to Laurens county, S. C., in 1773, and settled upon Little river. He early espoused the patriot cause, and was active in raising troops and defending the territory of the "Ninety-Six" District, abounding with many evil-disposed loyalists.

He first appears as a Colonel of militia in April, 1778. In the spring of 1779, he went into actual service, and was probably at the siege of Savannah. He was with Gen. Sumter in 1780, and in the early part of that year he was in the battle of Musgrove's Mill, on the Ennoree river. After that engagement he went to Hillsboro, where he raised a corps of cavalry, and returned to South Carolina. During Ferguson's movements, after crossing the Wateree with the intention of embodying the loyalists, and intercepting the "Mountain Men," Col. Williams continually hovered around his camp, prepared to strike a blow when he could, and cripple his advance.

Colonel Williams was a worthy member and Elder of the Presbyterian Church, and was highly esteemed by all who knew him. It is to be regretted more has not been preserved of his efficient military services.

COLONEL WILLIAM GRAHAM.

Colonel William Graham was the son of Archibald Graham, of Scotland. He was born in Augusta county, Va., in 1742. He emigrated to North Carolina several years previous to the Revolutionary War, became the owner of much valuable land, and finally settled on First Broad river, then Tryon county, but now in Cleaveland. His patriotic principles soon became known, and were called into active service at the commencement of the Revolution. As the commanding officer, he had the general surperintendence of several Forts, erected on and near the frontier settlements, as protections against the hostile Cherokee Indians. Whilst in command of Fort McFadden, near the present town of Rutherfordton, he formed the acquaintance of Mrs. Susan Twitty, widow of William Twitty, and, as the "darts of Cupid" are often irresistible, he married her, and the union proved to be a happy one.

In the Provincial Congress which met at Halifax on the 12th of Nov., 1776, when the first State Constitution was formed, Colonel Graham was one of the delegates from Lincoln county, his colleagues being Joseph Hardin, Robert Abernathy, William Alston and John Barber.

In the expedition which marched in 1776, under General Rutherford, against the Cherokee Indians, Colonel Graham commanded the regiment which went from Lincoln and Rutherford counties. This expedition, as is well known, was completely successful, and caused the Indians to sue for peace.

In the expedition which marched for the relief of Charleston, in the spring of 1780, from Charlotte, the place of renndezvous for several counties, Colonel Graham led the regiment from Lincoln county. On the arrival of the several forces at Charleston, they found the city so completely invested by the British army that they could not render assistance to the American garrison.

Soon after his return home, Colonel Graham again marched with his regiment, General Rutherford commanding, against a large body of Tories assembled at Ramsour's Mill under Lieut. Colonel John Moore, (son of Moses Moore) near the present town of Lincolnton. General Rutherford, with some Mecklenburg troops, crossed the Catawba river at Tuckaseege Ford, on the evening of the 19th of June, 1780, and camped at Colonel Joseph Dickson's plantation, three miles northwest of the ford. On the morning of the 20th, Gen. Rutherford marched, at an early hour, with the expectation of co-operating with Colonel Locke, of Rowan county, in making a combined attack against the Tories, but failed to reach the battle-ground until about two hours after the close of that sanguinary engagement, in which the Tories were signally defeated.

When a call was made upon the commanding officers of the militia of Lincoln county (under its old limits) in September, 1780, for troops to oppose the boasting Ferguson, Colonel Graham marched with his regiment, and joined Colonels Campbell, Sevier, Shelby and others at the "Cowpens," where, a little more than three months afterward, General Morgan gained a brilliant victory;

but, it is known, in consequence of severe sickness in his family, Colonel Graham did not participate in the battle which took place on King's Mountain on the afternoon of the 7th of October, 1780, and which resulted so gloriously for the American arms.

During the year 1775, the Province of North Carolina, ever in the van of early patriotic movements, formed "Associations" throughout her territory, mainly as *tests of patriotism*. The county of Cumberland formed an Association on the 20th of June, 1775. The county of Tryon (embracing Lincoln and Rutherford) formed a similar "Association" on the 14th of August following, which was signed by the "Committee of Safety," and ordered to be "signed by every freeholder in the county." Among the forty-eight signatures may be conspicuously noticed those of William Graham, Charles McLean, (who at one time commanded the Lincoln regiment), Frederick Hambright, (see sketch of his services in this volume) John Walker, Jacob Forney, (father of Gen. Peter Forney), Thomas Espey, (brother of Capt. Samuel Espey, severely wounded at the battle of King's Mountain), Andrew Neal, Joseph Neal, John Dellinger, George Dellinger, Joseph Hardin, Jacob Costner, Valentine Mauney, Peter Sides, Joseph Kuykendall, James Coburn, James Miller and others. One of the signers, Peter Sides, (properly Seitz) belonged to a family from Switzerland—all true Whigs, and worthy representatives of the land of William Tell.

Colonel William Graham died in April, 1835, in the eighty-seventh year of his age, and is buried at the old homestead, on First Broad river, in Cleaveland county, N. C.

LIEUTENANT-COLONEL FREDERICK HAMBRIGHT.

Lieutenant-Colonel Hambright was born in Germany in 1727, emigrated to Pennsylvania about 1740, and after re maining there a short time removed to Virginia about 1755, where he married Sarah Hardin, with whom he lived happily until her death during the Revolution. A few years after his marriage he moved to Tryon county in North Carolina, being accompanied by his brothers-in-law, Colonel Joseph Hardin, John Hardin and Benjamin Hardin; also, by James Kuykendall, Nathaniel Henderson, Robert Leeper, and others. He first settled at the Fort, erected near the mouth of the South Fork of the Catawba river, as a protection against the attacks of the Indians. From that place he soon afterward moved to Long Creek, in the same county, and was living there when the battle of King's Mountain took place, in which he so gallantly participated. A short time previous to that battle he had purchased a tract of land on King's Creek, and had built a cabin upon it, preparatory to a future removal of his family.

Colonel Hambright was twice married. By the first marriage to Sarah Hardin, previously noticed, he had twelve children, of whom six were raised, viz: 1. John H. Hambright, who fought at King's Mountain. 2. Elizabeth. 3. Frederick. 4. Sarah. 5. Benjamin, and 6. James Hambright. Of these, Elizabeth married Joseph Jenkins, and Sarah Peter Eaker, both of whom have worthy descendants.

By the second wife, Mary Dover, whom he married in 1781, he had ten children, of whom eight were raised. Mrs. Susannah Dickson, the tenth child by the second wife, and the youngest of the twenty-two children, is still living and retains in her memory many interesting traditions of the Reveolution.

Colonel Hambright early displayed a fervent patriotic zeal for the independence of his adopted country. In 1777 he received the appointment of Lieutenant-Colonel, and was throughout the war an active and courageous officer. He was constantly watching the movements of the Tories, whose malicious influence and plundering habits seriously disturbed the peace and welfare of society. His name soon became a "terror to the Tories, who well knew the determination of his character and the vigilence and prowess of his arms in arresting disaffected persons, and defeating their designs.

At the battle of King's Mountain Col. William Graham, having charge of the Lincoln regiment, not being present on account of sickness in his family, the command devolved on Col. Hambright and most nobly and courageously did he sustain the responsible position. No portion of the advancing Whig columns evinced more irresistible bravery, and suffered more severely than the troops under his immediate command. Major William Chronicle, one of his most efficient and gallant officers, fell early in the action. There, too, Captain John Mattocks, Lieutenants Robb and Boyd, and others, all from the same neighborhood, lost their lives in that fiercely contested battle, which resulted so gloriously for the cause of liberty.

In this conflict Colonel Hambright was severely wounded by a large rifle ball passing through the fleshy part of the thigh. It was soon discovered by the soldiers near him that he was wounded and bleeding profusely. Samuel Moore, of York county, South Carolina, requested him to to be taken from his horse; he refused by saying, "he knew he was wounded but was not sick or faint from the loss of blood—said he could still ride very well, and therefore deemed it his duty to fight on till the battle was over." And most nobly did he remain in his place, encouraging his men by his persistent bravery and heroic example until signal victory crowned the American arms.

At the close of the action, when Colonel Hambright alighted from his horse, the blood was running over the top of the boot on the wounded leg. He was then conveyed to the cabin erected on his own land, as previously stated, before the war, where he was properly cared for until he was partially recovered. Although the wound, in-process of time, seemed to have healed, yet its deep-seated injury caused him to falter in his walk during the remainder of his life. The reason he assigned for refusing to be taken from his horse when severely wounded does honor to his exalted patriotism. He said if he had complied his men would neglect to *load* and *fire* as often as they should; would gather around him to administer to his wants, and thus fail to do their whole duty in opposing and conquering the enemy.

Such true devotion to the cause of freedom is worthy of our warmest admiration, and forcibly illustrates the heroic spirit which animated the band of patriots who achieved, on King's Mountain, one of the most important and decisive victories af the American Revolution.

Colonel Hambright was long a worthy member and elder of the Presbyterian church at Shiloh, in the present limits of Cleaveland county. On his tombstone we have this plain inscription:

"In memory of Colonel Frederick Hambright, who departed this life, March (figures indistinct) 1817, in the ninetieth year of his age."

CHAPTER VIII.

BURKE COUNTY.

Burke county was formed in 1777 from Rowan county, and was named in honor of the celebrated orator and statesman, Edmund Burke, an Irishman by birth, and possessed of all the warm and impetuous order of his countrymen. He early employed his pen in literature, and his eloquence in politics. Having been introduced to the Marquis of Rockingham, he made him his secretary and procured his election to the House of Commons. He there eloquently pleaded the cause of the Americans. During his political career he wrote much, and his compositions rank among the purest of English classics. This true friend of America died on the 8th of July, 1797, in the seventieth year of his age.

At the commencement of the Revolutionary war the territory now lying on and near the eastern base of the "Blue Ridge," or Alleghany chain of mountains, constituted the borders of civilization, and suffered freqently from marauding bands of Cherokee Indians, the great scourge of Western North Carolina. The whole country west of Tryon county (afterward Lincoln) was sparsely settled with the families of adventurous individuals, who, confronting all dangers, had carved out homes in the mountains and raised up hardy sons, deeply imbued with the spirit of liberty, prepared to go forth, at a moment's warning, to fight the battles of their country.

BATTLE OF THE COWPENS.

"There was Greene in the South; you must know him,—
Whom some called a "Hickory Quaker;"
But he ne'er turned his back on the foemen,
Nor ever was known for a *shaker*."

After the unfortunate battle of Camden, on the 16th of August, 1780, where Gen. Gates lost the laurels he had obtained at Saratoga, Congress perceived the necessity of appointing a more efficient commander for the Southern army. Accordingly Gen. Washington was directed to make the selection from his well-tried and experienced officers. Whereupon the commander-in-chief appointed General Nathaniel Greene, late the Quartermaster General, on the 30th of October, 1780, who, in a few days afterward, set out for his field of labor. As he passed through Deleware, Maryland and Virginia, he ascertained what supplies it was likely could be obtained from those States; and leaving the Baron Steuben to take charge of the defence of Virginia he proceeded to Hillsboro, then the temporary seat of government for North Carolina. Gov. Nash received him with much joy, as the safety of the State was in imminent danger. After a short stay in that place he hastened on to Charlotte, the headquarters of the Southern army. Gen. Gates there met him with marked respect, without displaying any of those feelings which sometimes arise from disappointed ambition, and immediately set out for the headquarters of Washington, then in New Jersey, to submit to an inquiry into his conduct, which had been ordered by Congress.

Gen. Green took charge of the Southern army in the town of Charlotte on the 3rd day of December, 1780. After surveying his troops and supplies he found himself at the head of about two thousand men, one half of whom were militia, with only a sufficiency of provisions for three days, in an exhausted country, and with a scanty supply of ammunition. With the quick eye of military genius, he determined at once to divide his army, small as it was, and provide the needful supplies in different localities. Relying upon Gen. Davidson's militia, as a central force and protection, to be called out upon emergencies from the surrounding counties, he led the largest portion of his army under himself, and encamped on Hick's Creek, opposite Cheraw, and about seventy miles to the right of Cornwallis, who was then at Winsboro, South Carolina. While encamped at this place he was joined by the legionary corps of cavalry under Lieutenant-Colonel Henry Lee, more familiarly known as "Light Horse Harry," and father of the late distinguished Gen. Robert E. Lee, of the Confederate army, whose memory the Southern people and an *impartial world* will ever delight to honor! The other detachment of the army, about one thousand strong, under Brig. Gen. Morgan was placed about fifty miles to the left to disperse bands of Tories and protect the country between the Broad and Pacolet rivers. Gen. Morgan's division, near the close of 1780, consisted of four hundred of Continental infantry under Lieutanant-Colonel Howard, of the Maryland line, two companies of the Virginia militia under Captains Triplett and Tate, and about one hundred dragoons under Lieutenant-Colonel William Washington. This force, at the time just mentioned, was considerably augmented by North Carolina militia under Major McDowell—"Mountain boys," ever reliable, and some Georgia militia, under Major Cunningham. Gen. Morgan encamped on the northern bank of Pacolet river, and near Pacolet Springs. From this point Col. Washington frequently sallied forth to disperse bodies of Tories who assembled at different places and plundered the Whig inhabitants. He attacked and defeated two hundred of them at Hammond's store, and soon afterward a section of his command dispersed another Tory force under the "bloody Bill Cunningham."

Cornwallis, who was still at Winnsboro, perceived these successes with alarm, and fearing an attack upon his important post at Ninety-Six, determined to diperse the forces under Morgan or drive them into North Carolina before he should rally the Mountain Men in sufficient numbers to cut off his communication with his post at Augusta. He accordingly dispatched Tarleton with his legion and a strong force of infantry, with two field pieces, to compel Morgan to fight or hastily retreat. Tarleton's entire force consisted of about eleven hundred well-disciplined men, and in every respect he had the advantage of Morgan.

It is related of Tarleton that when he heard of Morgan's forces being encamped near the post of Ninety-Six, he begged of Lord Rawdon the privilege of attacking the American officer. "By Heaven, my lord, said he, I would not desire a finer feather in my cap than Colonel Morgan. Such a prisoner would make my fortune." Ah, Ban, (contration of Banastre, Tarleton's christian name) replied Rawdon, you had better let the old wagoner alone." As no refusal would satisfy him, permission was given, and he immediately set out with a strong force in pursuit of Morgan. At parting Tarleton said to Rawdon with a smile, "My lord, if you will be so obliging as to wait dinner, the day after to-morrow, till four o'clock, Colonel Morgan shall be one of your lordship's guests." "Very well, Ban, said Rawdon, we shall wait; but remember, Morgan was brought up under Washington."

Tarleton commenced his march from Winnsboro on the 11th of January, 1781, Cornwallis following leisurely in the rear with the main army. He crossed Broad river near Turkey creek, and advanced with all possible speed in the direction of Morgan's camp. That officer was at first disposed to dispute Tarleton's passage of the Pacolet river, but being informed of the superiority of his numbers, and that a portion of the British army had already crossed above him, he hastily retreated northward, and took post for battle on the north side of Thicketty Mountain, near the Cowpens. Tarleton pressed eagerly forward in pursuit, riding all night, and making a circuit around the western side of the mountain. At eight o'clock in the morning he came in sight of the advanced guard of the patriots, and fearing that Morgan might again retreat and get safely across Broad river, he resolved to attack him immediately, notwithstanding the fatigued condition of his troops. Tarleton was evidently disposed to view Morgan as "flying game," and he therefore wished to "bag him" while clearly within scope of his vision. The sequel will show how sadly he was mistaken.

The Americans were posted upon an eminence of gentle ascent, covered with an open wood. They were rested and refreshed after their retreat from the Pacolet. And, now expecting the enemy, they were drawn up in battle order. Tarleton was rather disconcerted when he found that Morgan was prepared to fight him, for he expected to overtake him on a flying retreat. It was now about nine o'clock. The sun was shining brightly over the summits of Thicketty Mountain, and imparted a glowing brilliancy to the martial array in the forests below. On the crown of the eminence were stationed two hundred and ninety Maryland regulars, and on their right the two companies of Virginia militia under Major Triplet. These composed the rear line of four hundred and thirty men under Lieutenant-Colonel Howard. One hundred and fifty yards in advance of this line was a body of about three hundred militia under Colonel Andrew Pickens, all experienced riflemen, and burning with a spirit of revenge on account of numerous cruelties previously inflicted by the British and Tories. This brave officer had arrived during the night, with his followers, and joined Morgan. About one hundred and fifty yards in advance of this first line, were placed the best riflemen of the corps under McDowell and Cunningham. The action soon commenced. At a signal from Tarleton, his advance gave a loud shout and rushed furiously to the contest, under cover of their artillery, and a constant discharge of musketry. The riflemen under McDowell and Cunningham delivered their fire with terrible effect, and then fell back to the flanks of the first line under Pickens. The contest was close and severe, with alternate wavings of the British and American lines, under successive attacks of the bayonet, which the prescribed limits of this work forbid to be presented in all their annimating details. Suffice it to say, Tarleton here met a "foeman worthy of his steel;" and the Americans, at the Cowpens, on the 17th of January, 1781, gained one of the most triumphant victories of the Revolutionary War. Almost the whole of the British infantry, except the baggage guard, were either killed or taken. Two pieces of artillery, eight hundred muskets, two standards, thirty-five wagons and one hundred dragoon horses fell into the hands of the Americans. Notwithstanding the cruel warfare which Tarleton had waged against the Americans, to the honor of the victors it is said not one of the British prisoners was killed, or even insulted after they had surrendered.

The loss of the Americans in this decisive battle was twelve killed and about sixty wounded. The loss of the British was ten officers and ninety privates killed, and twenty-three officers and five hundred privates taken prisoners. At the close of the action, Washington, with his cavalry, pursued Tarleton, who now in turn, had become "flying game." In his eagerness of pursuit of that officer, Washington had dashed forward considerably in advance of his squadron, when Tarleton and two of his aids turned upon him, and just as an officer on Tarleton's right was about to strike him with his sabre, his sergeant dashed up and disabled the assailant's sword arm. An officer on Tarleton's left was about to strike at the same moment, when Washington's little bugler, too small to wield a sword, wounded the assailant with a pistol ball. Tarleton, who was in the center, then made a thrust at him, which Washington parried, and wounded his enemy in the hand. Tarleton wheeled, and, as he retreated, discharged a pistol, wounding Washington in the knee. During that night and the following morning, the remnant of Tarleton's forces crossed Broad river at Hamilton's Ford, and reached the encampment of Cornwallis at Turkey creek, about twenty-five miles from the Cowpens.

This *hand-wound* of Tarleton, inflicted by Washington, gave rise, on two different occasions, to sallies of wit by two American ladies, daughters of Colonel Montford, of Halifax county, North Carolina. When Cornwallis and his army were at Halifax, on their way to Virginia, Tarleton was at the house of an American citizen. In the presence of Mrs. Willie Jones, Tarleton spoke of Colonel Washington as an illiterate fellow, hardly able to write his name. "Ah! Colonel," said Mrs. Jones, "you ought to know better, for you bear on your person proof that he knows very well *how to make his mark!*" At another time, Tarleton was sarcastically speaking of Washington in the presence of her sister, Mrs. Ashe. "I would be happy to see Colonel Washington," he said, with a sneer. Mrs. Ashe instantly replied: "If you had looked behind you, Colonel Tarleton, at the battle of the Cowpens, you would have enjoyed that pleasure." Stung with this keen wit, Tarleton placed his hand on his sword with an inclination to use it. General Leslie, who was present, remarked, "Say what you please, Mrs. Ashe, Colonel Tarleton knows better than to insult a lady in my presence."

The victory of the Cowpens gave great joy to the friends of liberty throughout the whole country. Congress received information of it on the 8th of February following, and on the 9th of March voted an award of a gold medal to Morgan; a silver medal to Howard and Washington; a sword to Col. Pickens, and a vote of thanks to the other officers and men engaged in the battle.

At this time, Cornwallis was advancing triumphantly in the direction of North Carolina, having placed South Carolina and Georgia, as he thought, in submission at his feet. The defeat and death of Ferguson, one of his most efficient officers, at King's Mountain, and now of Tareton, his favorite partisan, greatly withered his hopes of strong Tory cooperation. His last hope was the destruction of Greene's army by his own superior force, and, with that design in view, he broke up his encampment near Turkey creek, and like Saul, "yet breathing out threatenings and slaughter" against Morgan's little army, he commenced that pursuit of the "hero of the Cowpens," who, encumbered with his five hundred prisoners, under various Providential interpositions, made good his retreat into Virginia, constituting one of the most thrilling and successful military achievements of the American Revolution.

GENERAL DANIEL MORGAN.

General Daniel Morgan was born in Bucks county, Pennsylvania, in 1737, and moved to Virginia in 1755. He was a private soldier under General Braddock, and after the defeat of that officer returned to his occupation of a farmer and a wagoner. When the war of the Revolution broke out, he joined the army under General Washington, at Cambridge, and commanded a corps of riflemen. He was with General Montgomery at Quebec, and with General Gates at Saratoga, in both of which battles he greatly distinguished himself. For his bravery he was promoted to the rank of Brigadier General, and joined the army in the South. After the battle of Camden, when General Greene assumed the chief command, General Morgan was detached to raise troops in the western part of the State and in South Carolina. He soon became distinguished as a partisan officer, inspiring confidence and arousing the despondent Whigs to a more active sense of duty. His victory at the Cowpens was justly considered as one of the most brilliant and decided victories of the Revolution, and Congress accordingly voted him a gold medal. At the close of the war, he returned to his farm. In 1794 he was appointed by General Washington to quell the Whisky Insurrection in Western Virginia, and after the difficulties were settled, he was elected a member of Congress and served from 1797 to 1799. His health failing, he declined a re-election. His farm in Clarke county, a few miles from Winchester, Va., was called *Saratoga*. In 1800, he removed to Winchester, where he died on the 6th of July, 1802, in the sixty-seventh year of his age.

In early life, General Morgan was dissipated; yet the teachings of a pious mother always made him reverential when his thoughts turned toward the Deity. In his latter years he professed religion and became a member of the Presbyterian Church in Winchester. "Ah!" he would often exclaim when talking of the past, "people said old Morgan never feared—they thought old Morgan never prayed—they did not know old Morgan was miserably afraid." He said he trembled at Quebec, and in the gloom of early morning, when approaching the battery at Cape Diamond, he knelt in the snow and prayed; and before the battle at the Cowpens, he went into the woods, ascended a tree, and there poured out his soul in prayer to the Almighty Ruler of the Universe for protection.

COLONEL CHARLES M'DOWELL AND BROTHERS.

(Condensed from Wheeler's "Historical Sketches.")

Colonel Charles McDowell and his brothers, Joseph and William, were sons of Joseph McDowell and Margaret O'Neal, who emigrated from Ireland and settled in Winchester, Va. Here, Charles and Joseph were born, the former in 1743. Soon afterward, Joseph McDowell, Sr., moved to Burke county, N. C.

In June, 1780, Colonel Charles McDowell being joined by Colonels Isaac Shelby and John Sevier from Tennessee, and by Colonel Clarke, of Georgia, near the Cherokee Ford on Broad river, in South Carolina, he determined to attack a post held by the enemy on Pacolet river, in Spartanburg county. The position was strongly fortified under the command of Captain Patrick Moore, a distinguished loyalist. On being surrounded, the enemy, after some parley as to terms, surrendered as prisoners of war. One British Sergeant Major, ninety-three loyalists, two hundred and fifty fire-arms and other munitions of war were the fruits of this victory. Soon afterward Col. McDowell detached Shelby to watch the movements of Ferguson, and attack him. On the 1st of August, 1780, Shelby met the advance guard of Ferguson at Cedar Spring, about six-hundred strong, when a spirited contest commenced; but on the enemy being reinforced, Shelby made good his retreat, carrying off from the field twenty prisoners, including two British officers.

On learning that a body of five hundred Tories had assembled on the south side of Enoree river, near Musgrove's Mill, Colonel McDowell detached Colonels Shelby, Williams and Clarke to attack them. Colonel Ferguson, with his whole force, lay encamped between them. They left the camp on the 18th of August at Smith's Ford on Broad river, and taking a circuitous route through the woods, avoided Ferguson's forces. They rode hard all night, and at daybreak encountered a strong patrol party of the enemy. A skirmish immediately ensued and the Tories retreated. They then advanced on the main body of the Tories. At this juncture a countryman living near, a friend of liberty, came to Shelby and informed him that the enemy had been reinforced the evening before, by six hundred regular troops, and the Queen's American regiment from New York, commanded by Colonel Innis, marching to join Ferguson. Here was a position that would have tried the talent and nerve of the most skillful and brave officer. Advance was hopeless, and retreat impossible. But Shelby was equal to the emergency. He immediately commenced forming a breast-work of brush and old logs, while he detailed twenty-five tried men to reconnoiter and skimish with the enemy as soon as they crossed the Enoree river. The drums and bugles of the enemy were soon heard marching upon this devoted band. Captain Inman had been ordered to fire and retreat. This stratagem, suggested by Captain Inman himself, was successful in its object. The enemy advanced in rapid pursuit and in great confusion, believing that the whole American force was routed. When they approached the rude breast-work of Shelby, they received from his riflemen a most destructive fire, which carried great slaughter among them. This was gallantly kept up; all the British officers were killed or wounded, and Hawsey, the Tory leader, shot down. The enemy then began a disorderly retreat. The Americans now in turn pursued, and in this pursuit the brave Captain Inman was killed, fighting hand to hand with the enemy. Colonel Shelby commanded the right wing, Colonel Clarke the left, and Colonel Williams the center.

The British loss in this brilliant and well-planned battle, was sixty-three killed and one hundred wounded and prisoners; the American loss was only four killed, including Captain Inman, and Captain Clarke wounded.

The triumphant victors were about to remount and advance on the British post at Ninety Six, when an express arrived from Colonel McDowell, with a letter from Governor Caswell, informing them of the defeat of General Gates at Camden on the 16th of August, and advising the retreat of our troops, as the British, flushed with victory, would advance in strong force and cut off all detachments of our people. With Ferguson near him, Colonel Shelby, encumbered with more than two hundred prisoners, acted with energy and promptness. He distributed the prisoners among the companies, each behind a private, and without stopping day or night, retreated over the mountains to a place of safety.

This rapid movement saved his men and himself. On the next day Major DePeyster, of Ferguson's forces, with a strong body of men, made an active but fruitless search.

In consequence of the panic after Gates' defeat on the 16th of August, 1780, and the surprise and dispersion of Sumter's forces at Fishing creek by Tarleton's cavalry on the 18th following, Colonel McDowell disbanded, for a time, his little army, and he himself retreated over the mountains.

This was a dark and doleful period of American history. The British flag floated in triumph over Charleston and Savannah. The troops of Lord Cornwallis, with all the pomp and circumstance of glory, advanced from the battle-field of Camden to Charlotte, with the fond expectation of soon placing North Carolina under his subjection. Many of the brave had despaired of final success, and the timid, and some of the wealthy, to save their property, had taken "protection" under the enemy. Colonel Ferguson, with chosen troops, was ravaging the whole western portion of upper South Carolina, subduing in his progress to western North Carolina, all opponents of English power, and encouraging, by bribes and artifice, others to join the royal standard.

Under all these discouraging circumstances the brave "Mountain Boys," and other kindred spirits of the west never despaired. On the mountain heights of North Carolina, and in her secure retreats, like Warsaw's "last champion," stood the stalwart soldiers of that day:

> "Oh Heaven! they said, our bleeding country save!
> Is there no hand on high to shild the brave?
> What though destruction sweep these lovely plains!—
> Rise, fellow-men! our country yet remains;
> By that dread name, we wave the sword on high,
> And swear for her to live! for her to die!"

If the sky was then gloomy, a storm was gathering in these mountain retreats which was soon to descend in all its fury on the heads of the enemies of our country. In a short time afterward the battle of King's Mountain was fought and won by the patriots, which spread a thrill of joy throughout the land.

Colonel Charles McDowell was elected the first Senator to the State Legislature from Burke county in 1778, and successively from 1782 to 1790. From 1791 to 1795, he was succeeded in the same position by his brother, Major Joseph McDowell. About this period, at three or four different times, all three of the members of the Assembly to which the county was entitled were of this family, which proved their great popularity and worth. Major Joseph McDowell also served as a member of Congress from 1793 to 1795, and from 1797 to 1799. He lived on John's river, and died there. His family returned to Virginia, where some of his descendants may still be found. One of his sons, Hugh Harvey, settled in Missouri, and Joseph J. McDowell, in Ohio, who was a member of Congress from that State from 1843 to 1847.

General Charles McDowell married Grace Greenlee, the widow of Captain John Bowman, who fell at the battle of Ramsour's Mill. By this union he had several children, one of whom was the late Captain Charles McDowell, who resided on the Catawba river, near Morganton.

General Charles McDowell died on the 31st of March, 1815, aged about seventy-two years.

CHAPTER IX.

WILKES COUNTY.

Wilkes county was formed in 1777, from Surry, and named in honor of John Wilkes, a distinguished statesman and member of Parliament. He was a fearless political writer, and violently opposed to the oppressive measures of Great Britain against her American Colonies. In 1763 he published in the "North Briton" newspaper a severe attack on the government, for which he was sent to the Tower. Acquitted of the charge for which he was imprisoned, he sued for and recovered five thousand dollars damages and then went to Paris. In 1768 he returned to England and was soon after elected a member of Parliament. In his private character he was licentious, but his eminent talents, energy, and fascinating manners made him a great favorite with the people. He died at his seat in the Isle of Wight in 1797, aged seventy years.

COLONEL BENJAMIN CLEAVELAND.

Colonel Benjamin Cleaveland, one of the distinguished heroes of King's Mountain, and in honor of whom Cleaveland county is named, lived and died in Wilkes county at a good old age.

In 1775 he first entered the service as Ensign in the second regiment of troops, and acted a brave and conspicuous part in the battle's of King's Mountain and Guilford court house. A serious impediment in his speech prevented him from entering public life. He is

SKETCHES OF WESTERN NORTH CAROLINA. 343

frequently spoken of in the mountain country as the "hero of a hundred fights with the Tories." He was for many years the Surveyor of Wilkes county and resided at the "Little Hickerson place."

Among other singular incidents in his remarkable career, as preserved by General William Lenoir, and recorded in Wheeler's "Historical Sketches," we give place to the following:

"Riddle Knob, in Watauga county, derives its name from a circumstance of the capture of Colonel Benjamin Cleaveland, during the Revolution, by a party of Tories headed by men of this name, and adds the charm of heroic association to the loveliness of it unrivaled scenery. Cleaveland had been a terror to the Tories. Two notorious characters of their band, (Jones and Coil) had been apprehended by him and hung. Cleaveland had gone alone, on some private business, to New river, and was taken prisoners by the Tories, at the "Old Fields," on that stream. They demanded that he should furnish passes for them.

Being an indifferent penman he was some time in preparing these papers, and he was in no hurry as he believed that they would kill him when they had obtained them. While thus engaged Captain Robert Cleaveland, his brother, with a party followed him, knowing the dangerous proximity of the Tories. They came up with the Tories and fired on them. Colonel Cleaveland slid off the log to prevent being shot, while the Tories fled, and he thus escaped certain destruction.

Some time after this circumstance the same Riddle and his son, and another were taken and brought before Cleaveland, and he hung all three of them near the Mulberry meeting-house, now Wilkesboro. The depredations of the Tories were so frequent, and their conduct so savage, that summary punishment was demanded by the exigencies of the times. This Cleaveland inflicted without ceremony."

COLONEL JOHN SEVIER.

Colonel John Sevier was born in Shenandoah county, Virginia, in 1734. His father descended from an ancient family in France, the name being originally spelled Xavier.

About 1769 young Sevier joined an exploring and emigrating party to the Holston river, in East Tennessee, then a part of North Carolina. He assisted in erecting the first fort on the Watauga river, where he, his father, his brother Valentine, and others settled. Whilst engaged in the defence of the Watauga fort, in conjunction with Captain James Robertson, so known and distinguished in the early history of Middle Tennessee, he espied a young lady, of tall and erect stature, running rapidly towards the fort, closely pursued by Indians, and her approach to the gate cut off by the savage enemy. Her cruel pursuers were doubtless confident of securing a captive or a victim to their blood-thirsty purposes; but, turning suddenly, she eluded the savages, leaped the palisades of the fort at another point, and gracefully fell into the arms of Captain John Sevier. This remarkably active and resolute woman was Miss Catharine Sherrill, who, in a few years after this sudden leap and rescue, became the devoted and heroic wife of the gallant Captain and future Colonel, General, Governor and people's friend, John Sevier. She became the mother of ten children, who could gratefully rise up and call her blessed.

During Sevier's visit to his family in Virginia in 1773, Governor Dunmore gave him a Captain's commission. Through his own exertions he raised a company and was in the sanguinary battle of Point Pleasant, on the

Kenhawa, in which James Robertson and Valentine Sevier actively participated.

The first settlers on the Holston, Watauga and other tributary streams, were so far beyond the influence of the State laws of North Carolina as to induce them in 1772 to form a temporary government for their better protection and security. The people enjoyed the advantages of this "Watauga government," as it was called, from 1772 until 1777, at which date Colonel Sevier procured the establishment of courts and the extension of State laws over "Washington District," then in North Carolina, embracing an interesting section of country in waich he and other pioneers of civilization had cast their lots. These hardy pioneers opened roads across the mountains, felled the forests, built forts and houses, subdued the earth, and began rapidly to replenish it, for they married and were given in marriage. The State of North Carolina, several years afterward) with a motherly forgiveness, passed laws to confirm marriages and other deeds of these wayward children in the wilderness.

Colonel Sevier served in the expedition under Colonel Christian to chastise the Indians for their numerous murders and depredations. In 1779, he raised troops, entered the Indian territory, and fought the successful battle of Boyd's creek. A few days after this battle, he was joined by Colonel Arthur Campbell with a Virginia regiment, and Colonel Isaac Shelby with troops from Sullivan county, then in North Carolina. These active officers scoured the Cherokee country, scattered hostile bands, destroyed most of the Indian towns, and, after inflicting this severe chastisement, returned to their homes with greater assurance of peace and security.

The former part of the year 1780, was one of gloom and despondency in the Southern States. Charleston surrendered, Gates defeated, and other minor reverses; Tories becoming daring and insolent; the British overrunning

South Carolina and Georgia; the Indians upon the borders, bribed and inflamed against the Americans—all tended to increase the gloom and darken the prospect of achieving our independence. But amidst all the obscurity which shrouded the sun of American independence, there was a gallant band of patriots in the mountains of North Carolina and upper South Carolina, who never quailed in duty before the enemy, struck a severe blow at every opportune moment, and never despaired of final success.

In the brilliant victory of King's Mountain, Col. Sevier, with his regiment, displayed the most consummate bravery. In June of the same year, he marched into South Carolina and assisted Col. McDowell and other officers in the successful battle of Musgrove's Mill.

In 1781, Colonel Sevier was appointed by General Greene a commissioner to treat with the chiefs of the Cherokees and other tribes of Indians, which trust he faithfully performed. During the years 1781 and 1782, he was almost constantly engaged in leading expeditions into the Cherokee country.

On the 14th of December, 1784, a convention of five delegates from each county of the extreme western portion of North Carolina, met at Jonesboro, now in Tennessee, of which body Col. Sevier was made President. They formed a constitution for a new State, to be called "Frankland," which was to be received or rejected by another body of similar powers, "fresh from the people," to meet at Greenville in November 1785. This anomolous state of things, as might be expected, caused Governor Caswell, who was both a soldier and a statesman, to issue his proclamation "against this lawless thirst for power."

The prescribed limits of this sketch forbid a full recital of all the angry discussions and violent acts of the opposing parties which unfortunately, for about three years, seriously disturbed the peace and welfare of Western North Carolina.

In 1789, Colonel Sevier was elected the Senator from Greene county to the Legislature of North Carolina. In 1790, he was elected a member of Congress. He was twice elected Governor of Tennessee. In 1811, he was elected a Representative to Congress, and in 1813, re-elected to the same position. In 1815, he was appointed by President Madison a commissioner to adjust difficulties with the Creek Indians. Whilst engaged in the performance of this arduous duty, he was taken seriously ill, and soon thereafter died near Fort Decatur, Ala., on the 24th of September, 1815, aged about eighty-one years.

Gen. Gaines, then in command of the regular troops near that place, though quite ill at the time, paid the last sad tribute of respect to a brave fellow-soldier, and had him buried with the honors of war.

GENERAL WILLIAM LENOIR.

General William Lenoir was born in Brunswick county, Virginia, on the 20th of May, 1751. He was of French (Huguenot) descent, and the youngest of a family of ten children. When he was about eight years old his father removed to a place near Tarboro, N. C., where he resided until his death, a short time afterward. He received no other education than his own limited means and personal exertions enabled him to procure. When about twenty years of age he married Ann Ballard, of Halifax, N. C.— a lady possessing, in an eminent degree, those domestic and heroic virtues which qualified her for sustaining the privations and hardships of a frontier life, which it was her lot afterward to encounter.

In March 1775 Gen. Lenoir removed with his family to Wilkes county (then a part of Surry) and settled near the place where Wilkesboro now stands. Previous to leaving Halifax he signed the paper known as the "Association," containing a declaration of patriotic principles and means of redress, relative to the existing troubles with Great Britain. Soon after his removal to Surry he was appointed a member of the "Committee of Safety" for that county. He took an early and active part in repelling the depredating and murderous incursions of the Cherokee Indians upon the frontier settlements. In this kind of service he was actively engaged until the celebrated expedition, under Gen. Rutherford, completely subdued the Indians, and compelled them to sue for peace. From the termination of this campaign, in which he acted as a Lieutenant under Captain Benjamin Cleaveland, to the one projected against Major Ferguson, he was almost constantly engaged in capturing and suppressing the Tories, who, at that time, were assuming great boldness, and molesting the persons and property of the Whig inhabitants.

In the expedition to King's Mountain Gen. Lenoir held the appointment of Captain in Colonel Cleaveland's regiment, which united with the other Whig forces at the head of the Catawba river. When it was ascertained it would be impossible to overtake Ferguson, now evidently showing signs of fear, with the footmen, it was decided by a council of the officers, that as many as could procure horses should do so, and thus, as mounted infantry, advance rapidly upon the retreating enemy. Accordingly, Gen. Lenoir and his company offered their services, joined the select Spartan band of *nine hundred and ten* brave spirits, and pressed forward without delay to the scene of action.

In the brilliant achievement on King's Mountain, Gen. Lenoir was wounded in the arm and in the side, but not severely, and a third ball passed through his hair, just above where it was tied. He was also at the defeat of Col. Pyles, on Haw River, where his horse was shot and his sword broken. At a later period he raised a company and marched towards Dan river with the hope of joining

General Greene, but was unable to effect a junction in time. He performed many other minor but important services, which it is here unnecessary to enumerate.

General Lenoir served as Major General of the militia about eighteen years. In a civil capacity he also discharged many high and responsible duties.

He filled, at different times, the offices of Register, Surveyor, Commissioner of Affidavits, Chairman of the County Court, and Clerk of the Superior Court for Wilkes county. He was one of the original Trustees of the State University, and the first President of the Board. He was also a member of both the State Conventions which met for the purpose of considering the Constitution of the United States. He served for many years in both branches of the State Legislature. During the last seven years of his services in the Senate, he was unanimously chosen Speaker of that body, and performed the duties of that important station with great satisfaction, firmness and impartiality.

In private life General Lenoir was no less distinguished for his moral worth and generous hospitality than in public life for his unbending integrity and enlarged patriotism. His mansion was open at all times, not only to a large circle of friends and relatives, but to the stranger and the traveller. To the poor he was kind and charitable, and in his will made liberal provision for those of his own neighborhood.

During his last illness he suffered much pain which he bore with Christian resignation. He often said " he did not fear to die—death had no terrors for him. He died, with calm composure, at his residence at Fort Defiance, on the 6th of May, 1839, aged eighty-eight years.

His remains were interred in the family burying ground which occupies the spot where Fort Defiance was erected during the Revolutionary war.

CHAPTER X.

MISCELLANEOUS.

LORD CORNWALLIS.

The readers of American history, and more particularly those of the Southern States, will doubtless be gratified to know something of *the end*—the closing career, and "shuffling off of this mortal coil" of Lord Cornwallis and Colonel Tarleton, the two British officers, who remained the longest time among them; sometimes conquering all before them, and again retrograding, until their capture and surrender at Yorktown, in Virginia, on the 19th of October, 1781.

Charles Cornwallis, son of the first Earl of Cornwallis, was born in Suffolk on the 31st of December, 1738. He was educated at Westminster and St. John's College, Cambridge. He entered the army in 1759, and succeeded to the title and estates of his father in 1761. He was the most competent and energetic of all the British generals sent to America during the Revolution, but the cruelties exercised by his orders on a few occasions, have left an indelible stain upon his character. It was in pursuance of one of his orders, issued soon after the battle of Camden, that the unfortunate Colonel Isaac Hayne was executed by that tyrannical British officer, Lord Rawdon. Notwithstanding this cruel tragedy, which might have resulted otherwise had he been present, Cornwallis possessed some fine traits of character, had an amiable disposition, was greatly beloved by his men, and was bitterly opposed to *house-burning* when the fortunes of war were in his favor. In 1770, he and three other young peers, joined Lord Camden in protesting against the taxation of the American colonies. Mansfield, the Chief Justice, is said to have sneeringly remarked: "Poor Camden could only get four boys to join him." Although opposed to the course of the British Ministry, yet, when hostilities commenced, he did not refuse to accept active employment against America. Soon after the war he was appointed Governor-General of the East Indies, which position he held for six years. During that time, he conquered the renowned Tippoo Sultan, for which service he was created a marquis and master of the ordnance. He was Lord Lieutenant of Ireland from 1798 to 1801, and was instrumental in restoring peace to that country, then distracted by rebellion. He signed the treaty of Amicus in 1802, and in 1804 was again appointed Governor General of India. On his arrival at Calcutta, his health failed and he died at Ghazepore on the 5th of October, 1805, aged sixty-seven years.

COLONEL TARLETON.

Colonel Banastre Tarleton was born in Liverpool, England, on the 21st of August, 1754. He commenced the study of the law, but when the war in America broke out he entered the British army and came to this country with Lord Cornwallis. He served with that officer in all his campaigns in the South, and by his daring intrepedity, and indomitable energy, greatly contributed to the success of the British arms at Camden. He possessed a sanguinary disposition, as was exhibited in the cruel massacre of Col. Buford's regiment at the Waxhaws. In tracing his history in America, we look in vain for any redeeming traits in his character. The ardor of his temper and military ambition received a severe check at the battle of the "Cowpens" on the 17th of January, 1781. The capitulation of the British army at Yorktown, closed his military services in America. On his return to England, he received, as might be expected, numerous honors.

In 1798, he married the daughter of the Duke of Ancaster. He died on the 25th of January, 1833, in the seventy-ninth year of his age, *without* issue, and *without* any lingering affection of the American people.

THE CHEROKEE INDIANS.

> "We, the rightful lords of yore,
> Are the rightful lords no more;
> Like the silver mist, we fail,
> Like the red leaves in the gale—
> Fail, like shadows, when the dawning
> Waves the bright flag of the morning."

In every history of the United States the different tribes of Indians—the native "sons of the forest" and "rightful lords of the soil," from Main to Florida and from the Atlantic ocean to the great Mississippi valley—justly claim conspicuous notice, whether considered as prowling enemies or warm-hearted friends.

As the Tuscaroras of eastern and middle Carolina were one of the most powerful of the Indian tribes, exercising a dominant sway over much of its undulating and semitropical territory early in the last century, so the Cherokees were the most powerful tribe of western Carolina and the adjoining region, preceding and during our Revolutionary war, frequently requiring the strong arm of military force to chastise them and teach them, by dear experience, the superiority and growing destiny of their "pale faced" neighbors.

The native land of the Cherokees was the most inviting and beautiful section of the United States, lying upon the sources of the Catawba and Yadkin rivers—upon Keowee,

Tugaloo, Etowah, Coosa and Flint, on the east and south, and several of the tributaries òf the Tennessee, on the west and north. If to this list be added the names of Hiwassee, Enoree, Tallulah, Swannanoa and Watauga, all streams originating and flowing through this mountainous country in rapid, frolicksome mood, we have an assemblage of musical sounds, (omitting the hard-sounding *Flint*,) only equaled in beauty and soft cadence upon the ear, by the grand and picturesque scenery with which they are surrounded.

According to Adair, one of the earliest settlers of South Carolina, and who wrote of the four principal tribes, (Cherokees, Shawnees, Chickasaws and Choctaws,) in 1775, "the Cherokees derive their name from *Cheera*, or *fire*, which is their reputed lower heaven, and hence they call their *magi*, *Cheera-tah-gee*, men possessed of the divine fire.

Within twenty miles of old Fort Loudon, built on the Tennessee in 1756, says the same authority, "there is a great plenty of whetstones for razors, of red, white and black colors. The silver mines are so rich that by digging about ten yards (thirty feet) deep, some desperate vagrants found at sundry times, so much rich ore as to enable them to counterfeit dollars to a great amount, a horse load of which was detected in passing for the purchase of negroes at Augusta." "A tradition, says Dr. Ramsey, (Annals of Tennessee,) still continues of the existence of the silver mine mentioned by Adair. * * * After the whites had settled near, and began to encroach upon the "Over-Hill Towns," their inhabitants withheld all knowledge of the mines from the traders, fearing their cupidity for the precious metals might lead to their appropriation by others, and the ultimate expulsion of the natives from the country." The history of the Cherokees is closely identified with that of the early settlements of the frontiers of the Carolinas, Georgia, Virginia and Tennessee, and all suffered from their vigorous and frequent hostile and murderous incursions. They were formidable for their numbers, and passionate fondness for war. They were the mountaineers of Aboriginal America, and like all other inhabitants of an Alpine region, cherished a deep affection for their country, and defended it with a lasting devotion and persevering tenacity. Little of their early history can be gathered from their traditions, extending back scarcely a century preceding the Revolution. *Oko-na-sto-ta*, one of their distinguished chiefs, visited England during the reign of George the Second. From his time they date the declension of their nation. His place of residence was at *Echota*, one of the Over-Hill Towns. Of the *tumuli*, or mounds scattered through the country, and other ancient remains, they know nothing, and considered them, when they took possession of the country, as vestiges of a more numerous population than themselves, and farther advanced in the arts of civilization. The several Indian tribes in America have been compared to the fragments of a vast ruin. And though these vestiges of a remote period in the past may not awaken the same grand associations in the mind of the beholder as the majestic ruins of Greece and Rome, yet they cannot fail to excite feelings of veneration for the memory of a numerous people, whose lingering signs of greatness are widely visible from the western borders of North Carolina to the Gulf of Mexico, and throughout the Mississippi valley.

As early as the year 1806, two Deputations attended Washington City from the Cherokee nation; one from the lower towns, to make known to the President their desire to remove west of the Mississippi, and pursue the hunter's life; the other Deputation, representing in part the Cherokees belonging to the above settlement, to make known their desire to remain in the lands of their fathers, and become cultivators of the soil. The President answered their petitions as follows: "The United States, my children, are the friends of both parties. As far as can be reasonably asked, they are willing to satisfy the wishes of both. Those who remain may be assured of our patronage, our aid, and good neighborhood."

The treaties formed between the United States and the Cherokee Nation, in the years 1817 and 1819, made provision for those desiring to remain, agreeably to the promise of the President; and they thus became citizens of the United States, each family being allowed a reservation of six hundred and forty acres of land. The whites claimed the same lands under a purchase made of the State. Suits were instituted in favor of the Indians, and by our Courts were decided in their favor. Afterward they sold their reservations to the Commissioners of the State, and purchased lands in the white settlement, and in the neighborhood of the hunting grounds reserved for them by treaties concluded with the Cherokee nation between the years 1790 and 1799; which privilege as a part of their nation they now enjoy.

The Cherokees now own in Haywood county, a tract of seventy-two thousand acres of land, well adapted in the vallies for farming, and on the mountains for wild game and sports of the chase. *Qualla Town*, their metropolis, is chiefly inhabited by the former sovereigns of the country, among whom are a few Catawbas. The Qualla Town people are divided into seven clans or divisions, over each of which a chief presides.

About the year 1830 the principal chief of this settlement, by the name of "Drowning Bear" (or You-na-guskee) becoming convinced that *intemperance* would destroy himself and his people, determined, if possible, to bring about a work of reform. He accordingly directed his clerk to write in the Indian language an agreement which translated reads as follows: "The undersigned Cherokees, belonging to the town of Qualla, agree to abandon the use of spirituous liquors." This instrument of writing was immediately signed by the old and venerable chief, and the whole town. This wise proceeding has worked a wonderful change for the better in their condition. They are now a temperate, orderly, industrious and peaceable people.

One of the most wonderful achievments of our age is the invention of the Cherokee alphabet. The invention was made in 1821 by *Guess*, (Se-qua-yah) *a half breed* Indian, his father being a white man and his mother a Cherokee. He was at the time not only perfectly unacquainted with letters but entirely so with every other language except his own. The first idea of the practicability of such a project was received by looking at an old piece of printed paper and reflecting upon the very singular manner (to him) by which the white people could place their thoughts on paper and communicate them to others at a distance. A thought struck him that there surely must be some mode by which the Indians could do the same. He first invented a distinct character for each word, but soon found the number so great that it was impossible to retain them in the memory. After several months' labor he reduced his original plan so as to give to each character a *syllabic sound*, and ascertained there were but eighty-six variations of sounds in the whole language; and when each of these was represented by some particular character or letter, the language was at once reduced to a system, and the extraordinary mode of now writing it crowned his labors with the most happy success. Considerable improvement has been made in the formation of the characters, in order that they might be written with greater facility. One of the characters, being found superfluous, has been discarded, reducing the number to eighty-five.

Guess emigrated to the West in 1824. It has been much regretted that he did not remain in North Carolina to witness the advantages and blessings of his discovery.

The Bible, newspapers and other literature are now published in the *musical* Cherokee language.

The Catawba Indians, contiguous to our southern borders, and once so numerous and powerful, have dwindled down to a diminutive remnant—mostly half breeds. They inhabited in their palmiest days much of the territory south of the Tuscaroras, and adjoining the Cherokees. For their general adherence to the patriots in the Revolution they have always received the fostering care of the State. They own a tract of land ten miles square in the south-east corner of York county, South Carolina. They speak a different language from the Cherokees, but possessing a similarity of musical sounds. They gave origin to the name of the noble river along whose banks, in its southern meanderings and its larger tributaries their lingering signs of former habitation are frequently visible, informing us here they once flourished in their simple avocations and enjoyments of the forest, and now excite our commiseration in their gradual decay and probable future extinction.

CONCLUSION.

In conclusion, the author would remark that other historic materials are on hand, in a partial state of preparation, which may hereafter be published. The history of "liberty's story" in the "Old North State," with all its grand array of early patriotic developments, has never been fully presented to the world. The field of research is still far from being exhausted, and it is hoped others—descendants, it may be, of our illustrious forefathers, will prosecute the same line of investigation as herein attempted.

For the present, this series of sketches, with their unavoidable omissions and imperfections, craving indulgent criticism, will come to an end.

ERRATTA.

Page 29, fourth line of third paragraph, for "Mayor" read "Major."
" 69, bottom line, for "$4,000" read "£4,000."
" 329, eighteenth line from top, for "Cherokee" read "Charlotte."

www.ingramcontent.com/pod-product-compliance
Lightning Source LLC
Chambersburg PA
CBHW031959220426
43664CB00005B/80